COMPASS AMERICAN GUIDES
An imprint of Fodor's Travel

★ YOSEMITE ★
and Sequoia / Kings Canyon National Parks

BY **SARA BENSON**
UPDATED BY **CHERYL CRABTREE** · PHOTOGRAPHY BY
CHRIS FALKENSTEIN AND **ROBERT HOLMES**

D1590759

Tuolumne
Meadows

1

2

Tenaya
Lake

Yosemite
Falls

Tioga Road

Big Oak Flat
Road

1 Mt. Conness
2 Lembert Dome
3 Mammoth Peak
4 Cathedral Peak
5 Half Dome
6 Washington Column
7 Glacier Point
8 Sentinel Dome
9 El Capitan
10 Leaning Tower
11 Cathedral Spires
12 Dewey Point
13 Valley View
14 Tunnel View

PANORAMIC VIEW OF
YOSEMITE NATIONAL PARK,
LOOKING EAST

CATHEDRAL RANGE

LITTLE YOSEMITE VALLEY

TENAYA CANYON

Nevada Falls

Vernal Falls

Curry Village

Yosemite Village

Glacier Point Road

YOSEMITE VALLEY

Bridalveil Fall

Wawona Road

El Portal Road

BERANN

Sunset over Tuolumne River.

A skier on Dewey Point takes in the vista of Yosemite Valley and the High Sierra.

COMPASS AMERICAN GUIDES: YOSEMITE AND SEQUOIA/KINGS CANYON NATIONAL PARKS

PUBLISHER: Stephen Horowitz, *General Manager*
EDITORIAL: Douglas Stallings, *Editorial Director;* Jill Fergus, Amanda Sadlowski, *Senior Editors;*
Brian Eschrich, Alexis Kelly, *Editors;* Angelique Kennedy-Chavannes, *Assistant Editor*
DESIGN: Tina Malaney, *Design and Production Director;* Jessica Gonzalez, *Senior Designer;* Erin Caceres,
Graphic Design Associate
PHOTOGRAPHY: Viviane Teles, *Senior Photo Editor;* Namrata Aggarwal, Neha Gupta, Payal Gupta,
Ashok Kumar, *Photo Editors;* Eddie Aldrete, *Photo Production Intern;* Kadeem McPherson, *Photo
Production Associate Intern*
MAPS: Rebecca Baer, *Senior Map Editor;* Mark Stroud (Moon Street Cartography), *Cartographer*
PRODUCTION: Jennifer DePrima, *Editorial Production Manager;* Elyse Rozelle, *Senior Production Editor;*
Monica White, *Production Editor*
BUSINESS & OPERATIONS: Chuck Hoover, *Chief Marketing Officer;* Robert Ames, *Group General Manager*
PUBLIC RELATIONS AND MARKETING: Joe Ewaskiw, *Senior Director of Communications and Public Relations*
FODORS.COM: Jeremy Tarr, *Editorial Director;* Rachael Levitt, *Managing Editor*
TECHNOLOGY: Jon Atkinson, *Director of Technology;* Rudresh Teotia, *Associate Director of Technology;*
Alison Lieu, *Project Manager*

EDITOR: Laura M. Kidder
PRODUCTION EDITOR: Elyse Rozelle
DESIGNERS: Tigist Getachew, Nora Rosansky, Chie Ushio
PRODUCTION DESIGNER: Tina Malaney
ILLUSTRATIONS: William Wu

COVER PHOTO: Josh Miller/Cavan Images RF/Getty Images [Description: Cathedral Peak reflected in lake at sunset, Yosemite National Park, California].

7th Edition

ISBN 978-1-64097-578-1
ISSN 1943-0086

SPECIAL SALES
This book is available at special discounts for bulk purchases for sales promotions or premiums. For more information, email SpecialMarkets@fodors.com.

PRINTED IN CHINA

10 9 8 7 6 5 4 3 2 1

Giant sequoias in Mariposa Grove, Yosemite National Park. ▶ ▶

DEDICATION:
To all the NPS employees, especially the hardworking seasonal staff who protect the Sierra Nevada region.

Contents

SPOTLIGHTS

TOPICAL ESSAYS AND SIDEBARS

MAPS AND CHARTS

Introduction

High in the glacier-carved Sierra Nevada mountain range in California near the western edge of the North American continent, there is a place of incredible beauty and heart's solace called Yosemite Valley. There, waterfalls leap from the edges of cliffs into grassy meadows nourished by bubbling streams. The valley is overhung by natural masterpieces of weather-worn granite, including world-famous Half Dome and El Capitan. Above the timeless valley, the craggy peaks of the Sierra Nevada high country rise, liberally scattered with pristine alpine lakes, wildflower-strewn meadows, and rugged hiking trails that make you feel as if you are walking on the rooftop of the world. Both the high altitudes and the imperial panoramas will steal your breath away and make your blood course like a waterfall rushing with spring snowmelt.

Before there were any artificial boundaries, these Western lands were inhabited by Native American nations, including the Miwok, Paiute, and Mono tribespeople who staked out summer camps in the elevated valleys and beat trading routes on foot over high mountain passes. Beginning in 1848, the California gold rush brought miners, ranchers, and pioneers into the American West. Slowly the lands began to lose their rich natural resources, especially as grazing livestock denuded meadows and many of the largest living trees on earth—giant sequoias—were cut down by loggers. In 1890, Yosemite and Sequoia National Parks were established to preserve these lands, from the snowy heights of Tuolumne Meadows to the cloaked depths of the Giant Forest. That same year, General Grant National Park (which was later expanded into Kings Canyon National Park) was created to protect the General Grant Tree, a legendary giant sequoia that still stands. Today, these national parks together stand guard over a large swath of epic landscape and natural ecosystems along the spine of the Sierra Nevada, including Mt. Whitney (elevation 14,505 feet), the tallest peak in the United States outside of Alaska.

Even if you have only a brief time to experience the Sierra Nevada, it's worthwhile to visit these parks. Wildlife watchers, outdoor enthusiasts, photographers, and countless tourists return to the parks many times over to explore them in all four seasons. The best time to visit is in late spring or early summer, when wildflowers bloom in the high country, rushing streams feed the verdant valleys and mountain meadows, and sunlight dapples the groves of giant sequoia trees. You can watch black bears and their cubs foraging for berries and acorns during the day, then see the stars of the Milky Way shine with startling clarity at night. Or just laze away an entire afternoon swimming in an alpine lake until sunset casts an alpenglow on skyscraping Sierra Nevada peaks. The opportunities for adventure are endless here.

Editor's Note: Although most COVID-19 travel restrictions, including vaccination and masking requirements, have been lifted across the United States, some local mandates still exist. Individual national park websites have details on what to expect during your park visit. In addition, many national parks have instituted policies (e.g., timed-entry systems, mandatory reservations at campgrounds and for certain activities) to manage crowds and keep everyone safe and well. Staffing shortages have also affected park offerings and amenities, from shuttle services and tours to operations at entrances, visitor centers, and in-park restaurants, hotels, and campgrounds. It's important to plan ahead, be flexible, and remain patient.

"Climb the mountains and get their good tidings. Nature's peace will flow into you as sunshine flows into trees. The winds will blow their own freshness into you, and the storms their energy, while cares will drop off like autumn leaves."

–John Muir, *Our National Parks,* 1901.

HOW TO USE THIS BOOK

Our guidebook opens with Best Experiences, a photo-rich introduction to the most outstanding sights, activities, and places to stay in the three national parks. Our contributors share their favorite experiences and hope to inspire your trip planning. Next is a short overview of the history of the region, starting with its early Native American inhabitants and leading up to the political and environmental issues that the parks face today.

Each of the main regional chapters is devoted to an individual national park. These three park chapters are each subdivided into Sights and Other Activities. The Sights sections follow the key driving routes around the parks. The Other Activities sections cover the most popular outdoor pursuits, listing them alphabetically. Star icons in these park chapters highlight the must-see attractions, which are especially useful to keep in mind if your time is limited.

Following the regional chapters are our recommendations for where to stay and eat in and near the national parks. Here, too, we star our top choices. The Geology, Flora, and Fauna chapter showcases the natural history of the region and includes a handy reference to the most noteworthy local plants and animals. Finally, our Practical Information chapter rounds up essential tips and contacts, plus a short list of recommended further reading.

RESTAURANTS

The following price categories apply for the average price of most main course dishes:

$ = under $17	$$ = $17–$26	$$$ = $27–$36	$$$$ = over $36

HOTELS

The following price categories apply for the average price of a single night's peak-season rate for a standard double room:

$ = under $150	$$ = $150–$250	$$$ = $251–$350	$$$$ = over $350

Hetch Hetchy
A glacier-carved valley that's now a reservoir.

Tuolumne Meadows
A lush meadow that's a favorite for wildlife watchers, hikers, and rock climbers.

ORIENTATION TO YOSEMITE AND SEQUOIA/KINGS CANYON NATIONAL PARKS

0   40 Miles

0   60 Kilometers

Mono Lake

Tioga Pass Entrance   Lee Vining

YOSEMITE NATIONAL PARK

INYO NATIONAL FOREST

NEVADA
CALIFORNIA

Big Oak Flat Entrance

Arch Rock Entrance

El Portal

Tioga Road
Incredibly scenic route through the high country, but open only from roughly June through October.

Mammoth Lakes

INYO NATIONAL FOREST

Yosemite Valley
The awe-inspiring heart of the park. Crammed with the iconic El Capitan and Half Dome granite monoliths, waterfalls, hiking trails, and the visitor facilities in Yosemite Village.

South Entrance
Fish Camp

SIERRA NEVADA

Owens

Bishop

Wawona and Mariposa Grove
The visitor hub of Wawona is smaller and quieter than Yosemite Village, with a strong historic vibe. Nearby Mariposa is the largest grove of giant sequoias.

SIERRA NATIONAL FOREST

Oakhurst

Big Pine

Kings Canyon Scenic Byway
Terrific views as you drive into one of the continent's deepest canyons.

Cedar Grove
In the heart of Kings Canyon, highlighted by Zumwalt Meadow and the Mist Falls trail.

River

395

Grant Grove
The busiest part of the park. The village is in the shadow of the huge General Grant giant sequoia.

SEQUOIA NATIONAL FOREST

KINGS CANYON NATIONAL PARK

Kings

Independence

Fresno

Big Stump Entrance

River

Giant Forest
The world's biggest concentration of giant sequoia trees—including the world's largest giant sequoia, General Sherman.

Crystal Cave
Enormous marble cavern filled with stalactites, stalagmites, and a diverse crowd of subterranean bugs.

Generals Hwy

SAN JOAQUIN VALLEY

Ash Mountain Entrance

SEQUOIA NATIONAL PARK

INYO NATIONAL FOREST

Three Rivers

99

Lookout Point Entrance

Mt. Whitney
The highest peak in the lower 48 states; a popular backpacking challenge.

Visalia

198

Welcome to Yosemite, Sequoia, and Kings Canyon National Parks, the wild heart of the Sierra Nevada mountain range. We want to share some of our favorite places in the parks with you, from thundering waterfalls and giant sequoias to hidden trails and backcountry vistas. Whether you're looking for a serene retreat or an adrenaline fix, here are experiences we think you'll love as much as we do. It's time to get ready for unforgettable adventures.

–Sara Benson, *author*
–Chris Falkenstein, *photographer*
–Robert Holmes, *photographer*

BEST EXPERIENCES

BEST
Scenic Drive

Tioga Road, Yosemite; *see p. 114*

"This route takes you up to Yosemite's high country, with **knockout** views at every turn.

You'll wind through thick forests, pass Tenaya Lake (a perfect place to swim and picnic), and finally crest at Tioga Pass." —*Chris Falkenstein*

Splashy views from Tioga Road. ▶▶

INSIDER'S PICK

Kings Canyon Scenic Byway

"With sharp turns and drop-offs, this road dives into a canyon deeper than even the Grand Canyon. In spring, whitewater spray from the Kings River splashes my car!"

—Sara Benson, *see page 240*

BEST
Family
Adventures

Swimming and Rafting, Merced River; see p. 153
Skiing, Badger Pass Ski Area; see p. 155

"**While Yosemite can be** a strikingly rugged place, Mother Nature's gentler side also emerges. The bubbling Merced River is one such place—take the kids on a dreamy summertime float. From the vantage point of an inflatable raft, you can crane your neck up at granite monoliths like Half Dome. In winter, join the generations of families who've learned to ski down the pint-sized slopes of Badger Pass Ski Area, near Glacier Point."

—Sara Benson

Rafting on the Merced River in Yosemite National Park. ▶▶

BEST
Day Hikes

Half Dome, Yosemite; see p. 134
Tuolumne Meadows, Yosemite; see p. 137
Mist Falls, Kings Canyon; see p. 256

"If you're up for a challenging hike, **iconic** Half Dome is the ticket. It's a long day's effort but worth every step. Don't forget to take plenty of water, as there's none on the mountain." —Robert Holmes

Half Dome, as viewed from the south. ▶▶

"If you crave a real wilderness experience, away from the hordes of tourists in Yosemite Valley, head for the high country. Polished granite domes in a pristine mountain landscape provide a spectacular backdrop for a hike in this alpine wonderland. Black bears abound in forests of Tuolumne, and while they rarely present a problem make sure you make enough noise to let them know you are coming."

—*Robert Holmes*

◂◂ Tuolumne Meadows.

"Almost no other trail in the Sierra Nevada gives you so much in so short a distance: a deep canyon gorge, mossy pine forest, granite talus slopes, and finally, Mist Falls. For the full dramatic effect, hike in April or May, when you'll move through mist so thick it obscures the trail itself. You'll have to stand back to admire nature's handiwork—as if the scene were a painting hanging in a museum."

—*Sara Benson*

◀◀ Midway point on Mist Falls trail.

⊕ INSIDER'S PICK

Zumwalt Meadow,
Kings Canyon

"Misty spring mornings are best for spotting black bears foraging for berries and wildflowers alongside the river. Canyon views and great birding make it worth the trip." —*Sara Benson, see p. 245*

BEST
Waterfalls

Vernal and Nevada Falls, Yosemite
see p. 133

"The slick, knee-knocking miles of hiking—either up from the valley or down from Glacier Point— are worth the singular experience of getting **up close** and personal with these mighty waterfalls." —*Sara Benson*

Vernal Fall, Yosemite National Park. ▶▶

"Yosemite's waterfalls peak in May, when clouds of mist often obscure the base of the valley's cliffside falls and rushing water sounds louder than an oncoming train. But as long as your footing remains as solid as a mountain goat's, you can walk right up the natural granite staircase beside twinned Vernal and Nevada falls, which appear mightier than the competition when hikers stand beside them."

—*Sara Benson*

◀◀ Hiking between twinned Vernal and Nevada falls.

INSIDER'S PICK

Wapama Falls, Yosemite

"In the hidden Hetch Hetchy Valley, a footpath thrillingly leads to the base of this triple cascade, which peaks in concert with the park's more famous falls in May." —*Sara Benson, see p. 128*

BEST
Extreme Thrill

Rock Climbing, Yosemite; *see p. 150*

"Climbers from all over the world seek the **challenging** routes in Yosemite Valley. There's a certain magic that develops as you climb here. Friendships are made and stories exchanged in our favorite home base, Camp 4."

—Chris Falkenstein

Legendary climber Ron Kauk works on a new route above Tuolumne Meadows. ▶ ▶

BEST
Campgrounds

High Sierra Camps, Yosemite; *see pp. 145 and 293*
Hume Lake, Kings Canyon; *see p. 242*

"**You don't have to** carry a heavy backpack to explore the High Sierra Camps—what conservationist John Muir called his 'high pleasure-ground.' This alpine wilderness circuit of summer-only tent villages provides plenty of creature comforts, including canvas-sided tents, hot meals, and sometimes showers. The camps also free you from carrying anything but the most essential gear on day hikes. Just don't forget bug spray!"

—*Sara Benson*

(right) Camping by a lake near Tuolumne Meadows. (above) High Sierra Camp. ▶▶

Best Viewpoints

Glacier Point, Yosemite; *see p. 102*

"It feels like you can touch the sky here. Spread beneath you is the jaw-dropping beauty of Half Dome, Nevada and Vernal falls, and the Yosemite Valley. I love to come here on full-moon nights, when it's easy to imagine the ghosts of John Muir and Teddy Roosevelt standing right beside me."   —*Sara Benson*

Olmsted Point, Yosemite; *see p. 119*

"This is one of my favorite places for watching sunsets. The view sweeps all the way from Half Dome to the domes of Tuolumne Meadows to the eastern high country. If you take the short nature trail south from the parking lot, you'll reach a small granite dome and even broader views of the surrounding mountains—a great photo op."
                                    —*Chris Falkenstein*

Best Hotels

The Ahwahnee, Yosemite *(left); see pp. 95 and 279*

"Nowhere else is Yosemite's natural splendor better matched by human craftsmanship. The hotel radiates a genteel, historic atmosphere— and let's not forget the spectacular views."
                                    —*Sara Benson*

Curry Village, Yosemite; *see pp. 89 and 282*

"For more than a century, families have been staying right here on the floor of Yosemite Valley. It's good old-fashioned summer-camp fun for everyone."   —*Sara Benson*

Best Backpacking

John Muir Trail, Yosemite (right); see p. 144

"Tracing the spine of the Sierra Nevada, this 210-mile route clambers through the high country that the namesake naturalist held so dear. If you go against the flow and hike north to south, it's easier to get a permit and you can finish triumphantly atop Mt. Whitney, the USA's highest peak outside Alaska." —*Sara Benson*

High Sierra Trail, Sequoia National Park; see p. 206

"If you've ever wanted to brag that you've walked across the Sierra Nevada, this trail is unquestionably the way to do it. Though not the shortest trans-Sierra route, this 70-mile-plus route has glorious alpine scenery, wildflower meadows, and glassy lakes. It's also a handy back door to climbing 14,505-foot Mt. Whitney." —*Sara Benson*

Best Sequoia Trees

Giant Forest, Sequoia National Park; see p. 183

"A wonderful way to get a handle on man's insignificance is to walk beneath the sequoias of the Giant Forest. It's impossible to grasp how massive these trees really are until you're standing beneath one of the centuries-old behemoths. Even if you're somehow jaded, this is an awe-inspiring, don't-miss experience." —*Robert Holmes*

Mariposa Grove, Yosemite; see p. 110

"Walking among these giant sequoias, you'll feel like a hobbit—the trees are that immense and magical. My favorite area is the upper grove. It takes a little more effort to reach it, but you'll be rewarded with a much quieter and more solemn experience." —*Chris Falkenstein*

History of the Parks

The sun sets on Half Dome and El Capitan

Today's battles over invasive tourism, wilderness management, indigenous land rights, water resources, and deforestation are, unfortunately, nothing new to the Sierra Nevada region and its big three parks. These are largely the same issues that have shaped the colorful, hardscrabble history of Yosemite, Sequoia, and Kings Canyon. One of the great aspects of visiting the region is the opportunity to trace the evidence of this past.

Bridalveil Fall flows year-round in Yosemite Valley, an area once home to the Ahwahneechees.

⊙ NATIVE AMERICANS

While relatively little is known about many of the native peoples who lived in the Sierra Nevada, we do know that various tribes have resided in the area since prehistoric times. Signs of these early inhabitants include *morteros* (grinding holes in rocks, where acorns were turned into flour) and rock art—mostly pictographs, but petroglyphs, too. You can spot the morteros in all three national parks: keep your eyes trained along the forest and valley trails for rocks with the telltale scooped depressions. The best place to spy prehistoric rock art is in the southern reaches of Sequoia National Park.

Evidence suggests seasonal relocation as part of the prehistoric peoples' lifestyle. They moved around to stay ahead of the cold as well as to hunt game and gather edible plants at higher elevations in the summer. Later tribes in the Sierra Nevada foothills also followed this movement pattern. On the east side of the mountain range, especially around Mono Lake and the Owens Valley, lived the Paiutes; to the west were the Southern Miwok. Though the tribes sometimes intermarried and had occasional alliances, skirmishes between them were frequent. Historians disagree about why the two warred, though it's typically assumed that common causes were hunting ground rights and a scarcity of resources, especially for the Paiutes, who had to contend with the east side's demanding desertlike conditions.

Farther south in what today is Sequoia National Park, the Monache (or Western Mono) tribe was divided into different bands, with the Wuksachi residing north of the Kaweah River and the Potwisha (Patwisha, or Balwisha) to the south. The Wobonuch band inhabited the foothills farther north at what is now Grant Grove in Kings Canyon National Park. In the lowest-elevation foothills and across California's Central Valley were the Yokut, whose role in the most significant event in the history of Yosemite, the engagement of the Mariposa Battalion, is described below.

In Yosemite Valley, a distinct band of Native Americans who called themselves the Ahwahneechee ("dwellers of the gaping mouth," referring to the valley itself) eventually emerged. A fierce debate continues over whether these people were more closely connected to Miwok or Paiute tribespeople. This conflict helps prevent either tribe from achieving federal recognition as an indigenous tribe with rights related to Yosemite Valley.

There can be no debate, however, that the Ahwahneechee ways of life showed significant cultural influences from both sides of the Sierra Nevada. This is demonstrated, for example, in their mixed artistic styles of basketry. The baskets reflect different traditional designs, interpretations, and materials. It's possible to see some of this basketry, which is often made with willow, maple, dogwood, or hazelnut, at the museum in Yosemite Valley, as well as other park interpretive centers.

You can literally walk in the footsteps of some of these tribes. Still in existence are footpaths more or less as they were centuries ago, crossing formidable mountain passes. They're snowbound for most of the year but clear for a couple of months in summer.

EARLY EXPLORERS AND A RUSH FOR RICHES

On January 6, 1805, a Spanish expedition came across the great canyon of the Kings River, named by them in honor of the royals who stopped in Bethlehem for the Feast of Epiphany. However, it is not known for certain who the first European-Americans to set foot in Yosemite Valley were. It may have been a bunch of frontiersmen led by Joseph Reddeford Walker, who crossed the Sierra Nevada in 1833 and stumbled upon what the group described as a vast valley with nearby groves of giant sequoia trees.

Early inhabitants of the Sierra Nevada wove baskets. You can see demonstrations at the Yosemite Museum, near Yosemite Valley Welcome Center.

In the 19th century, pioneers came
to hunt in the area that would
become Yosemite National Park.

It wasn't until 1848, when James W. Marshall successfully panned for gold at Sutter's Mill, that the pioneer boom really began. As word of the riches hidden in the Sierra Nevada spread eastward, gold seekers traveled by wagon train across the United States and many more arrived by ship in the San Francisco Bay. Perhaps in part because of the gold in them thar hills, California was quickly granted statehood in 1850.

Encounters between miners (for gold as well as mineral resources) and Native Americans were seldom friendly. The miners and other newcomers to the West, including the military, ranchers, and homesteading pioneers, introduced such foreign diseases as smallpox, influenza, and measles that decimated tribal populations, much as earlier Spanish Catholic missions had done elsewhere along the California coast. The U.S. federal government supposedly wanted to negotiate the peaceful relocation of local tribes, but Native Americans resisted being forcibly removed to reservations in California's Central Valley.

THE MARIPOSA BATTALION

In 1851, a militia called the Mariposa Battalion led by prospector James Savage entered Yosemite Valley, hell-bent on avenging an attack on trading posts by Miwok and Yokut tribespeople who had been working for immigrant miners. After successive campaigns, this militia captured Chief Tenaya, the leader of the Ahwahneechee people then living in Yosemite Valley.

The Ahwahneechee were taken to a reservation outside Fresno. Soon afterward, Chief Tenaya left the reservation to live with Paiutes near Mono Lake before returning in 1853 to Yosemite Valley, where he died violently during a confrontation with Southern Miwok tribesmen, allegedly over stolen horses. These events swung the pendulum from Native American dominance in the Yosemite region in favor of the expansion of the Western frontier. Today, the conflict's impact is signaled by the many landmarks bearing Native American names, such as Tenaya Lake in the Tuolumne Meadows highlands of Yosemite National Park.

HUNGRY FOR PROFIT

No rich veins of mineral ore were ever discovered in Yosemite Valley or Kings Canyon, although mining operations were set up at Tioga Pass and Mineral King in the Sierra Nevada high country. After the mid-19th century, once it was clear mining was not paying off, California immigrants became interested in exploiting the more abundant natural resources in the region, trying their hand at ranching—ranchers grazed herds of cattle and sheep in the mountain meadows and valleys—as well as logging.

The loggers found themselves in a no-win situation. They hacked down giant sequoias, but never profited from their labors because the wood of these trees becomes more brittle as the trees age, often causing them to break apart into useless pieces after being felled. Loggers didn't know that the trees would splinter until they started cutting them down, and even after the logged trees disintegrated, the loggers kept hoping they could profit by transforming the wood into different products (like mulch or toothpicks) or by trying

Frustrated by shattering giant sequoias, some 19th-century loggers tried to turn the wood into toothpicks.

different techniques. But ultimately, nothing proved profitable. Ugly fields of giant-sequoia stumps in Kings Canyon National Park and the Giant Sequoia National Monument of the Sierra National Forest testify to this brief, destructive period of local history.

PRESERVING THE PARKS

Not everyone who visited the Yosemite region during the late 19th century was just trying to make a buck. Painters and photographers soaked up the natural beauty of the uniquely shaped and unusually lush Yosemite Valley, while scientists and surveyors measured, observed, and cataloged the flora and fauna. After concerns were raised by early visitors and budding conservationists, President Abraham Lincoln signed the Yosemite Land Grant of 1864, which gave the Yosemite Valley and the Mariposa Grove of giant sequoias to the state of California to better protect them as a natural resource.

In 1866, Wawona-area pioneer Galen Clark was appointed as the guardian of the grant, an ill-defined job that came with little authority and no official tasks. His duties consisted of welcoming visitors and providing them with some guidance. He in effect served as both an early park interpreter and an ad hoc law

Conservationist
John Muir called Kings Canyon
"a rival of the Yosemite."

enforcement ranger, albeit one without power to enforce regulations. He was able to educate visitors on how to better preserve the wild-lands in their natural state, even as ranchers, sheepherders, home-steaders, and tourism entrepreneurs continued to wreak havoc on the natural ecosystem of the area. Fragile meadows were eroded by graz-ing livestock and a burgeoning tourism infrastructure.

Fortunately today you cannot see the effects of this damage, as these areas have long since been restored within the national park boundaries. Nevertheless, the carelessness of the past is still felt by visitors confronting the fact that there are limited places to camp in Yosemite Valley.

John Muir, Father of Our National Parks

In 1868, Scottish-born naturalist and conservationist John Muir took his first life-changing trip into the Sierra Nevada. He saw firsthand how grazing livestock (which he referred to as "hoofed locusts") and the logging of giant sequoias were ruining this mountainous region. Muir soon became an advocate of the need to further protect these public lands for future generations. His efforts were popular with the U.S. public, but not so much with the state and federal government or private entre-preneurs.

Muir invited politicians and other well-known people of influence to accompany him on camp-ing trips into the high country, including at Tuolumne Meadows and in Kings Canyon, which Muir called "a rival of the Yosemite." At the same time, partly in response to these grass-roots efforts, Visalia newspaperman George Stewart had been campaigning for federal protection of the Giant Forest from timber-logging interests. In 1890, the federal govern-ment established not only Yosemite National Park but also Sequoia National Park, encom-passing the Giant Forest, and General Grant National Park, surrounding the General Grant Tree in Grant Grove, now part of Kings Canyon National Park. Two years later, Muir founded the Sierra Club.

Theodore Roosevelt and John Muir stand at Glacier Point in Yosemite National Park.

Kitty Tatch and Katherine Hazelston, both waitresses at hotels in the park, dance on Yosemite's overhanging rock at Glacier Point around 1900. **Top Right:** Ice skaters enjoy Mirror Lake. **Bottom Right:** A stagecoach takes visitors through Yosemite Valley.

⊙ TOURISM TAKES ROOT

Visitors could pass through the Wawona Tunnel Tree between 1881, when the hole was carved out, until 1969, when, weakened by the hole and the compaction of its roots, it toppled under a heavy load of snow. What's left of the felled tree lies in Mariposa Grove, Yosemite National Park.

Even before the national parks were established, pleasure-seeking visitors had started frequenting the Yosemite Valley, Giant Forest, Kings Canyon, and Mt. Whitney (named after Josiah Whitney, the leader of the ambitious California Geological Survey, begun in 1860).

The first tourists arrived on foot or by horseback. Starting in 1886, a horse-drawn stage service reached Yosemite Valley from Wawona. The stage operated until 1907, when a railroad between Merced and El Portal allowed visitors access to the valley from the west. Tourist camps were built in both Yosemite Valley and in the Giant Forest of Sequoia National Park, while atop Glacier Point in Yosemite National Park a tourist hotel appeared that was accessible by hiking or on horseback via a 4-mile toll trail up from the valley below. The detrimental effects of this early tourism were slowly erased once the area came under the administration of the National Park Service.

By the turn of the 20th century, tourism in both parks, as well as in the nearby Kings Canyon, was well established. In 1906, the state of California gave back Yosemite Valley and Mariposa Grove to the

BUFFALO SOLDIERS: THE FIRST PARK RANGERS

Although Native Americans were the original protectors of the land, it was the U.S. military that was assigned to protect the new Sierra Nevada national parks that Congress created in 1890. African-American regiments of "buffalo soldiers" (so called out of respect by Native Americans in honor of their fierce fighting style, as well as the color of their skin and the feel of their hair) that had been established during the Civil War were assigned this peacetime duty.

Starting from San Francisco's Presidio, it took the soldiers about two weeks to journey overland into the mountains, where they set up camp during the summer in the Wawona area of Yosemite National Park and also in the giant sequoia groves farther south.

While most of the officers in charge of these black regiments were white, Captain Charles Young, the African-American son of freed slaves, was in charge of the soldiers assigned to Sequoia National Park as well as General Grant National Park (which would later be incorporated into Kings Canyon). In defense of the parks, these infantry and cavalry regiments chased off poachers, sheepherders, loggers, and miners until civilian rangers took over after 1914.

Unfortunately, few photos or other documents remain today to tell us more about this unique period in the parks' history.

(above) Buffalo soldiers of the 25th Infantry.

federal government, thus expanding Yosemite National Park. The ever-increasing popularity of Yosemite, Sequoia, and General Grant national parks exerted pressures on the natural ecosystem as tourist development continued unchecked.

All that changed after the National Park Service (NPS) was founded in 1916. Under Director Stephen T. Mather and his successor, Horace Albright, the parks were judiciously developed. Many in-holdings (privately owned parcels of land within the national park boundaries) were eliminated; park concessionaire businesses were consolidated; a network of trails and roads was built; and the tradition of ranger-led campfire programs and guided interpretive hikes began.

LESSONS OF HETCH HETCHY

The NPS was too late, however, to save the Hetch Hetchy Valley of Yosemite National Park from being environmentally affected by the building of a dam, which had been approved by Congress three

Yosemite's Hetch Hetchy Valley held a special place in John Muir's heart, but try as he did, he was not able to stop it from being dammed. The flooded valley provides water and energy for San Francisco.

years before the NPS was founded. When it was completed in 1923, the O'Shaughnessy Dam flooded the Hetch Hetchy Valley and began supplying water and generating power for the rapidly growing San Francisco Bay Area. John Muir had tirelessly campaigned against the dam, but lost out to political interests from the city of San Francisco before he died in 1914.

Also in the 1920s, a similarly alarming plan by the city of Los Angeles proposed damming the nearby Kings River watershed.

However, conservationists had begun advocating not only for the enlargement of Sequoia National Park (to which the Kern River canyon and Mt. Whitney were successfully added in 1926), but also for legal protection of Kings Canyon from logging and ranching interests. Much political wrangling over all of these environmental concerns ensued.

The controversy over the creation of the third national park in the Sierra Nevada ended in 1940, when Congress established Kings Canyon National Park, which swallowed up smaller General Grant National Park. In 1965, the proposed dam sites of Cedar Grove and the Tehipite Valley were also safely added to the new national park, saving them from Hetch Hetchy's fate.

Building Up the Parks

The advent of automobile travel sparked the greatest changes to the national parks. Paved roads quickly connected the parks to towns and

President Teddy Roosevelt stands with some companions at the base of the Grizzly Giant tree in Yosemite National Park's Mariposa Grove, 1903.

cities in California's Central Valley and provided greater access to the parks' interiors.

The first cars entered Yosemite Valley in 1913. Soon afterward, NPS director Mather purchased the privately owned Tioga Road, a historic wagon route across Yosemite's high country. Then, in 1926, Generals Highway opened between the Sierra Nevada foothills and the Giant Forest area of Sequoia National Park. In the 1930s, convict labor was used to build a stunning scenic byway into Kings Canyon to connect

FREE FOR ALL

"There is nothing so American as our national parks. The scenery and wildlife are native. The fundamental idea behind the parks is native. It is, in brief, that the country belongs to the people, that it is in process of making for the enrichment of the lives of all of us. The parks stand as the outward symbol of this great human principle."

"It took a bitter struggle to teach the country at large that our national resources are not inexhaustible and that, when public domain is stolen, a twofold injury is done, for it is a theft of the treasure of the present and at the same time bars the road of opportunity to the future."
—President Franklin D. Roosevelt in a radio address, 1934.

Grant Grove with Cedar Grove along the South Fork of the Kings River. Because of its hairpin turns and sheer cliff drop-offs, it was a hazardous byway to build as well as drive. The breathtaking, twisting road is still used today by drivers going from Grant Grove to Cedar Grove.

In the same decade, President Franklin D. Roosevelt created the Civilian Conservation Corps (CCC), which employed 3 million young men mostly on forestry and flood-control projects, some of which were in the national parks during the Great Depression. The CCC brought hundreds of thousands of workers into the American West to create an infrastructure that would enable more people to visit the national parks.

Yosemite was no exception. CCC workers paved over the park's road to Glacier Point and the historical stagecoach route between Wawona and Yosemite Valley. In Sequoia National Park, the CCC extended the Generals Highway from Giant Forest all the way to Grant Grove, built a stone stairway up Moro Rock, and installed the Spider Gate, shaped like the arachnid's web, at Crystal Cave.

As the network of roads increased in the parks, so did tourism, especially once the all-weather highway from Merced into Yosemite Valley was completed in 1926. The next year the famous Ahwahnee Hotel opened in Yosemite Valley. This luxurious hotel, another brainstorm from director Mather, attracted VIP visitors, which aided the park's continuing preservation efforts by ensuring popular support from celebrities, high-society movers and shakers, and even U.S. presidents.

During World War II, visitation to the parks dropped, especially as areas of Yosemite came under military control. Security was increased at Hetch Hetchy Reservoir, and the grand Ahwahnee served as a military hospital. Nevertheless, after the war, tourism boomed again, thanks to postwar euphoria and a strong U.S. economy. The birth of the classic American driving vacation in the late 1940s and early '50s, during the heyday of Route 66, increased park visitation many times over.

Unfortunately, federal funding for the parks failed to keep pace with increasing tourism. By the early 1950s, the park infrastructure was sadly lacking, having fallen behind the ever bigger crowds who came to visit each year. The buildings constructed by CCC workers in the 1930s became overwhelmed by tourists, and there were not enough NPS rangers to help control the crowds, resulting in widespread damage to some of the country's most-prized national parks.

MIDCENTURY MANEUVERS

In 1955, NPS director Conrad Wirth proposed a solution to the crisis: Mission 66, a federally funded program that aimed to overhaul the parks. Over the next 10 years, the Mission 66 program poured more than $1 billion into rescuing national parks and improving their visitor facilities, most memorably by creating more than 100 new national-park visitor centers. It was during the Mission 66 era that the Tioga Road through Yosemite's high country was realigned and paved, and

The breathtaking, twisting road is still used today by drivers going from Grant Grove to Cedar Grove.

Cedar Grove was finally added to Kings Canyon National Park.

As these Sierra Nevada national parks became increasingly developed and accessible to tourists, Congress wisely passed the Wilderness Preservation Act of 1964, which set aside more than 9 million acres of public lands across the country to remain forever untrammeled by roads or motor vehicles. This important act was passed after the Leopold Report of 1963, which recommended that national parks work to restore the native ecosystems of the areas they protect.

The legislation resulted in widespread NPS policy changes, such as allowing wildfires to burn after decades of fire suppression, and working to hold population levels of wild animals steady. In Yosemite Valley, traffic was curtailed by a system of one-way roads, and a shuttle-bus service was implemented. Restoration of the Giant Forest in Sequoia National Park is an ongoing project.

As national-park visitation increased further after 1970—the year of the Stoneman Meadow riots in Yosemite, when hippies and park rangers clashed on July 4th over public use of fragile meadow areas—the NPS limited national-park campsites and placed a cap on the number of people who could use wilderness trails.

The government also sent a strong message about preservation in 1978 when it put the kibosh on the Walt Disney Company's plans for a ski resort in the Mineral King Valley, which was added to Sequoia National Park that same year. Mineral King continues today to be a flashpoint for debate, as many rustic mountain cabins there have been in the same family for generations, and private in-holdings remain inside the national-park boundaries.

⊙⟶ THE PARKS TODAY

Like many national parks, those in the Sierra Nevada are generally underfunded and overwhelmed, a fact that is quite visible during most visits. Bumper-to-bumper vehicles and the pollutants they emit are the unfortunate by products of popularity, especially at Yosemite, which receives between 3 and 4 million visitors each year.

Sequoia and Kings Canyon National Parks also teem with vehicles, especially along the Generals Highway, though in a perverse take on dumping trash in your neighbor's yard, most of the air pollution that hazily obscures viewpoints and mountain peaks of those parks drifts up from California's Central Valley. Noise from frequent military overflights of these parks is regulated but still may intrude upon your wilderness experience. More dangerously for the environment, the Sierra Nevada foothills region has become a prime area for illegal marijuana plant cultivation, a harsh mix of terraced landscaping, irrigation pipe systems, and toxic pesticides that seep into the river systems of Sequoia and Kings Canyon National Parks.

In response to the underfunding, crowding, and pollution, but more broadly in keeping with the legacy of the Wilderness Act, the NPS is trying to restore more parkland to its natural state. Individual parks are doing their best to improve the visitor experience. A free shuttle-bus service now runs in the Giant Forest area of Sequoia National Park, for example. In Yosemite, the Merced River Management Plan (which has been under environmental impact discussion for many years) aims to eventually restore hundreds of acres of meadow in Yosemite Valley, in part through the reorganization of parking and expanded shuttle service. Similarly, the Mariposa Grove Restoration project, completed in 2018, improved the habitat of the giant sequioas through the removal of some roads and a parking lot.

A rainbow after a storm arcs over the mountains of Kings Canyon National Park.

Yosemite National Park

Sunrise at North Dome

No other place in the Sierra Nevada stirs up the soul and can jump-start wild imaginations like Yosemite National Park. For many nature lovers, it's one of the American West's ultimate outdoor destinations, and it's open year-round. You could visit Yosemite in every season for a decade and still not wholly penetrate its wild heart. It's worth fighting the crowds to see this famous place because it's one of those rare things: a wonder of the world that actually lives up to the hype, time and again.

The ethereal beauty of Yosemite, with Half Dome, below right.

TUOLUMNE RIVER

COLD CANYON

Pacific Crest Trail

White Mountain

Ragged Peak

Glen Aulin

Gaylor Peak

Gaylor Lakes

Bennettsville
Tioga Pass Entrance

Mt. Dana

Dana Meadows

Parsons Memorial Lodge

Dog Lake

Pothole Dome

Lembert Dome

Soda Springs

TUOLUMNE MEADOWS

Tioga Road

Mt. Gibbs
12,764 ft

Fairview Dome

Tuolumne Meadows Visitor Center

Mammoth Peak

Mono Pass
10,604 ft

Medlicott Dome

KUNA CREST

Parker Pass

Cathedral Peak

Elizabeth Lake

Unicorn Peak

Cathedral Lakes

Tresidder Peak

Echo Peaks

Johnson Peak

LYELL CANYON

Koip Peak
12,962 ft

Tenaya Lake

John Muir Trail

Sunrise

Vogelsang

Vogelsang Lake

KONA CREST

Pacific Crest Trail and John Muir Trail

Donohue Peak
12,023 ft

Merced Lake

Mt. Florence

Mt. Lyell
13,114 ft

Donohue Pass

Merced Lake

Mt. Clark

Mt. Ansel Adams
11,760ft

Foerster Peak
12,057ft

Mt. Ritter

Gray Peak

Long Mountain
11,502 ft

CLARK RANGE

Red Peak

Isberg Peak

Isberg Pass

Merced Peak

Post Peak Pass

Triple Divide Peak

CREST

Merced Pass

ANSEL ADAMS
WILDERNESS

Fernandez Pass

Gale Peak
10,693ft

Sing Peak
10,552ft

Chiquito Pass

SIERRA
NATIONAL FOREST

Mono Basin
Scenic Area
Visitor Center

Lee Vining

To Bridgeport

Mono Lake

To Mammoth Lakes
and Bishop

Mono Lake Tufa State Reserve

120

395

158

June Lake

Legend

Ranger / Information

Food Service

Picnic Area

Lodging

Campground

Gas Station

P Parking Area

John Muir Trail /
Pacific Crest Trail

Other Trails

YOSEMITE
NATIONAL PARK

0 — 5 Miles

0 — 7.5 Kilometers

In early spring, waterfalls burst from sheer granite cliffs as the snow melts off the skyscraping, high-country peaks. As summer arrives, wildflowers fill delicate alpine meadows with a joyful palette of colors, and icy mountain passes become trekable once more. The hottest days of summer invite swimming in the park's lazy rivers and hidden, high-elevation lakes. Summer is also the most active time for the park's wildlife, so there are plenty of opportunities to photograph delicate hummingbirds or to follow the trails of brawny black bears.

Fall is a more peaceful time, as the wilderness transitions into winter and the crowds begin to thin. However, golden afternoons and snow-free trails tempt plenty of off-season explorers to the park. Winters are cold (regularly dipping below freezing at night) and long (usually lasting from November through April), but there's a freshness in the crisp air and beauty in the powdery layers of snow that blanket the park from peak to valley, beckoning to snowshoers, skiers, and those seeking solitude.

Yosemite National Park comprises almost 1,200 square miles of mountainous terrain. The park has four main tourist areas: Yosemite Valley, Glacier Point, Wawona/Mariposa Grove, and Tuolumne Meadows, and two minor areas, Hetch Hetchy Valley and Crane Flat. The regions are only an hour or two apart by car, so it's theoretically possible to stop at all of them, however briefly, in just one day. But then you would miss out on some of Yosemite's most spectacular moments that justify lingering longer, from walks beside the Merced River and its dew-drenched meadows while dawn breaks over Yosemite Valley, to watching the moon rise above the Sierra Nevada's jagged peaks as you sit on ancient rocks atop Glacier Point. Make more time to absorb the awesome experiences this singular wilderness offers. Stay overnight in a campground, at an in-park lodge or hotel, or in a gateway town (*see* the Where to Stay and Eat chapter).

Alpine scenery stretches along Tioga Road.

Yosemite and Sequoia / Kings Canyon National Parks

Water flowing through Yosemite Valley. (top left) Catching the view from Glacier Point. (bottom left) A deer wades through the Tuolumne River.

Planning Your Time

If you've come for a weekend, spend the first day exploring Yosemite Valley. Free yourself from the confines of your car by leaving it behind in a day-use parking lot. Ride the free shuttle bus from point to point, or, during warmer months, rent a bicycle to explore at your own pace. First, visit the Yosemite Valley Welcome Center in Yosemite Village. Then walk to the nearby museum and theater, and Ansel Adams Gallery, where you can see iconic black-and-white photography of the park's well-known landmarks. Afterward, ride out to view the valley's famous waterfalls, especially Yosemite Falls and Vernal Fall, the latter of which is near the family-friendly Happy Isles Art and Nature Center, where you learn about the park's unique ecology. Just before sunset, drive up to Glacier Point; you may wish to stay for the excellent stargazing.

On your second day, drive the scenic Tioga Road through the Sierra Nevada high country that John Muir and others worked so hard to preserve. The road is open only during summer, when you can relish sunny walks around Tuolumne Meadows and Tenaya Lake. Or, head south from the valley to Wawona, with its historical sites and the nearby Mariposa Grove of giant sequoias. Anyone with more time

(bottom) Fern-covered black rocks frame 317-foot-tall Vernal Fall; rainbows often play in the spray at its base.

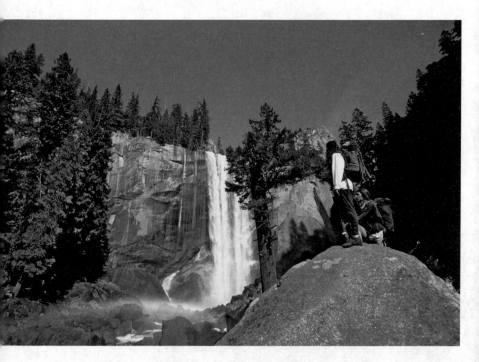

to spend in the park can tour at a more leisurely pace, taking time out for more day hikes to waterfalls, craggy granite formations, and photo-worthy viewpoints.

Things to Know

COVID-19

The COVID-19 pandemic shut down Yosemite National Park for several months in 2020 and resulted in many changes when the park reopened, including the temporary and intermittent closure of lodges, campgrounds, restaurants, pools, stores, shuttles, and tours in the valley. Before visiting, check the park website to determine operating status. Notices about the overall NPS response to COVID-19, including safety measures, are updated regularly on *www.nps.gov/coronavirus*.

YOSEMITE CAMPING RESERVATIONS

At one time, some of Yosemite's campgrounds were first-come, first-served, and you could get same-day camping reservations at the others. **As of 2022, advance reservations (*www.recreation.gov*) are required for all campgrounds. Do not come to Yosemite without a reservation if you intend to camp in the park.**

YOSEMITE DAY VISITS

In response to the pandemic, the park instituted a reservation system to limit the number of cars entering Yosemite between 6 am and 4 pm. Although this policy, which required day visitors to buy a pass ($35 per vehicle) via *www.recreation.gov*, was expected to continue indefinitely during peak season (mid-May through September), the park announced that it would be discontinued in the summer of 2023. In December of 2022, however, the park also announced that passes would be required for busy weekends in February 2023. **Before you travel, check the park website for the latest announcements about the day-pass reservation system.**

You do not need a day pass if you have reservations at an in-park campground, lodge, or vacation rental; you have a wilderness or Half Dome permit; or you enter the park using the local public transit system (YARTS) or on a tour with one of the local businesses that have commercial use authorizations (CUAs).

Rising more than 350 stories above Yosemite Valley, El Capitan (shown on both pages) is the largest exposed granite monolith in the world.

SIGHTS

YOSEMITE VALLEY

See the Yosemite Valley Floor map.

The wellspring of Yosemite National Park is the grand **Yosemite Valley** (elevation 4,000 feet). Ranchers, tourists, writers, and painters all began trickling into this idyllic valley after Native Americans were forced out in the mid-19th century. One early visitor, part of the Mariposa Battalion, described being moved to tears by the sight of the valley—a response that echoes over the centuries. Most of today's millions of annual visitors to Yosemite start by exploring the valley, that constant source of awe and wonder.

One way to see Yosemite Valley's key sights is by combining driving with walking—basically enjoying a scenic drive with several stops along the way. By car, there are a few ways to access the valley, but the southern approach provides the most thrills. In the park, Highway 41 becomes Wawona Road as it skirts north along the western edge of the Wawona region.

Once you've emerged from the almost mile-long **Wawona Tunnel**, which was bored through the mountainside by Civilian Conservation Corps (CCC) workers in the 1930s, pull over at ★**TUNNEL VIEW**. There awaits a framed postcard-perfect view of the entire Yosemite Valley. On your left stands mighty **El Capitan** (elevation 7,569 feet), an iconic formation that issues a siren's call to rock climbers. Rising more than 3,000 feet above the valley floor, it is the world's largest granite monolith. The curved tooth of **Half Dome** (elevation 8,836 feet) rises, also more than 3,000 feet, in the central background. And off to the right, Bridalveil Fall plunges off the cliffside into the valley below.

Though the crowds can be daunting, and the parking lots fill up at peak times, there's a reason everyone is snapping photos from the large viewing area; some of the most iconic images of the park have been captured here.

Be forewarned that a confusing system of one-way roads flows through the 7-mile-long valley. A free national-park map handed out to visitors at the entrance stations will help you navigate the spottily signposted roads. When in doubt, go with the flow. You'll rarely get lost for too long.

(opposite) Taking in the view of Yosemite Valley near Wawona Tunnel.

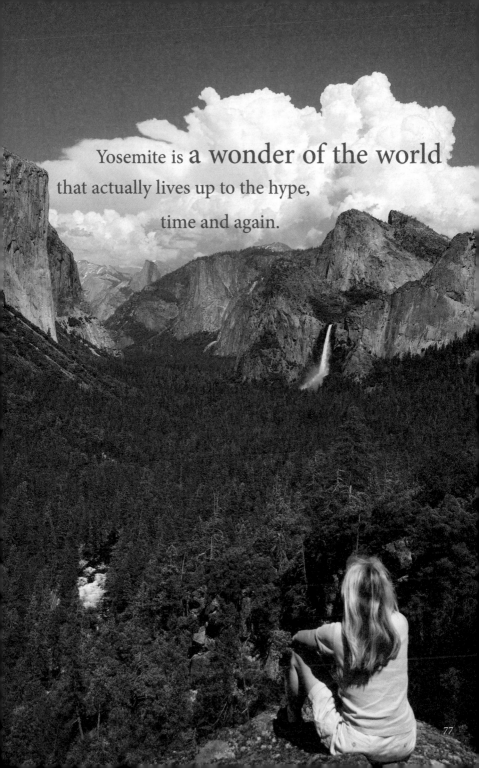

Yosemite is a wonder of the world that actually lives up to the hype, time and again.

Beyond Tunnel View, Wawona Road continues east deeper into the valley. Your next stop is **Bridalveil Fall**, a lacy waterfall that tumbles off the valley's steep cliffs for 620 feet. From the parking lot, you can walk to the waterfall on a ½ mile round-trip trail that ends with a climb up to the fall's base—if you're there during its peak flow, usually in May, be prepared to be sprayed. The trail to Bridalveil Fall is paved—except for the short climb at the end—so people in strollers and wheelchairs can experience this attraction as well (though it's an uphill trail, so it may still be a small challenge for those in nonmotorized wheelchairs). The fall flows year-round, though it may dry to barely a trickle in warmer months. In winter, icy conditions prevail, so the trail may be slippery.

Continue driving east on Wawona Road, which has now become Southside Drive (it switches en route between Tunnel View and here) past the twin **Cathedral Spires**, which jut skyward out of the valley's meadows off to the right. On the Merced River, which flows through the entire valley, **Cathedral Beach** on your left makes a good place to stop for a picnic and provides dead-on views of El Capitan, which towers above the treetops on the north side of the road. To the east of "El Cap," look for the **Three Brothers**, a trio of granite points more than 3,000 feet tall dominated by **Eagle Peak** (elevation 7,779 feet). Two more inviting picnic areas are found farther east along the river at **Sentinel Beach** and the **Swinging Bridge**. If you walk out into the middle of Swinging Bridge, you may glimpse Yosemite Falls on the opposite side of the valley.

YOSEMITE'S INDIAN WARS, NEW AND OLD

Yosemite Valley was first inhabited by Native American tribes, notably Southern Miwok people from the west side and Paiutes from the Mono Lake region to the east. Despite frequent battles (*Yosemite* is a Miwok word meaning "those who kill"), a rich cultural intermingling also took place between the tribes, resulting in intermarriage and a distinct set of religious rituals, political laws, and habits of everyday life. Descendants of both tribes continue to debate whose heritage is more closely linked to protecting Yosemite's vast parklands and fight for federal recognition accordingly.

At the time of initial contact with Europeans, Chief Tenaya led the mixed band of Native Americans living in Yosemite Valley. They called themselves the Ahwahneechee, or people of the Ahwahnee, which means "wide, gaping mouth," in reference to the valley. As the California gold rush began in 1848, miners invaded the Sierra Nevada, stirring up trouble with local tribes. In 1851, the state of California sent the Mariposa Battalion into Yosemite Valley to forcibly remove its indigenous peoples to a reservation outside Fresno. Chief Tenaya and his people were captured, and their village was burned. Today, a reconstructed tribal village with a short self-guided interpretive trail is set up behind the valley's Yosemite Museum.

Come in via Highway 41 and your first marvelous view in the valley is of Bridalveil Fall, a 620-foot filmy fall that is often diverted as much as 20 feet one way by the breeze.

The Mist Trail climbs
past the top of 317-foot
Vernal Fall. It flows
year-round but peaks in May.

The Merced River plunges out of the high country toward the eastern end of Yosemite Valley, creating 594-foot Nevada Fall.

Composed of three falls, Yosemite
Falls form the highest waterfall in
North America and the fifth-highest
in the world. The water from the top
descends 2,425 feet. When the falls
run hard, you can hear them thunder
across the valley.

The Yosemite Conservation Heritage Center, built in 1903–04 by the Sierra Club, is still in use as a library and educational center.

Southside Drive next passes the wooden **Yosemite Chapel** (*Southside Dr.; www.yosemitevalleychapel.org*), with its petite steeple stretching above the pine trees. A popular spot for weddings, the 1879 structure, the oldest in the park, is a serene spot to stop and reflect upon what John Muir described as nature's temple.

East of the chapel, the drive approaches a heavily trafficked intersection at the **Sentinel Bridge**. If you continue straight without crossing the Merced River, you'll find yourself on a one-way driving loop that takes you past the Housekeeping Camp and the unusual looking Tudor-style **Yosemite Conservation Heritage Center** (*formerly the LeConte Memorial Lodge; Southside Dr.; 209/372-4542; www.sierraclub.org*), a National Historic Landmark built of granite and wood. Operated by the nonprofit Sierra Club for more than a century, the lodge is open between May and September from 10 am until 4 pm Wednesday through Sunday. Family-friendly nature programs are offered throughout the day, with natural and cultural history presentations on some Fridays and Saturdays at 8 pm. Arrive early for evening presentations, as the lodge seats only 50.

Next, the one-way loop passes the "tent camp" ★CURRY VILLAGE (*Southside Dr.; 209/372–8333; www.travelyosemite. com*), a rustic family-friendly resort with canvas tents, cabins, and casual dining options started by an enterprising couple, David and Jenny Curry, in 1899. Back then at the village, "a good bed and clean napkin with every meal" cost just $2 a day. Today, Curry Village is a buzzing hub for outdoor activities in all four seasons. At its Mountain Shop, you can buy almost anything you need for an outdoor adventure, from clothing to all sorts of camping gear, climbing equipment, and dehydrated food.

Before looping around past the valley's main campgrounds—Upper Pines, North Pines, and Lower Pines—the one-way driving loop passes the **Happy Isles Art and Nature Center** (*Southside Dr.; 209/372–0631*), where, from April to October, kids can explore the valley's wildlife ecology and its forest, river wetlands, and granite talus environments through hands-on exhibits and interpretive trails. Bubbling brooks and streams bring their sounds to the air outside the center; it's a great place to sit on a cool boulder and simply breathe in the fresh air deeply.

The Mist Trail (*see* Best Day Hikes) climbs past the tops of 317-foot-tall **Vernal Fall** and 594-foot-tall **Nevada Fall**, from where daring hikers can continue to the summit of the park's most famous granite formation, **Half Dome,** perched high above the valley floor. The falls flow year-round but peak in May. From here the road continues looping around the valley past Happy Isles and the trailhead for the Mirror Lake hike before running into the Yosemite Village area.

AMONG THE LOVERS OF NATURE

"But no temple made with hands can compare with Yosemite. Every rock in its walls seems to glow with life. . . . Awful in stern, immovable majesty, how softly these rocks are adorned, and how fine and reassuring the company they keep: their feet among beautiful groves and meadows, their brows in the sky, a thousand flowers leaning confidingly against their feet, bathed in floods of water, floods of light, while the snow and waterfalls, the winds and avalanches and clouds shine and sing and wreathe about them as the years go by, and myriads of small winged creatures—birds, bees, butterflies—give glad animation and help to make all the air into music. Down through the middle of the Valley flows the crystal Merced, River of Mercy, peacefully quiet, reflecting lilies and trees and the onlooking rocks; things frail and fleeting and types of endurance meeting here and blending in countless forms, as if into this one mountain mansion Nature had gathered her choicest treasures, to draw her lovers into close and confiding communion with her."
—John Muir, *The Yosemite,* 1912.

In the village, the nonprofit **Yosemite Conservancy** (*209/379–2317; yosemite.org*) runs the worthwhile bookstore next to the impressive **Yosemite Valley Welcome Center** *(off Northside Dr.; 209/372–0200)*, where rangers orient visitors to the park's offerings. Stop by to peruse the exhibits for a quick overview of Yosemite's natural and cultural history, starting with its geological prehistory when glaciers that had slipped down from the uplifted Sierra Nevada and the Merced River worked together to carve this valley. The center's theater presents live performances and shows free films. The lineup of movies changes, but they usually deal with nature, history, and/or adrenaline-pumping pursuits in the park, such as rock climbing and mountaineering.

Beside the visitor center, the small **Yosemite Museum** *(off Northside Dr.; 209/372–0200)* focuses on park history, specifically the Native American cultures that once flourished here. Rotating exhibits on the native peoples who once lived here, the history of park tourism, and more are displayed in a building constructed from local rocks and trees, allowing it to blend into the landscape.

The Happy Isles Art and Nature Center is a great place to sit on a cool boulder and breathe the fresh air.

Demonstrations of native basket-weaving and flute-making techniques take place frequently. Behind the museum stands an interpretive reconstruction of what Yosemite Valley's Ahwahneechee village may have looked like in the mid-19th century, before it was destroyed by the Mariposa Battalion. A brochure available for a small fee describes a self-guided walking tour. Farther west across the street, you can stroll through the pioneer-era **Yosemite Cemetery**.

Just east of the museum is the **Ansel Adams Gallery** *(off Northside Dr.; 209/372–4413; www.anseladams.com)* and gift shop. Best known for his black-and-white photographs of the American West, Adams began visiting Yosemite Valley with his family in 1916, and he returned for many seasons to take photographs while trekking in the Sierra Nevadas. The gallery exhibits and sells both original Adams photographs and modern reproductions. The gallery also organizes

(top right) Earth Day in Yosemite Valley. (bottom right) A craft demonstration at the Yosemite Museum.

ANSEL ADAMS, AT HOME IN YOSEMITE

"I *knew* my destiny when I first experienced Yosemite," claimed Ansel Adams. One of the most revered photographers of the 20th century, Adams is inextricably linked with the Sierra Nevada, especially Yosemite National Park. He was Yosemite's most famous portrayer, and he worked tirelessly for its conservation.

Adams was born in San Francisco in 1902. His family lived by the Golden Gate beaches, so they were spared the worst of the Great Quake and fires of 1906. But during an aftershock, Adams fell and bashed his nose sideways, giving him his distinctive "earthquaked" profile.

His first trip to Yosemite was on a family vacation in 1916—and it was a momentous one. When he saw Bridalveil Fall for the first time, he realized that "a new era began." His parents gave him his first camera, a Kodak Box Brownie, and he started a visual diary of the landscape's wonders. For the rest of his life, Adams spent at least part of every year in Yosemite.

By 1919, Adams had joined the Sierra Club and was working for the group in Yosemite Valley. But he was also considering a career as a concert pianist, and in 1921 he began visiting an art and souvenir studio in the park to practice on its piano. There he met the owner's daughter, Virginia Best; they were married in the studio in 1928. (Years later, he and Virginia took over the space, selling special-edition prints and teaching photography workshops. Now the studio is the Ansel Adams Gallery.)

As the Sierra Club's photographer, Adams recorded a relatively pristine Yosemite throughout the late 1920s. One spring day in 1927, he set out to capture one of the park's most dramatic landmarks. During the climb to his vantage point, most of his glass plates were ruined. With just one plate left, he decided to use a red filter to retain the striking contrasts between light and shade. The result was his first iconic image: *Monolith, the Face of Half Dome*.

Monolith signaled a shift to a more personal, emotionally expressive photographic style. It also showed how Adams could use equipment and technique to realize an inner vision. Among photographers, Adams quickly became known for his technical brilliance and for sharing his innovations through writing and teaching. Meanwhile, his inspiring images of Yosemite and the Sierra Nevada sparked the American imagination.

These photos had a major material impact as well. In 1936, as one of the Sierra Club's board of directors, Adams went to Washington as the organization's representative. Lobbying to win Kings Canyon protection as a national park, he showed his photos to conservationist and Secretary of the Interior Harold L. Ickes, who in turn brought some of Adams's influential pictures to President Franklin Delano Roosevelt. In 1940, FDR signed the bill making Kings Canyon a national park.

For decades, Adams championed the importance of wilderness, the caretaking of national parks in general, and the protection of his beloved Yosemite. Although he wanted Yosemite, like other parks, to be accessible to the public, he fought against the "resortism" of concessionaires and other modern developments. He also contributed photos to *This Is the American Earth*, a Sierra Club book that became a classic of the conservation movement.

Although he photographed all over the country, Adams always considered Yosemite to be his spiritual home. His luminous black-and-white images have become enduring visions of the American West and the power of nature.

—Jennifer Paull

(opposite) Photographer Ansel Adams in 1943.

The Ansel Adams Gallery displays and sells original and reproduction prints and posters by Yosemite's most famous photographer.

photography workshops for visitors, and guided camera walks depart a few mornings a week (reservations required).

If you feel inspired to try your own hand at creating art during your sojourn in the park, the **Happy Isles Art and Nature Center** offers art classes and open studios several days a week from April through October in everything from landscape watercolor painting to pen-and-ink sketching. The center accepts reservations for some slots and reserves others for walk-ins. The center also sells art supplies if you didn't bring your own.

It's a short walk from the main Yosemite Village area to the **Yosemite Valley Lodge** *(Northside Dr.; 209/372-1274; www.travel yosemite.com)*, which offers an array of services, from bike rentals to a staffed tours-and-activities desk, in addition to a coffee shop, food court, restaurant and bar, and a gift shop. In summer, the outdoor amphitheater behind the lodge becomes the happening place, as rangers and naturalists lead frequent evening programs and occasionally screen nature-themed movies.

Although the lodge's early-20th-century buildings look bland, it's what you can view on the cliffside above that makes it worth a detour. At 2,425 feet high, the namesake **Yosemite Falls** comprises three waterfalls, with the Upper, Middle, and Lower Falls all bouncing off cliffs and plummeting into the valley below. If you hike the mile-long loop trail (which is partially paved for wheelchair access) to the base of the Lower Falls during the peak water flow in May, expect to get soaked. The trio of falls usually thunders from April through June, but typically runs dry between August and October. In winter, an ice cone forms at the base of the Upper Falls, presenting a unique opportunity for photographers. Farther west of the lodge is **Camp 4**, the famous campground that gets taken over by rock climbers every year. The trailhead for the hike to Upper Yosemite Falls (*see* Best Day Hikes) is nearby.

Before leaving the valley, take the side road east of Yosemite Village over to ★THE AHWAHNEE *(Ahwahnee Rd.; 209/372–1407; www.travelyosemite.com)*, now a National Historic Landmark. It was built in 1927 at the request of Stephen T. Mather, then the director of the NPS, who chose this site for its remarkable views, particularly of Half Dome. Unlike many of the rustic park lodges of its day, The Ahwahnee Hotel was not built of wood, which would make it vulnerable to fires, but instead of poured concrete that was treated to look like redwood. The interior design boldly mixes Native American, Arts and Crafts, and art-deco stylistic elements, but it's the sheer size of the public areas that impresses most. Peek inside the Mural Room, with its enormous wall painting of Yosemite's flora and fauna, then take a breather in the solarium while you contemplate Glacier Point, or just have a cocktail at one of the bar's outdoor tables, where you can watch Half Dome glow orange at sunset. Inside, in the Great Lounge, a fireplace blazes on chilly nights.

After backtracking to pick up your car from the day-use parking lot, join the westbound traffic leaving the valley via Northside Drive. You'll pass the Three Brothers trio of rock formations before reaching **El Capitan Meadow**, a favorite viewpoint for staring up at the vertical face of the meadow's eponymous monolith, which sets the standard for big-wall climbing.

On the east side of El Capitan Meadow, look for 1,000-foot-high **Horsetail Fall**, which usually flows from December

★ Souvenir Alert ★

Here's a place to flex your wallet. The Ahwahnee gift shop has an unmatched selection of artisan crafts, from wood carvings and Native American beadwork to fine-art nature photographs.

Laden with snow in winter and decked with color in the fall, oak trees stand guard at El Capitan Meadow; Middle Cathedral Rock hovers in the background.

In the latter half of February,
Horsetail Fall glows as
it reflects the setting sun . . .
it almost looks as if it has caught on fire.

Mist from Horsetail Fall blows over the east side of El Capitan.

At 1,612 feet, Ribbon Fall is the highest single fall in North America. The rainwater and melted snow that create the slender fall evaporate quickly at this height, making it the first of the valley waterfalls to dry up in summer.

through April. For a week or so in the latter half of February, the sun is at the right angle to illuminate the falls at sunset, so that it almost looks as if they have caught on fire. To the west of the meadow, the 1,612-feet-high **Ribbon Fall** peaks in May, but usually flows from March through June.

Driving west of El Capitan, pull over just short of the Pohono Bridge at the **Valley View** vista point for one last, lingering look at Yosemite Valley before reluctantly leaving it behind.

GLACIER POINT ROAD

See the Yosemite Valley Floor map.

Although Yosemite Valley is where visitors spend most of their time, taking the road to Glacier Point is also a must-do. Detouring here will give you an eagle-eye overview of the entire Yosemite Valley, plus gorgeous views of Half Dome, all from dizzying heights that you won't have to earn the hard way on hiking trails that are like steep granite stairways leading out of Yosemite Valley.

As you drive toward Glacier Point Road, keep a sharp eye out for the Chinquapin intersection. That is where you'll turn east to access Glacier Point Road. It climbs for 16 miles through pine and fir forests from Chinquapin to Glacier Point, winding past **Badger Pass Ski Area** (*see* Winter Sports); **McGurk, Summit, and Mono Meadows**, where wildflowers usually bloom in June; and **Bridalveil Creek Campground**, not too far from the trailhead for **Ostrander Lake**, where a rustic hut is open to experienced wilderness skiers and snowshoers in winter. Three miles before reaching Glacier Point, you find the trailhead for **Sentinel Dome**, one of the park's easiest hikes, taking you to the summit of this iconic granite formation (*see* Best Day Hikes). As you continue driving east on Glacier Point Road, you come to **Washburn Point**, which looks out at Half Dome as well as Nevada and Vernal falls. It's worth stopping for the view, because it's a different perspective than what you'll get at the road's end.

Finally, the road reaches its namesake destination, ★**GLACIER POINT** (elevation 7,214 feet), where you are rewarded with a stunning overlook of Yosemite Valley. To see it, you must pull into the parking lot and then take a short walk. Though the drive up is not bumper to bumper, you'll find that once you reach Glacier Point, the crowds are almost always thick during the day, as people tend to stay awhile. Also, as in Yosemite Valley, black bears are active

Glacier Point Road leads you to knockout views of Half Dome.

From **Glacier Point,**
the dead-on views of Half Dome
are unmatched by any other
roadside viewpoint in
Yosemite National Park.

in this area, so do not leave any food or scented items in your car. To discourage bear break-ins, either lock everything out of sight in the trunk or, better yet, use the food storage metal lockers provided around the lot.

From Glacier Point, the dead-on views of Half Dome are unmatched by any other roadside viewpoint in Yosemite National Park. It looks as if you could step right off the edge of the cliff and walk out onto the clouds and over to the dome. Also visible are Yosemite Falls tumbling into the valley below and many of the craggy peaks of the Sierra Nevada high country farther north toward Tioga Road and Tenaya Canyon, which appears to the left of the famous dome. The view from Glacier Point is so iconic that in 2005 it was commemorated on the California state quarter, which depicts John Muir standing atop the point and gazing at Half Dome, while incongruously a California condor flies overhead.

If the crowds are too crushing at Glacier Point, walk down the Panorama Trail to the right for about 20 minutes to have equally gorgeous vistas all to yourself. Look for the detour from the Panorama Trail about a half mile from Glacier Point, after you cross the bridge. Along the trail, watch for black bears foraging in the forest and ripping up fallen logs to uncover tasty insects beneath the bark. Observe wild bears from a distance and remember never to feed them. If you're feeling hungry yourself, walk back toward Glacier Point, where there is a snack bar and gift shop.

WAWONA

See the Wawona and Mariposa Grove map.

About an hour's drive south of Yosemite Valley is the remarkably peaceful enclave of Wawona (elevation 4,000 feet). Far less crowded than the valley, Wawona is steeped in the early pioneer history of the Sierra Nevada, and stopping here feels like walking backward in time.

Wawona offers a variety of outdoor activities, from forested and waterfall hikes, horseback rides, and swimming holes to, surprisingly, tennis and even golf. In winter, snowshoeing and cross-country skiing among the giant sequoia trees are hardy adventures for those with wilderness experience.

Just 5 miles north of the park's South Entrance Station, Wawona is a hub of vital visitor services, including an old-fashioned hotel with a restaurant, a gas station, a gift and sundries shop, a post office and an interpretive center for Mariposa Grove. A short distance down Chilnualna Falls Road, east of Highway 41, are a campground reservation office, a public library, a small market, and a cluster of private vacation-house rentals.

It is believed that the Wawona Road follows the same path taken by the Mariposa Battalion in 1851, when they ousted Native Americans from Yosemite Valley. The road, which became a stagecoach route for tourists in the 1870s, was paved over by CCC workers during the Great Depression. By that time, what had been merely a stagecoach stop run by pioneer

THE FIREFALL

Now discontinued, the old tradition of the Yosemite firefall dates from the late 19th century. An Irishman named James McCauley constructed a 4-mile-long trail from Yosemite Valley to Glacier Point, which hikers paid a toll to use. Soon McCauley also built the Mountain House hotel atop the point. According to legend, one night McCauley shoved a campfire right over the edge of the cliff, some say to entertain his guests while others say out of frustration over lack of tourist business. Whatever the motivation, the firefall became a much-anticipated ritual, occurring whenever enough people were willing to pay for it.

At first, McCauley charged tourists $1.50 to watch the spectacle. When he'd gathered enough interested viewers, he'd send his sons up the steep trail to Glacier Point from the valley below on pack animals to carry out the firefall.

In the early 20th century David Curry, the cofounder of Yosemite's Camp Curry, turned the firefall into a nightly event to attract more business. Crowds would gather in Camp Curry to hear the echoing yell "Let the fire fall!" shouted by those standing atop Glacier Point. During World War II, the firefall was suspended when the U.S. military assumed control of areas of the park. By the time the National Park Service stopped the firefall in 1968, due to its destruction of natural resources, uncountable visitors had witnessed the sight of thousands of sparks floating over the cliff.

WAWONA AND MARIPOSA GROVE

0 _____ 1 Miles
0 _____ 1.5 Kilometers

YOSEMITE

NATIONAL

PARK

Chilnualna Falls

▲ *Wawona Dome*

Wawona Campground

Chilnualna Falls Rd.

Pioneer Yosemite
History Center

Wawona Rd.

Ranger Station

Wawona Hotel

Wawona Visitor Center
at Hill's Studio

Wawona
Golf Course

Wawona

**Wawona
Meadow**

Meadow Circle Rd.

41

Chowchilla Mountain Rd.

Wawona Point
(8,810 ft.)

Galen Clark's
Cabin

Clothespin
Tree

California
Tunnel Tree

**Mariposa
Grove**

Grizzly
Giant

South Entrance

Mariposa
Grove
Welcome
Plaza

Mariposa Grove Rd.

Fallen Monarch

Summerdale
Campground

41

N
W   E
S

Forest Dr.

Yosemite Mountain Ranch Rd.

Fish Camp

To
Fresno ↓

Jackson Rd.

Galen Clark, appointed guardian of the Yosemite Grant from 1866 through 1889, had become a popular mountain resort visited by such dignitaries as U.S. presidents Ulysses S. Grant and Theodore Roosevelt. The name of the place had also been changed, from Clark's Station to Big Trees Station, referring to the nearby Mariposa Grove of giant sequoias. Later it became Wawona, which an early hotelier's wife believed meant "Big Trees" in a local indigenous dialect.

Guests today can unwind on the verandas and manicured lawns of the **Wawona Hotel** *(Forest Dr.; 209/375-6556; www.travel yosemite.com)*, a National Historic Landmark dating from 1879. The Victorian-era hotel where Grant and Roosevelt once stayed is a genteel getaway and a convenient enough base for exploring the park. Sipping a cocktail on the hotel's front porch or sitting in an Adirondack chair on the front lawn, you can gaze across the highway at **Wawona Meadow**, once used as a landing field for airplanes and now the site of a golf course that dates from 1918, making these the oldest greens in the Sierra Nevada. For some old-fashioned fun, stop by the hotel lobby any evening for cocktails and, most Tuesdays through Saturdays 5:30 to 9:30, a performance by longtime resident pianist Tom Bopp.

Adjacent to the hotel is the **Wawona Visitor Center at Hill's Studio** *(Forest Dr.; 209/375-9531)*, where you can get oriented to the park and check schedules of free ranger-guided programs and activities, including morning and twilight strolls and presentations on natural and cultural history at the Wawona Campground Amphitheater. The center stands inside the historic studio once

Built in 1879, the Wawona Hotel is an example of Victorian resort architecture.

occupied by late-19th-century landscape painter Thomas Hill, who worked alongside Hudson River School artists before moving to California, where he became closely acquainted with John Muir and photographer Carleton E. Watkins. Today, the center has a small collection of Hill's work.

Inspect the yesteryear trappings of the **Pioneer Yosemite History Center** *(Chilnualna Falls Rd.; 209/372–0200)*, which lies a short walk north of the hotel across a covered bridge that has been restored using hand-hewed timbers and 19th-century woodworking techniques. The history center is an amalgamation of buildings from different eras of the park's development, all of which were moved here during the 1950s and '60s. Included are a Wells Fargo office, once used by tourists to send telegrams and make phone calls out of the valley, and Degnan's Bakery, which supplied the valley with fresh-baked goods in the late 19th century. A highlight is a collection of historic conveyances that used to travel to Yosemite, from rough-hewn farm conveyances to plush upholstered passenger wagons. On summer weekend afternoons, park interpreters dressed in period costumes give blacksmithing demonstrations.

WAWONA VISITOR CENTER AT HILL'S STUDIO

TELEPHONE: 209/375–9531

ADDRESS: Forest Drive

Back on the south side of the river near the bridge is the historic Grey Barn, where stagecoaches were repaired and horses rested before making the eight-hour overland journey from Wawona to Yosemite Valley. The horse-drawn stage service was discontinued in 1914, when automobiles began flooding the valley. On summer weekends, you can try a short but bone-rattling ride on a horse-drawn stagecoach here for a small fee.

What brings most day visitors to the Wawona area of the park is the chance to wander among the giant sequoias of the monumental ★**MARIPOSA GROVE**, the largest of the park's three giant-sequoia groves (the other two are near Crane Flat). Standing beside one of these towering trees is an awe-inducing experience, especially early in the morning when dew is still glistening or at sunset as the changing colors of the sky create a painterly background to the trees' massive trunks. A major restoration project completed in 2018 improved access to the grove while taking steps to preserve the magnificent trees. Park at the Mariposa Grove Welcome Plaza, near the south entrance to the park, and take a shuttle to the arrival area. From there, a trail leads moderately uphill for three-quarters of a mile to the **California Tunnel Tree**, a still-living sequoia you can walk through—once upon a time carriages even passed through it.

(opposite) In Mariposa Grove, the Grizzly Giant stands 209 feet tall.

Numbered among the other famous giants in the grove are the **Wawona Tunnel Tree**, which toppled onto its side in the winter of 1968–69; the **Clothespin Tree**, which looks exactly as its name suggests, due to its hollowed-out trunk; and the **Grizzly Giant**, the largest giant sequoia tree in the grove, which scientists estimate to be almost 1,800 years old.

If you push onward and upward for another few miles, you'll reach **Wawona Point** (elevation 6,810 feet), from where you can peer

Standing beside one of these towering trees is an awe-inducing experience, especially at sunset as the changing colors of the sky create a painterly background to the trees' massive trunks.

out over thick forests, parted by the meandering south fork of the Merced River and the polished top of Wawona Dome (elevation 6,903 feet) to Wawona Meadow and its golf course.

CRANE AND BIG OAK FLATS

See the North Yosemite and Hetch Hetchy map.

Heading northwest from Yosemite Valley, Big Oak Flat Road leaves the canyon of the Merced River as it climbs uphill through the thick forest toward the busy **Crane Flat** intersection: although not a point of interest, Crane Flat is a crossroads for visitors driving between Yosemite Valley and the high country. If you need to refuel, Crane Flat has a small store and a service station with 24-hour gas pumps open year-round (you'll need a credit or debit card to buy gas after hours). Turning right at this intersection steers you onto Tioga Road (Highway 120), usually open from June through October, to reach White Wolf and Tuolumne Meadows (*see* the following section), eventually coasting by Tioga Pass (elevation 9,943 feet) over to the east side of the Sierra Nevada and otherworldly Mono Lake.

If you have some spare time and a desire to go hiking among more groves of giant sequoias, you can continue straight ahead on Big Oak Flat Road (Highway 120) to reach the trailhead for mercifully uncrowded **Merced Grove**. It's a moderate 3-mile round-trip hike to this petite grove surrounding a rustic cabin. Alternatively, from the Crane Flat intersection, you can drive east toward Tioga Pass for about a mile before pulling off into the parking lot for the more

A FEAST OF TREES

"And here let me renew my tribute to the marvelous bounty and beauty of the forests of this whole mountain region. The Sierra Nevadas lack the glorious glaciers, the frequent rains, the rich verdure, the abundant cataracts of the Alps; but they far surpass them—they surpass any other mountains I ever saw—in the wealth and grace of their trees. Look down from almost any of their peaks, and your range of vision is filled, bounded, satisfied, by what might be termed a tempest-tossed sea of evergreens, filling every upland valley, covering every hillside, crowning every peak but the highest, with their unfading luxuriance. . . . Steep mountain-sides, allowing them to grow, rank above rank, without obstructing each other's sunshine, seem peculiarly favorable to the production of these serviceable giants. . . . Their extremities gracefully bent down by the weight of winter snows, making them. . . the most beautiful trees on earth. . . I never before enjoyed such a tree-feast as on this wearing, difficult ride."

—Horace Greeley, *An Overland Journey from New York to San Francisco in the Summer of 1859.*

(above) Tuolumne Meadows.

heavily used trail to **Tuolumne Grove**, which follows Old Big Oak Flat Road (closed to vehicular traffic but open to cyclists and pedestrians). It's a moderate downhill 1-mile walk to the Tuolumne Grove, where few can resist the chance to walk through the "Dead Giant," a tunneled-out stump that seems almost as big as a house. Because both of these giant-sequoia groves are less visited than the Mariposa Grove near Wawona, they offer a more serene experience of the giant trees.

From the Merced Grove trailhead parking lot, Big Oak Flat Road (Highway 120) continues northwest to the park's **Big Oak Flat Entrance Station**, which has a small visitor center, open May to October. If you want to visit the Hetch Hetchy area, you should exit the park here.

TIOGA ROAD AND TUOLUMNE MEADOWS

See the North Yosemite and Hetch Hetchy map.

Driving north of Yosemite Valley along the curvy ★**TIOGA ROAD** is like riding on the rooftop of the planet. Riding so high among the jagged peaks of the Sierra Nevada feels otherworldly, and around almost every twist and turn in the road lies another jaw-dropping viewpoint or a gentle trailhead issuing a siren's call. Most people visit during July and August, when alpine wildflowers bloom at Tuolumne Meadows and paddlers and brave swimmers rush to the shores of cool Tenaya Lake.

Unless the most recent winter has been unusually harsh, vehicle traffic is allowed on the Tioga Road (Highway 120) east of Crane Flat between June and October, with most visitor services staying open from late June until early September. It's a 46-mile trip from the Crane Flat intersection with Big Oak Flat Road east to the Tioga Pass, where cars are usually lined up at the park's eastern entrance station. In winter, cross-country skiers and snowshoers may attempt to traverse sections of Tioga Road.

Realigned and paved over in 1961, the Tioga Road follows an old Native American traders' trail and later the Great Sierra Wagon Road, which was built in 1882 to service a short-lived mining district near Tioga Pass. Today, you can still follow sections of the old wagon road; for example, east of White Wolf on the way south to Yosemite Creek Campground or from Tioga Road north to the May Lake trailhead, west of Olmsted Point. The modern highway is more a pleasure, however, simply for its epic scenery, and there are plenty

A drive up Tioga Road (Highway 120) to the high country will reward you with gorgeous scenery, including crystal-blue lakes and high alpine peaks.

NORTH YOSEMITE
AND HETCH HETCHY

0   5 Miles
0   5 Kilometers

Twin Lakes

eye Pass

SAWTOOTH RIDGE

Slide Mountain

Burro Pass

Matterhorn Peak

Whorl Mountain

Virginia Peak

Virginia Pass

Green Lake

HUMBOLDT-TOIYABE
NATIONAL FOREST

To Bridgeport

167

Benson Pass

Peak
8 ft.

McCabe Lakes

North Peak

Saddlebag Lake

Lundy Lake

167

Mono Lake

INYO
NATIONAL
FOREST

395

Mono Basin
Scenic Area
Visitor Center

Lee Vining

120

Mono Lake Tufa
State Reserve

To
Mammoth Lakes
and Bishop

White Mountain

Ragged Peak

Parsons Memorial Lodge

Glen Aulin

Tuolumne Meadows
Wilderness Center

Dog Lake Trailhead

Pothole Dome

Soda Springs
Lembert Dome

Gaylor Peak

Bennettsville
Tioga Pass Entrance

Mt. Dana

Dana Meadows

Mt. Gibbs
12,764 ft.

Pacific Crest Trail

COLD CANYON

MATTERHORN CANYON

VIRGINIA CANYON

RS CANYON

UMNE RIVER

Tuolumne River

TUOLUMNE MEADOWS

Fairview Dome

Medlicott Dome

Cathedral Peak

Unicorn Peak

Echo Peaks

Johnson Peak

Tuolumne Meadows
Visitor Center

Mammoth Peak

Mono Pass
10,604 ft.

Parker Pass

Koip Peak
12,962 ft.

Tioga Road

Cathedral Lakes

Tresidder Peak

Tenaya Lake

John Muir Trail

CATHEDRAL RANGE

Sunrise

Vogelsang

KUNA CREST

LYELL CANYON

KOIP CREST

Donohue Peak
12,023 ft.

Donohue Pass

Pacific Crest Trail and John Muir Trail

Merced Lake

Merced Lake

Mt. Lyell
13,114 ft.

Mt. Florence

158

N

W   E

S

Legend

- Ranger / Information
- Food Service
- Picnic Area
- Lodging
- Campground
- Gas Station
- P Parking Area
- ⋯ John Muir Trail / Pacific Crest Trail
- ⋯ Other Trails

of panoramic viewpoints along the way. The road is also a major point of departure into the wilderness for hikers, backpackers, rock climbers, and equestrians. Before setting out along the Tioga Road, be sure to fill up your gas tank at Crane Flat, because the next gas station doesn't appear until Tuolumne Meadows, almost 40 miles away across the mountains.

East of Crane Flat, the thickly forested road ascends a ridge that divides the basins of the Tuolumne and Merced rivers. Once you rise above 7,000 feet in elevation (markers note this along the road), look for towering stands of red fir trees, which are conifers with blue-green, needlelike leaves. Evergreens like these are commonly sought after as Christmas trees. As the 1940s-era *Yosemite Road Guide* dryly notes, these national-park specimens "are not, of course, available for home use."

Next, petite **Siesta Lake** appears on the south side of the road, where the shoreline is bordered by stalky green rushes in summer and golden ferns in autumn. About 15 miles east of Crane Flat is a turnoff for the short side road north to **White Wolf**, which has a campground and a lodge with canvas tents, wooden cabins, and a dining room that's open during the summer season (*see* the Where to Stay and Eat chapter). Despite the area's name, wolves are not found in Yosemite (although visitors commonly mistake the coyotes that are frequently spotted in the park for wolves).

Continuing eastward, the road climbs through windy forests of western juniper and quaking aspen trees. As the road curves around past Porcupine Flat Campground, the often snow-covered summit of **Mt. Hoffmann** (elevation 10,850 feet), where John Muir once rambled, comes into view. So does iconic Half Dome, overshadowing the Yosemite Valley far below. If you take the 2-mile side road north toward **May Lake**, a moderate 2.4-mile hike brings you to the pretty alpine lake itself, backed by massive Mt. Hoffmann. It's an ideal spot for a picnic, with the shores often lined with wildflowers and patchy snow, even in July.

Although the literally breathtaking Tioga Road is full of classic Sierra Nevada high-country scenery, the best roadside viewpoint along Highway 120 is ★OLMSTED POINT. From here you can gaze out at Little Yosemite Valley below Half Dome and peer into the rugged canyon of Tenaya Creek. From the parking lot, it's a short walk down to the point itself. Interpretive signs examine the distinctive geology of the Yosemite region, from places that show evidence of glacial polish (where glaciers once carried pebbles across the surfaces of rocks, making them smoothed or grooved) to the weathering process of exfoliation, in which massive granite domes like Yosemite's Half Dome and North Dome slough off their concentric outer layers, much like a peeling onion. Just to the east is **Clouds Rest Vista Point**, which also frames views of Half Dome.

A couple of miles farther east, the Tioga Road hugs the shoreline of majestically beautiful **Tenaya Lake** (elevation 8,149 feet). Named for Chief Tenaya, the leader of the Native American band living in the Yosemite Valley who was captured by the Mariposa Battalion in 1851, this is the largest natural lake in all of Yosemite National Park. Its beautiful basin was carved by glaciers, and its waters, which reflect the clouds and the craggy peaks all around, are clear enough that you can see the rounded granite rocks on the lake bottom. Small ice floes may partially cover the lake's surface in early summer, while later in the season, mosquitoes swarm picnickers who follow the hiking path around to the west end of the lake.

All the beauty that you've witnessed so far still does not prepare you for arriving at ★TUOLUMNE MEADOWS (elevation 8,600 feet). Called "the most . . . delightful high pleasure-ground I have yet seen," by John Muir after his first summer in the Sierra Nevada, Tuolumne Meadows is especially magical after the mountain snowpack melts in early summer, when a watercolorist's palette of alpine wildflowers is in bloom and deep-blue lakes draw day-trippers. Unlike the Yosemite Valley, where the spiring walls of granite can evoke claustrophobic feelings, here the Sierra Nevada high country

Tuolumne Meadows is especially magical after the mountain snowpack melts in early summer, when a watercolorist's palette of alpine wildflowers is in bloom.

Tuolumne Meadows is
the Sierra Nevada's largest
subalpine meadow.

is a lush, wide-open meadow fed by the Tuolumne River and several streams. It's so idyllic that all you want to do is just lie on your back in the tall grasses, inhaling the pine-scented fresh mountain air and soaking up the brilliant high-altitude sunshine.

Tuolumne Meadows has limited visitor services, including a post office, a small market, a lodge with canvas-tent cabins, a restaurant, and a fast-food grill. Park your car in one of the day-use lots, then hop on the free Tuolumne Meadows shuttle, which loops around the meadows area and over to Olmsted Point and Tenaya Lake, usually operating from mid-June through mid-September. At the **Tuolumne Meadows Visitor Center** *(Tioga Rd.; 209/372–0263)*, have your questions answered and learn about glacial geology and the delicate ecology of these meadowlands, which come alive during the high country's all-too-brief summer season. You can buy maps and self-guided interpretive trail brochures here or at the **Tuolumne Meadows Wilderness Center**, farther east on Tioga Road, near the Tuolumne Meadows Lodge.

TUOLUMNE
MEADOWS
VISITOR CENTER

TELEPHONE:
209/372–0263

ADDRESS:
Tioga Rd.

To truly experience the wonder of the meadows, you must explore them without a car. Opposite the visitor center, a short interpretive trail leads across the biggest meadow to **Soda Springs**, named for the naturally carbonated water that bubbles up out of the ground here to form reddish pools that look almost as if they were colored by volcanic cinders. Nearby the springs, which are not safe to drink from, the **Parsons Memorial Lodge** has diverting exhibits about the human history of the Tuolumne Meadows, including when Native American tribes roamed here and the days when John Muir and Robert Underwood Johnson, then-editor of the influential *Century* magazine, plotted out their campaign to protect these meadows as national parklands. The lodge itself was built of granite stone in 1915; for many decades it was a meeting place for the environmental organization Muir founded, the Sierra Club.

Several well-marked trails thread through the valley floor along the meadow. We've mentioned the most important ones here. You can't freely roam around the meadows themselves—they are too fragile! So be sure to stay on the trails.

At the west end of the main meadow, a short scramble up **Pothole Dome** will reward you with expansive views over the entire Tuolumne Meadows area. It's especially photo-worthy when the sun sinks over the surrounding peaks, which sometimes blush with alpenglow. At the east end of the main meadow, a more difficult hike

MONO LAKE

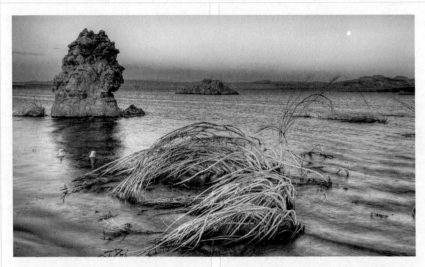

East of Tioga Pass, Highway 120 dramatically descends through a forested canyon to the town of Lee Vining on the shores of Mono Lake, which straddles the transition zone between the Sierra Nevada and the Great Basin Desert. The most fascinating thing about the lake is its towering tufa formations, made up of odd spires and knobs of calcium carbonate formed when freshwater springs bubbled up to mix with the alkaline lake water. The tufa look almost like undersea coral castles with their towers poking above the shimmering surface of the lake.

Mono Lake was once threatened with extinction by dropping water levels and increased salinity after the city of Los Angeles diverted most of the water out of Mono Basin. But today, environmental restoration efforts are successfully under way. These efforts include regrowing riparian forests,

raising the waters of the lake to a healthy level, and clearing invasive vegetation that blocks tributary streams. That's especially good news for more than 100 species of birds who depend upon the lake as a breeding ground and migratory stopover.

Off U.S. Highway 395, you can walk, canoe, or kayak alongside the alien-looking tufa towers at **Mono Lake Tufa State Reserve**, where interpretive tours are offered three times a day from late June to Labor Day. Birding walks depart Friday and Sunday mornings mid-May to Labor Day. North of Lee Vining, the **Mono Basin Scenic Area Visitor Center** *(off U.S. Hwy. 395; 760/647-3044)*, open Friday through Sunday, offers beautiful views of the lake—including white Paoha Island and black Negit Island—along with interesting natural-history exhibits.

ascends **Lembert Dome**, from where you can glimpse the mammoth Sierra Crest poised to the east and the Cathedral Range stretching to the south. The dome is named after John Baptist Lembert, an eccentric pioneer homesteader, butterfly collector, and goat herder who resided here until winter storms drove him out at the same time Yosemite National Park was created in 1890. The dome's summit hike is 2.8 miles round-trip starting from the Dog Lake trailhead, across Tioga Road from the lodge.

Leaving Tuolumne Meadows, Tioga Road heads east for 7 more miles to **Tioga Pass** (elevation 9,945 feet). Along the way it passes forests of lodgepole pine trees and lush **Dana Meadows**, the origin point for the Tuolumne Glacier that flowed westward from here as an ancient river of ice. To the east of the highway, the signature peaks of 13,061-foot-high **Mt. Dana** and 12,773-foot-high **Mt. Gibbs** dominate the horizon. Near Tioga Pass, a gravel side road leads north to the mining ghost town of **Bennettsville**, which spurred construction of the original Tioga Pass road in the late 19th century. There you can wander around the atmospheric town ruins, including some rustic wooden cabins that have withstood more than a century's worth of harsh mountain winters.

Hetch Hetchy

See the North Yosemite and Hetch Hetchy map.

Although John Muir won the war to protect the high country of Yosemite National Park in 1890, he lost the battle to save Hetch Hetchy in 1913, when Congress authorized construction of a dam on the Tuolumne River. Once the O'Shaughnessy Dam was completed in 1923, the resulting reservoir flooded Hetch Hetchy, which Muir described as "one of nature's rarest and most precious mountain temples."

The name Hetch Hetchy comes from a Miwok word for a type of food that once grew in the valley and that Native Americans used to harvest when camping there. Although not quite as grand as the Yosemite Valley, Hetch Hetchy is still a beautiful glacier-carved valley that some environmentalists would like to see restored to its natural state. The dam is still in operation. It supplies water and power to the city of San Francisco and the surrounding Bay Area.

A couple of miles west of the Big Oak Flat Entrance Station on Highway 120, you can turn right onto Evergreen Road, then drive through the thick forest north to Hetch Hetchy Road, which leads east toward the dam. For security reasons, all incoming traffic is required to stop at the **Hetch Hetchy Entrance Station**, where the ranger will take down your license plate number when you pick up a day-use permit and parking pass. The entrance is open daily 7 am to 9 pm from May to Labor Day, with reduced hours (corresponding roughly to daylight hours) the rest of the year.

The paved drive winds for about 8 miles from the entrance station northeast to the **O'Shaughnessy Dam**. Along the way you'll see evidence of the 2013 Rim Fire, one of the most devastating forest fires in California history. Although 20th-century preservationists could not prevent the dam from being built, similar campaigns to prevent dams in California's Kings Canyon, as well as the Grand Canyon in Arizona, did succeed, in part because of the dramatic example set by Hetch Hetchy. You can park off the road above the dam, then walk back downhill and out onto the top of the dam

The controversial Hetch Hetchy Reservoir supplies water and power to San Francisco. According to the Department of Water Resources, to take the dam down now would cost billions of dollars.

itself, where interpretive signs tell about this controversial project that drowned the valley's once-healthy meadows and drastically changed its ecosystem. Like a watery finger pointing toward the east, the **Hetch Hetchy Reservoir** accounts for about 85% of San Francisco's total reservoir-based water supply.

Rising above the north shore of the reservoir is **Hetch Hetchy Dome** (elevation 6,173 feet). Facing off against it on the south shore is **Kolana Rock** (elevation 5,772 feet), an often-photographed granite formation easily recognized by its pyramidal shape. Tumbling off the cliffs on the north side of the reservoir, just west of Hetch Hetchy

Dome, is the triple cascade of ★WAPAMA FALLS (elevation 1,400 feet), which flows year-round but peaks in May.

After walking across the top of the dam to its far side, hikers can continue through an eerie tunnel and onto a moderate 5-mile round-trip trail leading along the north shore past slim **Tueeulala Falls**, which appears only in spring, and beyond to the imposing base of Wapama Falls, where the footbridges crossing Falls Creek may be dramatically cut off by rushing water in spring. If the footbridges are passable, it's another challenging 4.2 miles each way to **Rancheria Falls**, a pretty collection of cascades that flow through a narrow canyon and is best viewed in spring.

⊶ BEST DAY HIKES

For day hikers, the wealth of trails inside Yosemite National Park ranges from easy nature walks around the valley floor to steep descents from Glacier Point past rushing waterfalls to excursions off Tioga Road and from Tuolumne Meadows into the Sierra Nevada high country, blessed with alpine lakes and meadows where wildflowers bloom. The best of these are detailed *below*. (For forested hikes to giant sequoia groves in the Crane Flat and Big Oak Flat areas, *see* that section of Sights.)

Check current schedules of ranger-guided hikes in the free park newspaper *Yosemite Guide* or at the main visitor centers in Yosemite Valley and Tuolumne Meadows, where you also can buy hiking maps and self-guided interpretive trail brochures.

Poppies and Indian paintbrush.

Yosemite Valley

As the most visited part of the park, Yosemite Valley has all sorts of trailheads for day hikers and nature walkers. Most popular in late spring and early summer are easy, short strolls to waterfall viewpoints in the area. The gentle **Valley Loop Trail** stops at scenic bridges overlooking the Merced River and wanders beside lush meadows and forests, providing great views of Bridalveil Fall and Yosemite Falls. You can do as much or as little of the 13-mile loop trail as you feel like walking, a refreshing alternative to driving in heavy traffic. Even just a ½-mile walk makes for a relaxing amble.

Catching a view of Yosemite Falls
while hiking in Leidig Meadow.

You'll walk through rainbows when you visit Vernal Fall.

Hikers on the John Muir Trail trek near Vernal Fall at Clark Point, with views of Glacier Point and Yosemite Valley. Right: Taking a break in Long Meadow.

Another easy walk in the Yosemite Valley is the paved 2-mile round-trip trail out to tiny **Mirror Lake**, which fills up in spring and early summer, when it occasionally reflects the peaked cliffs above, including Half Dome. The rest of the year, the lake is more of a meadow alongside Tenaya Creek, which the trail follows for a good distance. You can extend this hike into a moderate 5-mile loop around the lake and into Tenaya Canyon for wildlife watching.

It's the grandeur of Yosemite Valley that inspires even the most casual tourists to attempt more hiking than they've ever done before in their lives. The steep switchbacks required to climb out of the valley don't seem to deter anyone, either. Starting at Happy Isles, the **Mist Trail** climbs steeply upward for 1½ miles via a granite staircase of more than 600 steps to the top of ★**VERNAL FALL,** then continues another 2 miles to the brink of ★**NEVADA FALL.** The trail can be treacherous during late spring, when you should expect to get drenched by spray from the thunderous waterfalls.

A route to the falls that is longer but with a more gradual slope follows the **John Muir Trail**, also starting from Happy Isles. Hardy hikers tackle the **Upper Yosemite Falls Trail**, starting near Camp 4. It's a strenuous, 3.6-mile climb to the top of the falls. Many people hike just the first 1.5 miles of the trail to Columbia Rock, which affords gorgeous views of the entire valley.

HALF DOME: A SURVIVAL GUIDE

Hiking up Half Dome is thrilling—there's good reason it's considered a once-in-a-lifetime adventure—but it should never be undertaken lightly. It's not appropriate for anyone with a fear of heights or who isn't in top physical shape. Fatal accidents have occurred along this trail, so it's vital to take every precaution.

First, you'll have to acquire a coveted Half Dome permit. For the past few years, hopefuls have been instructed to submit an application to the lottery between March 1 and March 31 specifying their preferred dates for the upcoming season. Those who were unsuccessful or didn't plan in advance could apply to the daily lottery two days before their planned climb for a shot at a limited number of last-minute permits. The system, however, is subject to change, so visit *www.recreation.gov* or call *209/372-0200* well in advance of your visit.

Next, consider your clothing and gear. Hiking boots with excellent treads and gloves with good grips are essential. A rock-climbing harness with carabiners to attach yourself to the cables is also a good idea. Wearing sunglasses and a hat will help cut down on the glare of the sun on the rocks. Bring plenty of water, too.

Before your journey begins, get a good night's rest and arise early. Some attempt this as part of an overnight trek on the John

Muir Trail (*see* Backpacking, *p. 144*), but day hikers who want to ascend this most famous of all Yosemite's venerable domes should start out at sunrise or earlier. There are two paths to follow: either the 14-mile round-trip Mist Trail or the 16.4-mile round-trip John Muir Trail. Either route brings you to the 400-foot-long final leg of the ascent of Half Dome, which is accomplished only by cables bolted into the rock—this is where those carabiners come in handy.

In addition to a hiker's skill and stamina, the conditions of the trail and weather need to be taken into account. Like any granite dome, Half Dome should never be climbed when a thunderstorm is approaching or when the trail, rock, and cables are slick with recent rainfall. If you feel static electricity in the air or see lightning, get back down below the tree line immediately. The cables are up only from roughly late May through early October, depending on conditions, outside of which you should not attempt it.

Once you finally reach the top, you'll suddenly realize why this is considered the ultimate Yosemite day hike. The challenges of the summit fade with the heart-stopping payoff, standing atop this Sierra Nevada icon and gazing with eagles' eyes into nature's treasure box—meandering streams, meadows, and characterful spires—in the valley below.

GLACIER POINT ROAD

Starting from Glacier Point, the classic **Four-Mile Trail** (which is actually about 4.8 miles one way) follows steep switchbacks down into the valley, with dramatic views along the way that repay all of your knee-trembling efforts. Even more challenging is the 8.5-mile **Panorama Trail**, which visits lacy Illilouette Fall before descending along the **Mist Trail** (*see* the previous section) past Nevada Fall and Vernal Fall from Glacier Point. Both of these one-way hikes require first parking in the valley, then catching the tour bus up to Glacier Point.

A few miles west of Glacier Point are the signposted trailheads for **Sentinel Dome** and **Taft Point**. Each destination is a moderate 2.2-mile round-trip hike from Glacier Point Road, and the trails are usually not very crowded. The summit of Sentinel Dome (elevation 8,122 feet) gives 360-degree views of the valley that are even more sweeping than from Glacier Point. Here you'll find a Jeffrey pine that was made famous by an iconic 1940 Ansel Adams photograph. (Killed by drought in 1977, the tree toppled in 2003.) For more vertigo-inducing views without the safety of stone walls that hem in shutterbugs at Glacier Point, the trail to Taft Point passes over fissures, basically deep vertical cracks in the weather-worn cliff—watch your step! Taking children on this hike is not recommended.

Deer and wild iris in Tuolumne Meadow.

Farther back down Glacier Point Road, just west of the turnoff for Bridalveil Creek Campground on the opposite side of the road, a gentle 1.8-mile round-trip stroll leads through woodlands rife with birdsong out to **McGurk Meadow**, which looks prettiest in early summer when wildflowers bloom. From the meadow, you can continue 3 more miles each way to **Dewey Point** (elevation 7,385 feet) to get a dead-on look at El Capitan across Yosemite Valley and, to your right, the Cathedral Rocks and Half Dome.

WAWONA

Most visitors to this part of the park are here to hike in the impressive Mariposa Grove of giant sequoias. For a challenging day hike in the Wawona area, it's a moderately strenuous 4.2-mile ascent alongside Chilnualna Creek through a forest of ponderosa pine and incense cedar trees to **Chilnualna Falls** (elevation 2,200 feet). The waterfall trail starts from the east end of Chilnualna Road, past the Pioneer Yosemite History Center, off Wawona Road.

Tioga Road and Tuolumne Meadows

It's an easy walk from Tuolumne Meadows to Soda Springs and the **Parsons Memorial Lodge**. Nearby you can easily summit **Pothole Dome** or tackle the moderately difficult hike up Lembert Dome. (*See* the Tioga Road and Tuolumne Meadows section of Sights). Even more alluring trailheads in the Tuolumne Meadows area lead to pretty alpine lakes, any of which makes a pleasant half-day hike. Don't forget to carry insect repellent, which is an essential item in summer. Recommended meadows-to-lake trails include family-friendly **Dog Lake** (2.8 miles round trip), with its tree-lined shores and wide-open skies, and **Cathedral Lakes** (6.8 miles round trip, plus a mile-long spur trail), dramatically surrounded by Sierra Nevada peaks that rise above 10,000 feet in elevation.

Although **Glen Aulin** is primarily a backpacking destination along the High Sierra Camp circuit (*see* Backpacking), it's also a satisfying 12-mile round-trip day hike of moderate difficulty, following the canyon of the Tuolumne River and passing pretty cascades, including Tuolumne Fall (at 4 miles in). The Glen Aulin trailhead is on the east side of the main meadow near the Parson Memorial Lodge. Marathon hikers can continue beyond Glen Aulin to **Waterwheel Falls**, but this strenuous 17-mile round-trip excursion is best done as an overnight option.

Hiking by lower Cathedral Lake, with Tenaya Lake in the distance.

Taft Point has a rail so you can get close to the edge—but still be careful!

Gazing down from the summit of Mt. Hoffmann.

If sweeping vistas of Yosemite Valley are what you're after, both the challenging 14-mile round-trip hike to **Clouds Rest**, starting from Tenaya Lake west of Tuolumne Meadows, and the difficult up-and-down 10.4-mile round-trip hike to the summit of **North Dome** (elevation 7,540 feet) are unforgettable journeys through the high country. On the latter trail, which starts at the Porcupine Creek trailhead (not to be confused with Porcupine Flat Campground), the Indian Rock spur trail leads to Yosemite National Park's only natural arch. In between these two trailheads, a turnoff onto an old wagon road leads north to the trailhead for **May Lake**, an easy 2.4-mile round-trip hike, where energetic hikers can keep going through a rocky field of granite talus to reach the eroded summit of **Mt. Hoffmann** (elevation 10,845 feet). The views back over the lakes and the Sierra Crest are superb from the summit. Mt. Hoffmann, which happens to be the geographical center of the park, is a moderately difficult 4.8-mile round-trip trek from the May Lake trailhead.

East of Tuolumne Meadows along Tioga Road are a few more incredible high-altitude day hikes worth mentioning: the 3-mile round-trip journey to incredibly scenic and often forgotten **Gaylor Lakes**; the strenuous 7-mile round-trip ascent of **Mt. Dana** (elevation 13,061 feet); and the 7.4-mile climb up to **Mono Pass** and back, which follows an abandoned Native American trading route. To avoid potential parking hassles, all of these eastern trailheads are accessible via a free shuttle bus that in peak summer season makes four daily round-trip runs between the Tuolumne Meadows Lodge and Tioga Pass.

Keep in mind that all hikes beginning from Tioga Road are much easier when you're already acclimated to high altitudes. If you have symptoms of acute mountain sickness (*see* the Health and Safety section of the Practical Information chapter), the best remedy is immediate descent—which usually means returning to the trailhead and driving back down Tioga Road toward the valley.

HETCH HETCHY

If you're not up for hiking to the waterfalls that dramatically drop into the dammed valley of Hetch Hetchy (*see* the Hetch Hetchy section in Sights), take the moderate 3-mile round-trip trail instead to **Lookout Point**, atop which a few lone Jeffrey pines thrive. Photographers are rewarded with excellent views of the valley's falls and of the canyon of the Tuolumne River, with ideal lighting in the early morning.

Château du Sureau

Though many Yosemite visitors are happy to camp and live off granola and beef jerky, there are also options for those who prefer high-thread-count sheets to sleeping bags.

HIGH-END HOTELS
At **The Ahwahnee** (*209/372-1407; www.travelyosemite.com*), right in Yosemite Valley, grand public spaces take you back to an earlier era. If you had the foresight to reserve a year in advance (or the luck to find a last-minute cancellation), you'll have a hard time rousting yourself from the fireplace in the Great Lounge to hike all the trails outside the door.

More intimate (and even more luxurious) is the **Château du Sureau** (*559/683-6800; www.chateaudusureau.com*), a Relais & Châteaux property about 15 miles outside Yosemite's southern entrance. It's ideal for those in search of romance; just be sure to book well in advance. There are only 10 rooms and one two-bedroom villa, each furnished with fine antiques and equipped with lavish baths. The inn is also home to what is widely considered the best restaurant in the Sierras, **Erna's Elderberry House,** where French-inflected California cuisine is crafted from local ingredients.

GRAND TOURS

If you want someone else to do the planning (or haven't planned far enough out to snag a luxury-hotel room), consider one of the Yosemite hiking and walking trips offered by **Backroads** (*800/462-2848; www.backroads.com*), usually between mid-June and early October. Lodging is typically in the Tenaya Lodge, The Ahwahnee, or the Rush Creek Lodge (in Groveland), and packages include most meals. In general, the hikes and walks—all conducted by energetic and knowledgable trip leaders—aren't very difficult, but most days offer longer and/ or more difficult options, making the trip good for couples and groups with mixed abilities. Backroads also has family-oriented itineraries as well as "multisport" trips, which mix up days of moderate hiking with rock-climbing instruction and biking.

Far more strenuous is the eight-day trans-Sierra trek offered a few times between July and September by **Mountain Travel Sobek** (*888/831-7526; www.mtsobek.com*). Though you do camp by a lake instead of staying in a hotel, your trip fee includes transportation, experienced leaders who prepare your meals, and pack mules so you can literally (as well as figuratively) hike without any baggage. The company also offers private four-day trips in the valley, with stays in a park lodge after day hikes.

Yosemite 360 Bus Tours (*559/641-2208 or 559/692-8985; www.visittenaya.com/tours*) offers guided group and private tours and hikes. All excursions depart from the Tenaya Lodge in Fish Camp near the South Entrance. Trail lunches are provided.

SIERRA SPAS

Once you're done with all that activity, what could be better than a spa treatment? At The Ahwahnee, you can arrange in-room massages through the concierge. At the Château du Sureau, the small **Spa du Sureau** has one wet room as well as a spacious and romantic treatment room for two with a marble fireplace. **Ascent Spa** at Tenaya Lodge (*559/692-8954; www.tenayalodge.com*) is less intimate but better equipped, with steam rooms, saunas, indoor and outdoor swimming pools, fitness facilities, and a yoga room.

At the **Rush Creek Lodge & Spa** (*209/379-2373; www.rushcreeklodge.com/spa*), you can sit in a cove beneath warm waterfalls, relax in the aromatherapy steam room and Himalayan salt block sauna, and cool off in the mist and sensory rooms.

⊕ OTHER ACTIVITIES

Hiking and backpacking are the most popular activities in Yosemite National Park. But there are many more outdoor pursuits here for everyone to try as well, from guided horseback rides through the Sierra Nevada and whitewater-rafting to kayaking trips on the free-flowing Merced River to rock climbing Yosemite's massive granite walls and snowshoeing and skiing off Glacier Point Road in winter. There's even the 9-hole, pesticide-free **Wawona Golf Course** (*Wawona Rd.; 209/375–6572*), which is one of only a few organic golf courses in the United States and which is open spring through fall. Different tee positions allow it to be played in an 18-hole format. Call to set up a tee time.

Check the free newspaper *Yosemite Guide* for seasonal schedules of ranger-led programs and activities happening everywhere around the park, from daytime nature walks and waterfall hikes to old-fashioned campfire singalongs and after-dark stargazing programs. Ask at park visitor centers about the Junior Ranger program, which brings together arts-and-crafts activities, story time, and nature fun for families.

BACKPACKING

Even if you've scaled peaks in the Rocky Mountains before, or backpacked along long-distance trails in the Pacific Northwest, the sheer number and variety of overnight hikes and multiday backpacking routes in Yosemite cannot fail to impress. Although it takes more time and preparation than a day hike, a backpacking trip will immerse you in the beauty of the wilderness and let you find blissful solitude that Yosemite's roadside viewpoints and valley trails never can.

Although it is possible to take wilderness trips year-round, the ideal time is during summer, especially in the peak months of June and July, when access to the Sierra Nevada high country opens along Tioga Road. For an epic experience, venture forth on the ★JOHN MUIR TRAIL (JMT), which starts from Happy Isles in Yosemite Valley and runs over mountain passes for 211 miles through Kings Canyon and Sequoia national parks on its way to a dramatic finish atop Mt. Whitney (elevation 14,505 feet), the highest peak in the contiguous United States. A bit too much? No worries. There are scores of easier choices for weekend backpacking trips.

Starting from Yosemite Valley, the most popular overnight destination is **Little Yosemite Valley**, a moderate 4.7-mile hike up out of the valley along the JMT, which gives you a head start for climbing Half Dome (*see* Half Dome: a Survival Guide) the following day. A less crowded approach from Glacier Point follows the **Panorama Trail** to the top of Vernal Fall, then joins the main trail past Little Yosemite Valley to Half Dome, a tough 18.4-mile round trip. Along Tioga Road, there are two-dozen wilderness trailheads for backpackers to choose from. Starting from Tenaya Lake, the stunning **Sunrise Lakes Trail** leads over **Clouds Rest** (elevation 9,926 feet), one of the most inspiring viewpoints in the Sierra Nevada, then descends to Sunrise Creek and Little Yosemite Valley campgrounds; it's a moderately difficult 17.3-mile trip from Tenaya Lake to Yosemite Valley.

Other prime high-country destinations lie along the ★**HIGH SIERRA CAMPS** (*801/559–4909; www.travelyosemite.com*) circuit, where the lucky winners of a lottery (apply in October) get to stay in canvas tents and have all of their meals catered for them (for a cost, of course; the lottery just provides the opportunity to sign up). Otherwise, you'll have to procure a wilderness permit and haul all of your own backpacking gear along to visit the Grand Canyon of the Tuolumne River.

Many of the day hikes to alpine lakes described in the Best Day Hikes section also make great overnight backpacking destinations. Farther west, the Hetch Hetchy area of the park is the gateway for trips into the remote northern reaches of Yosemite National Park, which is 95% designated wilderness.

Backpackers pass through Yosemite's Tuolumne Meadows.

PERMITS

All trails inside Yosemite National Park are subject to a daily trailhead quota, and wilderness permits ($10 reservation plus $5/person via *www.recreation.gov*) are required for all overnight backcountry treks.

For hiking or climbing dates in late April through late October, you can enter the weekly permit reservation lottery from 24 weeks to three days in advance of the start of your trip (lotteries happen from mid-November to mid-May). Sixty percent of the reservations are distributed in these weekly lotteries. Of this portion, any reservations that remain become available on a first-come, first-served basis after the lottery process is complete for that week's reservations up until seven days in advance.

Seven days before a wilderness entry date, the remaining 40% of the reservation spots are released. Popular trailheads fill very quickly. Be ready to reserve promptly at 7 am (PDT) on Recreation.gov. The latest you can make a reservation is three days before a trip, subject to remaining availability.

From late October until late April, a wilderness permit is still required, but you can obtain it via self-registration at the Yosemite Valley Wilderness Center in Yosemite Village (in winter this is your only option), Tuolumne Meadows Wilderness Center on Tioga Road, Wawona Visitor Center at Hill's Studio on Wawona Road/Forest Drive, Big Oak Flat Information Station on Highway 120, and Hetch Hetchy Entrance Station on Hetch Hetchy Road.

All of these stations also rent food-storage canisters, which are required for wilderness travel. Those who hold valid permits can camp at designated backpacker campgrounds the night before and after their wilderness trip (no additional reservations are required.)

Wilderness trips starting outside the national park boundaries are often subject to trailhead quotas, too; you should check with other federal land-management agencies about permits and reservations.

FISHING

Good trout fishing is found along the Merced River near the national park boundary at El Portal and along the Tuolumne River near Hetch Hetchy. During summer, fishers also go boating on Tenaya Lake along Tioga Road, west of Tuolumne Meadows.

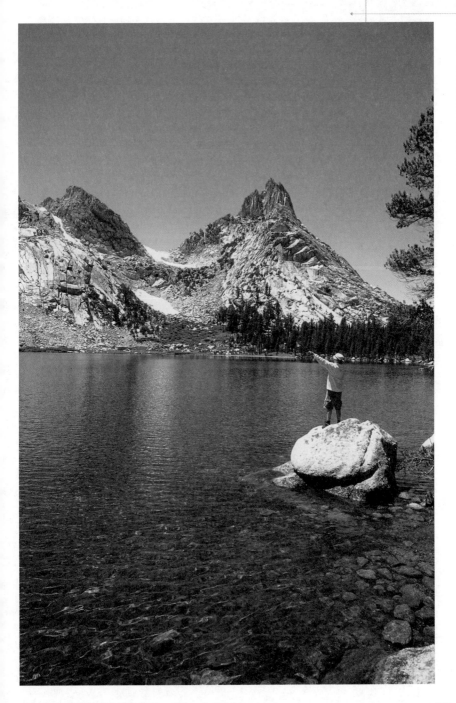

For half- and full-day guided fly-fishing trips, contact **Sierra Fly Fisher Tours** (*40872 Hwy. 41, Oakhurst; 559/683–7664; www.sierrafly-fisher.com*) or **Yosemite Fly Fishing** (*209/769–5534; www.yosemite-flyfishing.net*). Trips with the latter are led by conservationist and longtime local resident Tim Hutchins. All anglers ages 16 and older must carry a valid California fishing license, available for purchase at the Yosemite Village Sport Shop as well as at the general stores in Wawona, Crane Flat, and Tuolumne Meadows.

The season for stream and river fishing is open from late April until mid-November, while lakes and reservoirs remain open year-round. Additional restrictions apply inside the national park boundaries; ask at visitor centers for current regulations covering specific bait and hook types, daily limits, and catch-and-release requirements, which vary depending on your location and elevation within the park. The rules are strictest inside the Yosemite Valley. No fishing from bridges is allowed anywhere in the national park.

HORSEBACK RIDING

Rides range from a gentle two-hour trip around the Wawona area to six-day treks in the High Sierra.

Far easier than tackling Yosemite's often steep trails on foot, you can saddle up a sure-footed horse or mule and then relax and enjoy the scenery—with your animal hoofing it instead of you.

Horseback and mule rides within the park are run by Yosemite Hospitality, a subsidiary of Aramark (*www.travelyosemite.com*), the park's main concessioner. The most popular trip departs up to three times daily from the **Wawona Stable** (*209/375–6502*) in the Wawona area from late May to the end of September. The gentle two-hour ride follows the path of a historic wagon road and offers views of the Wawona Dome, a former Miwok encampment, and densely forested areas.

For overnight excursions in High Sierra, four- or six-day fully guided mule pack trips can be arranged. However, you must first enter the lottery and be awarded a reservation at the High Sierra Camps (*see* Backpacking). Once you have received a confirmation of your spot in the camps, you'll receive information about booking the guided pack and saddle trip.

Established in 1938, **Yosemite Trails** (*7910 Jackson Rd., Fish Camp; 559/683–7611; www.yosemitetrails.com*) offers half-day guided trail rides into the Mariposa Grove of giant sequoias, as well as shorter trips along a creek up to a vista point outside the park. In winter, sleigh rides are available on some weekends and holidays. The stables are in a small town outside the park's South Entrance Station.

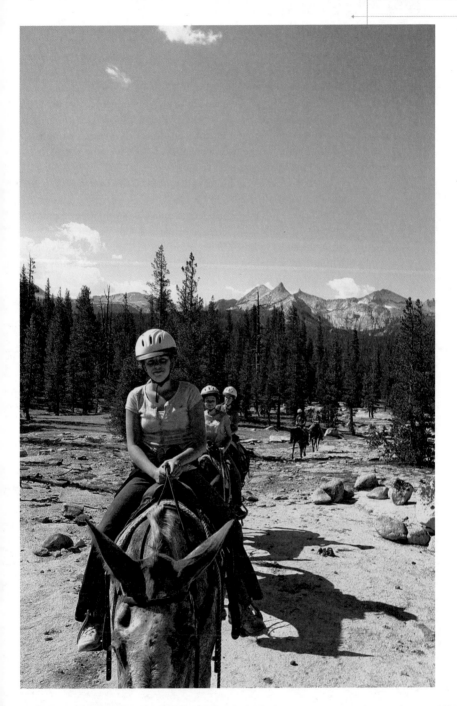

Rock Climbing

Yosemite is one of the premier rock-climbing and bouldering destinations in the United States. (*See* the Spotlight on: Rock Climbing in Yosemite.) Big wall climbs in the Yosemite Valley and crack climbs in the canyon of the Merced River present enough challenges for a lifetime. The buzzing center of activity for experienced climbers is **Camp 4**, a campground on the west side of the valley. During peak summer months, the encampment shifts to Tuolumne Meadows off Tioga Road in the park's high country.

Overshadowing Yosemite Valley, ★**EL CAPITAN** sets the standard for big wall climbs. El Capitan's "nose" (the prow connecting its two faces) was once considered impossible to climb until modern climbers initially conquered it during a 47-day assault in 1958. In 2018, the latest speed climbing record for El Cap was set at an astonishing 1 hour and 58 minutes. ★**HALF DOME**, meanwhile, offers classic slab climbing.

Experienced rock jockeys can free-climb up beside Yosemite Falls and to Glacier Point. Also popular are short- to medium-length dome climbs around Tuolumne Meadows, including several routes up Lembert Dome and **Stately Pleasure Dome** above Tenaya Lake.

For bouldering, head to **The Knobs** near Tuolumne Meadows or around Sentinel Rock and Camp 4, along the **Mirror Lake Trail**, or on the approach to Cathedral Rocks in the Yosemite Valley.

Certified guides from the **Yosemite Mountaineering School and Guide Service** (*209/372-8344*) lead a variety of classes at all skill levels, from introductory "Welcome to the Rock" workshops and basic anchoring for novices to advanced climbing techniques and self-rescue classes. Private lessons and guided climbs for small groups also can be arranged. Based at the Yosemite Mountain Shop, the school runs an additional branch at Tuolumne Meadows for the peak summer season.

Wilderness permits (*see* Backpacking) are not required for bivouacking overnight on any wall in the park, although climbers are required to follow minimum-impact guidelines, freely available from any wilderness center or permit-issuing station. Wilderness trailhead rangers also can let you know which areas are closed to climbing for safety reasons or to protect nesting peregrine falcons. Camping is not allowed at the base of any granite dome except Half Dome, for which a wilderness permit is still required.

Rock climber Tom Herbert tackles Death Crack, an overhanging climb near Tenaya Lake.

Rafting through Yosemite
Valley, past Yosemite Falls.

Swimming, Boating, Kayaking, and Whitewater Rafting

When the mercury spikes the thermometer above 90°F during summer, many park visitors can think about only one thing: where to get wet and cool down. With startlingly clear—but surprisingly cold—streams, rivers, and lakes all around, you'll find plenty of invigorating places to take a quick dip.

In summer, swimming is popular at sandy beaches that appear alongside the ★MERCED RIVER and Tenaya Creek in the Yosemite Valley; on the South Fork of the Merced River in the Wawona area, especially near the Swinging Bridge at the east end of Forest Drive; and along the Tuolumne River and at alpine lakes accessed via Tioga Road through the Sierra Nevada high country, especially near Tuolumne Meadows and at Tenaya Lake.

Keep in mind that winter snowmelt from the Sierra Nevada can turn rivers into a torrent of rapids, especially in late spring (a particularly dangerous time of year for a swim), so always exercise caution. Be prepared for chilly water conditions even during the dog days of August. Swimming is prohibited above all waterfalls, due to the serious risk of drowning, and also at Hetch Hetchy Reservoir.

For a nominal fee, the public is welcome to take a dip in the swimming pools at Curry Village and the Yosemite Valley Lodge in the Yosemite Valley. These pools are open from Memorial Day to Labor Day, weather permitting.

Also in summer (usually during June and July, although the exact times vary from year to year), daytime rafting and kayaking are allowed on the Merced River from the Stoneman Bridge near Curry Village down to the Sentinel Beach Picnic Area. You can rent a raft in Curry Village or bring your own equipment from home for kayaking and nonmotorized boating on Tenaya Lake. Wherever you swim, boat, kayak, or raft in the national park, be careful to approach the shoreline only from sandy beaches instead of cutting through grassy meadows and disturbing sensitive riparian areas.

YOSEMITE IN THE WINTER

Most people don't think of visiting Yosemite in winter, but independent-minded travelers who do will discover that it's a fairy-tale time, when the valley floor is hushed by powdery snowfall and waterfalls are partly frozen by ice. Not only is the park less crowded then, but its winter wonderland attracts families with young children and experienced winter-sports enthusiasts alike. Snowball throwing, ice skating, sledding, and skiing are among the most fun diversions this time of year.

Another big draw is a fizzing calendar of special seasonal events, including food and wine celebrations, old-fashioned holiday parties, and New Year's Eve celebrations (*see* the Festivals section in the Practical Information chapter).

Yosemite Valley is generally covered in snow from November to May. The Sierra Nevada high country usually stays snowed in most of the year, typically from late October through early June. Only the park's main roads remain open in winter:

Wawona Road (Highway 41), El Portal Road (Highway 140), Big Oak Flat Road (Highway 120), and Hetch Hetchy Road. Glacier Point Road is open only from the Chinquapin intersection east to Badger Pass Ski Area. All roads are subject to weather delays and snowplow closures. In the winter, always carry tire chains. For road conditions, call 209/372-0200.

Usually open from mid-December until late March, the family-friendly **Badger Pass Ski Area** (*Glacier Point Rd.; 209/372-8430; www.travelyosemite.com*) is one of California's oldest ski resorts. The two terrain parks are tame, so they're excellent places for novice skiers or snowboarders. Badger Pass, where kids revel in snow tubing and sledding, is also the gateway to groomed cross-country ski trails. The area has a first-aid station, a deli and fast-food cafeteria, and a shop that rents all types of winter-sports gear. In winter, there's a free shuttle bus between the Yosemite Valley lodgings and Badger Pass.

The **ski school** (*Glacier Point Rd.; 209/372-8430*) offers lessons for all skill levels, and guided cross-country ski tours can be arranged. Plan on taking all day to ski the more than 10 miles from Badger Pass out to the **Glacier Point Ski Hut**, where reservations for overnight stays are required. For experienced wilderness skiers only, the 10-mile one-way trip off Glacier Point Road out to

Ostrander Ski Hut (*209/379-2317; yosemite.org/experience/ostrander-ski-hut*), a two-story rustic stone building built by Civilian Conservation Corps workers in 1941, is a truly wild adventure. Reservations open for the season in November. The most popular dates fill up within minutes, so check the website in October to learn the exact date and mark your calendar.

In Yosemite Valley, rangers lead wintertime strolls focusing on the history, geology, and ecology of the park. At Curry Village, an **ice-skating rink** (*Southside Dr.; 209/372-8319*), where skate rental is available, is open from mid-November until early March, weather permitting. Purchase tickets at the Curry Village Tour and Activity Desk.

Snowshoeing is also popular in Yosemite. Snowshoe rentals are available in-season from the Nordic Center at Badger Pass Ski Area. The moderately difficult 7-mile loop out to Dewey Point is among the most popular snowshoe treks. Rangers lead guided snowshoe walks in both the Crane Flat and Badger Pass areas, including full-moon night outings at Badger Pass Ski Area only.

(opposite) Illilouette Creek in Yosemite National Park.

Spotlight on
ROCK CLIMBING
in Yosemite

It's no exaggeration to say that Yosemite National Park is not only the birthplace of American rock climbing but one of the best places to climb in the world. The breathtaking scale, beauty, and concentration of the rock formations here have inspired generations of climbers to develop new techniques, to invent equipment, and to set eye-popping records. The granite itself is polished by glaciers, fissured with vertical cracks, and often extremely steep. Most Yosemite routes involve traditional or "trad" climbing, which means finding routes and placing protective gear—a mental *and* physical challenge. Whether you're a veteran climber, starting out with an introductory class, or just watching from the ground, you're sure to be awestruck.

—Jennifer Paull

◄◄ On the West Ridge of Mt. Conness.

EPIC CLIMBS

Two of Yosemite's icons are also iconic rock-climbing locations: Half Dome and El Capitan. The breakthrough year was 1957, when each was tackled by a pioneering climber. Royal Robbins managed the first technical climbing route of Half Dome, up its northwest face. Meanwhile, Warren Harding, Wayne Merry, and George Whitmore started a fixed-rope route up the prow, or "Nose" of El Capitan. It took Harding's group more than a year of successive aid climbs before they summited in November 1958. In so doing, they established "seige" climbing, hauling up supplies and spending days at a time on the rock. Their feat also ushered in the era of climbing publicity by attracting hordes of reporters and wide-eyed tourists. There are now dozens of climbing routes up these monoliths. El Capitan's Nose has become a top route for speed-climbing.

ROUTE RATINGS

The American rating system used to gauge the difficulty of hikes and climbs is named for Yosemite: the Yosemite Decimal System. Routes get a numerical grade, from a flat trail (Class 1) to rock climbing using protective gear (Class 5). Class 5 climbs are then divided into more than a dozen subsets, from the relatively easy 5.0 on up.

Tackling a multiday climb up El Capitan.

El Capitan

Half Dome

YOSEMITE NATIONAL PARK

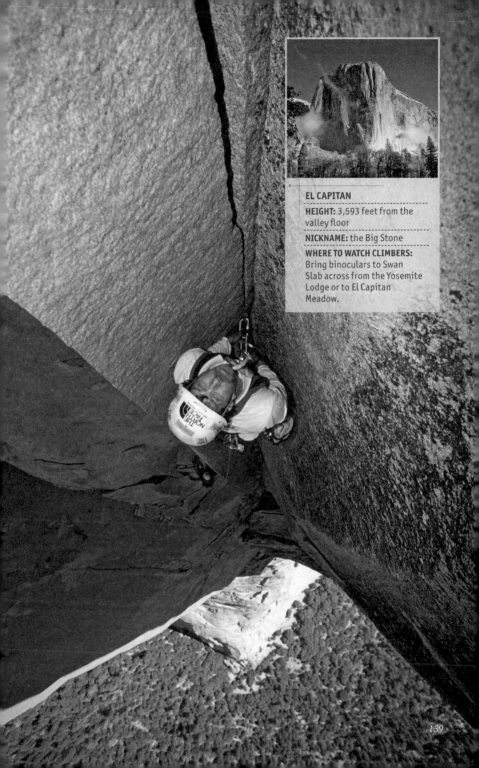

EL CAPITAN

HEIGHT: 3,593 feet from the valley floor

NICKNAME: the Big Stone

WHERE TO WATCH CLIMBERS: Bring binoculars to Swan Slab across from the Yosemite Lodge or to El Capitan Meadow.

HALF DOME

HEIGHT: 4,733 feet from the valley floor

WHERE TO WATCH CLIMBERS:
Bring binoculars to Mirror Lake or hike up to North Dome, which faces Half Dome.

OTHER BIG WALLS

"Big-wall climbing," or multiday aid climbs up huge rock faces, was literally invented here in Yosemite, when John Salathé and Ax Nelson spent five thirsty days on Lost Arrow Chimney in 1947. Beyond El Cap and Half Dome, other big walls include Leaning Tower (the steepest), Washington Column, Liberty Cap, Sentinel Rock, and Mt. Watkins.

Big walls are a serious undertaking—you need significant climbing experience, stamina, and advance planning. Not to mention the mental toughness to handle the nonstop work and exposure. The payoff? An indescribable climbing euphoria. If this kind of endurance test is for you, Yosemite's a goldmine of historic, world-renowned routes.

Lost Arrow Spire isn't a big wall, but the pinnacle is a unique draw.

BIVOUACKING

Don't panic if you see the specks of climbers staying put on a big wall for hours. They're (hopefully) not stuck but instead bivouacking, spending the night in midair. On multiday ascents, climbers sleep in a waterproof "bivy"sack on rock or portable ledges, affixed to the cliff hundreds or thousands of feet up.

Bivouacking: time to count birds instead of sheep.

EASIER ROUTES

When it comes to gauging easier climbs in Yosemite, remember that it's all relative. The nature of the rock here—smooth, steep, few handholds since the cracks run vertically instead of horizontally—means that there aren't a heck of a lot of introductory climbs rated 5.7 or less. Beginners usually start around Swan Slab in Yosemite Valley or at Tuolumne Meadows. Both areas are easy to access and usually have plenty of spectators cheering on new climbers. When considering the difficulty of a climb, don't forget to take into account how you'll get to the climbing site (for instance, whether there's a long hike).

GREAT INTRODUCTORY CLIMBS

After Six, in Yosemite Valley

Munginella, in Yosemite Valley

Oak Tree Flake or Claude's Delight, both on Swan Slab

Regular Route or Jamcrack, both on Sunnyside Bench

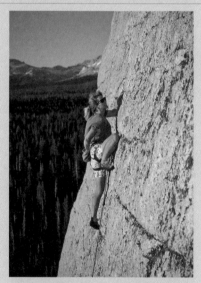

Tuolumne Meadows is a favorite for climbers.

A freshly hooked climber on the summit of Cathedral Peak.

Using friction on Zee Tree in Tuolumne Meadows.

BOULDERING

Not all Yosemite climbs are on a huge physical scale—the park is also a great place for bouldering. This form of climbing is usually done on large freestanding rocks, staying about 15 or fewer feet above the ground. Rather than using ropes and a harness, climbers put down a mat or crash pad and use a spotter in case of a fall. Otherwise, the only necessary tools are climbing shoes and hand chalk. Yosemite's bouldering routes, or "problems," were long used for training, but they've now become extremely popular in their own right. The granite boulders around Yosemite Valley's Camp 4 have some of the world's classic problems. Tuolumne Meadows is another boulder-rich area, and new favorites, like Candyland, emerge every summer.

Bouldering among giants in Yosemite Valley.

Going for the "Slap Shot" problem.

On the "Reach for a Peach" problem in Tuolumne Meadows.

WHERE TO LEARN

The Yosemite Mountaineering School and Guide Service (*209/372-8344; www.travelyosemite.com*) is the only in-park climbing school. There are daily beginners' sessions, plus specialized classes like crack climbing, big-wall techniques, and self-rescue. YMS guides will also take you out for private lessons or guided climbs. The school is based in Curry Village between April and October, with a temporary branch in Tuolumne Meadows during the height of summer. Costs start around $195 for a one-day class.

Southern Yosemite Mountain Guides (*800/231-4575 or 559/642-2817; www.symg.com*) offers private guides and classes at all levels June through September and several three- to five-day, small-group trips. Their routes are outside the national park, often in less trammeled backcountry. Costs start at $425 for a half-day class for one or two people.

WHEN TO GO

Late April through June and September through October are generally best in Yosemite Valley. The valley heat gets intense in July and August, with temperatures over 100°F on sunlit rock faces, so a better bet is Tuolumne Meadows. At a higher elevation, Tuolumne is much cooler. Be prepared for the occasional thunderstorm.

Tuolumne
Meadows

YOSEMITE
NATIONAL PARK

A Yosemite Mountaineering School instructor demonstrates knots.

QUICKDRAW
Used to attach ropes to bolt anchors or other protective gear in the rock.

HELMET
Protects during falls and deflects objects falling from above.

CARABINER
Aluminum loop with a spring-loaded opening. Locking carabiners are used for connections or belays.

HARNESS
Attaches rope to the climber and has loops to hold gear.

CLIMBING SHOES
Thin, tight-fitting shoes with a sticky rubber sole.

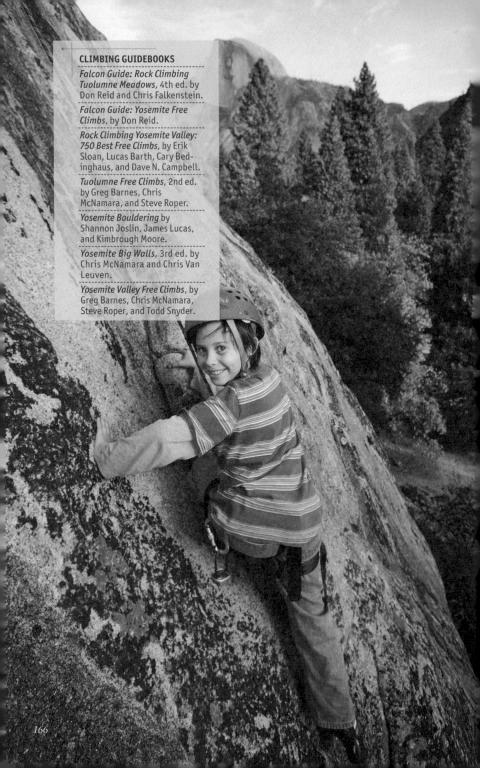

CLIMBING GUIDEBOOKS

Falcon Guide: Rock Climbing Tuolumne Meadows, 4th ed. by Don Reid and Chris Falkenstein.

Falcon Guide: Yosemite Free Climbs, by Don Reid.

Rock Climbing Yosemite Valley: 750 Best Free Climbs, by Erik Sloan, Lucas Barth, Cary Bedinghaus, and Dave N. Campbell.

Tuolumne Free Climbs, 2nd ed. by Greg Barnes, Chris McNamara, and Steve Roper.

Yosemite Bouldering by Shannon Joslin, James Lucas, and Kimbrough Moore.

Yosemite Big Walls, 3rd ed. by Chris McNamara and Chris Van Leuven.

Yosemite Valley Free Climbs, by Greg Barnes, Chris McNamara, Steve Roper, and Todd Snyder.

Early rock climbing in Yosemite was an under-the-radar and seat-of-your-pants experience. In 1875, George Anderson ascended Half Dome by creating a sort of ladder, drilling iron bolts into the granite and threading the bolts with rope. In 1934, three Bay Area Sierra Club members conquered Yosemite's Lower and Higher Cathedral Spires, using pitons and newly acquired alpine rope techniques to belay and rappel—opening a fresh world of possibilities. After World War II, a few climbers returned to Yosemite and tested out new equipment, the result of wartime technological advances. Most important, hemp

Dick Leonard, Jules Eichorn, and Bestor Robinson at their first ascent of Higher Cathedral Spire in 1934.

ropes were traded for sturdier nylon. Two more firsts occurred in the 1940s: the invention of hard steel pitons (handmade from a car axle!) and the first multiday, bivouacked climb.

If you travel through Mariposa on your way to or from the park, be sure to stop by the **Yosemite Climbing Museum and Gallery** (*5180 Hwy. 140; yosemiteclimbing.org; 209/742-1000*). It showcases area climbing history and the evolution of gear with an impressive collection of artifacts and historical photography.

Rappelling on Lower Cathedral Spire in 1935.

Camp 4

Cathedral Spires

YOSEMITE NATIONAL PARK

CAMP 4 AND THE CLIMBING BOOM

In the 1950s, a handful of eager rock climbers began gravitating to Yosemite Valley's Camp 4 campground. Mostly university students from the San Francisco area, they found ways to stay and climb daily from April to October. By the early 1960s, Camp 4 was the epicenter of American rock climbing. The site became legendary for its scruffy camaraderie, its parties, and, increasingly, a touchy hierarchy between hardcore, local climbers and weekenders. The campfire debates about technique and new equipment shaped the future of the sport. The first era of Camp 4 ended with the campground's renovation in 1970; the NPS renamed it Sunnyside. By then, the top climbers were winning international recognition, and the sport began to boom. The site quickly became one of the world's most famous climbing destinations. In 2003, it was added to the National Register of Historic Places, and the Camp 4 name was reinstated. Rock rats still flock to it as the ultimate "community center."

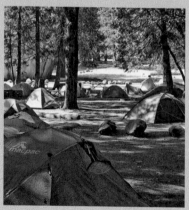

Sorting gear at Camp 4.

CLIMBING TERMS AND SLANG

Beta: Information about a climb, like a route's difficulty, length, and advice on holds.

Belay monkey: Someone who patiently belays for a long time (ensuring a cricked neck).

Crux: The toughest, most challenging part of a climb.

Elvis leg: When your leg quivers uncontrollably during a climb, usually due to nervousness plus taxed muscles. Also called sewing-machine leg.

Free climbing: When a climber moves up the rock using only his or her body (as opposed to **aid climbing,** in which climbers rely on equipment like pitons or nuts to advance). Free climbers use ropes and other protective equipment in case of falls.

Jamming: Wedging a body part, like your fingers, into a crack in the rock.

Smearing: Pushing the rubber soles of climbing shoes onto the rock to create friction.

CLIMBING WITH CARE

Climb clean by using nondamaging, removable gear.

Alongside the surge in rock climbing is a rising awareness of climbing's impact on the rocks themselves and the surrounding environment. Below are a few basic conservation rules.

Don't litter anywhere, whether on the rock or in a base area. That goes for "human waste," too. Pick up any litter you see and clean up your chalk marks.

Don't disturb any animals you might encounter. During peregrine falcon nesting season (typically March through July), certain rock-climbing locations will be closed. Check the Yosemite Mountain Shop or *www.nps.gov* for closure dates.

Be careful of any vegetation. Avoid walking on plants at the bases of climbing areas. Don't clear away plants from the rock (pulling up plants in Yosemite is illegal). Use established trails to reach and descend from your climbing area to reduce soil erosion.

Gathering trash at Camp 4.

Be careful not to crush or tear up vegetation on trails or rock faces.

Stretching from the dry, chaparral-covered foothills of the Sierra Nevada to the ferny meadows and groves of the Giant Forest, and even farther up into the glacially carved valley of Mineral King, Sequoia National Park offers a fully loaded menu of outdoor adventures. Whether you cruise along the Generals Highway through the tall trees to walk the Trail of the Sequoias or climb Moro Rock for views of the Great Western Divide, then dive underground into jewel-like Crystal Cave, this national park's variety of natural environments and landscapes makes it just as memorable as Yosemite.

Sequoia National Park

Sunset on the Forest Path,
Sequoia National Park

Fires in the parks leave burn marks on some of the sequoia trees, like this one. (right) Visitors snap photos of the General Sherman tree in the Giant Forest.

GENERAL SHERMAN

SEQUOIA TREES

AGE: Can live past 3,000 years.

HEIGHT: Can be greater than 250 feet.

WIDTH: Their diameters can exceed 30 feet.

FUN FACT: They grow faster than any other conifer.

Established by President Benjamin Harrison in 1890, Sequoia was created a week before Yosemite National Park, making it the United States' second-oldest national park after Yellowstone. And like Yosemite, Sequoia National Park flourishes with groves of majestic giant sequoias, but there's a reason the latter park has this beloved tree in its name: nowhere in the world do giant sequoias grow in such abundance as they do in Sequoia National Park's Giant Forest. So many, in fact, that they can't be counted. Even after all of the 19th-century logging efforts, it's safe to say they still number in the thousands.

Sequoia National Park lies just south of its friendly neighbor, Kings Canyon National Park. Together, these parks comprise even more wilderness territory than Yosemite National Park, which lies a hundred-odd miles farther north in the Sierra Nevada. Sequoia and Kings Canyon are managed jointly, connected by the lifeline of the Generals Highway, which winds from Grant Grove in Kings Canyon slowly south through the Giant Forest to the Sierra Nevada foothills area of Sequoia. Between Sequoia and Kings Canyon national parks lies the Giant Sequoia National Monument of the Sequoia National Forest, which wraps around the parks.

Here, dirt roads lead off into more remote wilderness areas. (Giant Sequoia National Monument is covered in the Kings Canyon National Park chapter.)

In addition to the towering sequoias, the park's top draws include Crystal Cave, where you can go underground to see a wealth of smoothly polished marble and unusual cave critters that have adapted to a subterranean environment found only in this park. Rounding off the trio of top attractions is Mineral King, an 1870s mining settlement. Here the jagged peaks of the Sierra Nevada rise all around you, without you even having to earn the panoramic views by hiking into the wilderness.

PLANNING YOUR TIME

A long day is enough time to see many of the park's highlights, but a longer sojourn allows for taking short hikes through the giant sequoia groves, joining a ranger-guided nature walk or talk, and perhaps traversing the rugged side road up to Mineral King.

If your time is limited, rise and shine early. Briefly stop at the Foothills or Lodgepole visitor center to get oriented and to purchase Crystal Cave tour tickets, then drive on the Generals Highway to the Giant Forest Museum, with its educational exhibits for all ages that unlock the ecological mysteries of the giant trees. With more time on your hands, you can explore the Native American history of the Foothills area of the park, where riverside walking trails and swimming holes are especially refreshing on hot summer days.

SIGHTS

See the Sequoia National Park map.

This suggested driving itinerary for exploring Sequoia National Park starts from the Ash Mountain Entrance Station near the Sierra Nevada foothills and climbs into the Giant Forest area, where you can lose yourself among the groves of giant sequoia trees. The southernmost area of the park, which is the Mineral King Valley, also happens to be the most remote and least visited area, so it appears at the very end of our tour.

(opposite) A sequoia's stump reveals the tree's age through its rings. The method of cross-dating trees by their rings points to a potential lifespan for sequoias of more than 3,200 years.

Diamond Peak
13,126ft

Rae Lakes

Independence

Charlotte Lake

Kearsarge Pass
11,823ft

KINGS CANYON
NATIONAL
PARK

University Peak
13,632ft

Mt. Bradley
13,289ft

KINGS-KERN DIVIDE

Junction Peak

Mt. Geneva
13,055ft

Table Mountain
13,630ft

Mt. Tyndall
14,018ft

Centennial Peak
13,255ft

GREAT WESTERN DIVIDE

Colby Pass

Tyndall
Creek

Mt. Barnard
13,990ft

Triple Divide
Peak

Whitney
Portal

Mt. Whitney
14,505ft

To
Lone Pine
& Hwy 395

John Muir
Trail

SEQUOIA
NAL PARK

Crabtree

Mt. Kaweah
13,802ft

High Sierra
Trail

Mt. Guyot
12,300ft

Mt. Langley
14,042ft

Rock Creek

Little Five Lakes

New Army Pass
11,475ft

Siberian Pass
10,950ft

Sawtooth Peak

ng Valley

KERN CANYON

INYO
NATIONAL
FOREST

Franklin
Lakes

Franklin Pass
11,800ft

Florence Peak
12,432ft

Kern Canyon

Coyote Pass

SEQUOIA
NATIONAL FOREST

Coyote Peaks
10,892ft

Legend

🚹	Ranger / Information
🍴	Food Service
⛱	Picnic Area
🛏	Lodging
⛺	Campground
⛽	Gas Station
🅿	Parking Area
····	John Muir Trail / Pacific Crest Trail
----	Other Trails

SEQUOIA
NATIONAL PARK

0   5 Miles

0   7.5 kilometers

FOOTHILLS

At the northern edge of Three Rivers township, Highway 198 memorably crosses the Kaweah River via the **Pumpkin Hollow Bridge,** a distinctive masonry arch structure built in 1922. Migratory swallows return from South America every year, usually around mid-March, to nest in the nooks and crannies of the bridge. You can often observe these twittering birds from the dining room of the town's well-located but tired Gateway Lodge, as they glide across the river's banks and hop from tree branch to tree branch.

It's half a mile past the historic bridge to the park's **Ash Mountain Entrance.** Just inside the national park boundary, on the right side of the road, is a hand-carved sign for Sequoia National Park that was created by Civilian Conservation Corps (CCC) artisans in the 1930s. What makes this antique sign notable is its unusual portrait of a Native American man, heralding the area's indigenous history, which is now protected in cooperation with the National Park Service. Until the mid- to late 19th century, these Sierra Nevada foothills were the exclusive territory of the Monache (Western Mono) tribespeople, with the Potwisha (also called Patwisha or Balwisha) band living south of the Kaweah River divide and the Wuksachi band inhabiting the upper valleys to the north. These peoples made seasonal migrations over high mountain passes to trade with the Paiutes living in the Owens Valley on the eastern side of the Great Western Divide.

About a mile past the entrance station, the **Foothills Visitor Center** *(47050 Generals Hwy.; 559/565–4212)* is a good place to stop and stretch your legs. Natural-history exhibits showcase the diversity of flora and fauna inhabiting the park's different ecological zones, which vary in elevation from the foothills to above the tree line. Although the surrounding foothills are hot and dry for much of the year, in spring they're carpeted in wildflowers, especially fields of orange California poppies. Those planning to visit Crystal Cave can purchase tour tickets inside the visitor center, along with trail maps, star guides, and books on the park's natural and human history.

Beyond the visitor center, the Generals Highway starts its long, winding journey up from the foothills to the Giant Forest by following the Kaweah River. Along the way, the highway offers scenic canyon views.

★ Did You Know? ★

The image of a Native American man on the Ash Mountain Entrance sign is most likely modeled after a profile used on early-20th-century U.S. "buffalo nickels," which are now collectors' items.

About 1.5 miles north of the visitor center, **Tunnel Rock** appears on the left side of the road. The tunnel itself was originally dug by CCC workers in the 1930s, which allowed park visitors to drive right through a giant granite rock. Standing here and looking upward at the narrow, twisting highway before you, imagine how much of an adventure it was to visit the national park during the early 1900s, when the road was even narrower and far more of a challenge for touring motorists, as it lacked many of the guardrails in place today and was more prone to landslides. It was CCC workers who first lined the highway with the rock work that you will see all along the way to the Giant Forest.

After another 1.5 miles, a side road leads left to **Potwisha Campground**. Driving north another few miles brings you to **Hospital Rock**. This Native American pictograph and mortero site is easy to access: it's just across the highway from the picnic-area parking lot, standing beside the road to Buckeye Flat Campground.

This Hospital Rock area was once the site of a Monache village housing up to 500 inhabitants who probably resided here beginning around AD 1350. Archaeologists believe the rock may have been a ceremonial gathering place. In 1860, pioneer John Swanson stayed here for three days while Native Americans treated his broken leg, but the place didn't get the nickname Hospital Rock until 1873, when an early Western pioneer and fur trapper named Alfred Everton lay here waiting while his friend went for help after Everton ironically injured himself with his own bear trap.

Immediately after Hospital Rock, the Generals Highway begins its squiggly ascent out of the gently rolling foothills. Just over 10 miles from the Foothills Visitor Center, look out for **Amphitheater Point** on the right side of the highway, just past a hairpin turn. Pull off to see what lies magnificently spread out before you: not only the Kaweah River as it meanders through the foothills, but also Moro Rock perching over the mixed conifer forests above, signaling the beginning of the giant sequoia's life zone. In the background, the often snow-topped Sierra Nevada high country of the Great Western Divide comes into view. All of this should whet your appetite for what lies just farther ahead up the vertiginous highway.

The Generals Highway climbs upward to **Deer Ridge**, where wide vistas open down into the Kaweah River canyon and out onto the flat plains of the San Joaquin Valley. The air is often especially fresh and crystal clear after a thunderous storm front moves through.

FOOTHILLS VISITOR CENTER

TELEPHONE:
559/565–4212

ADDRESS: A mile past Ash Mountain Entrance Station on Generals Highway

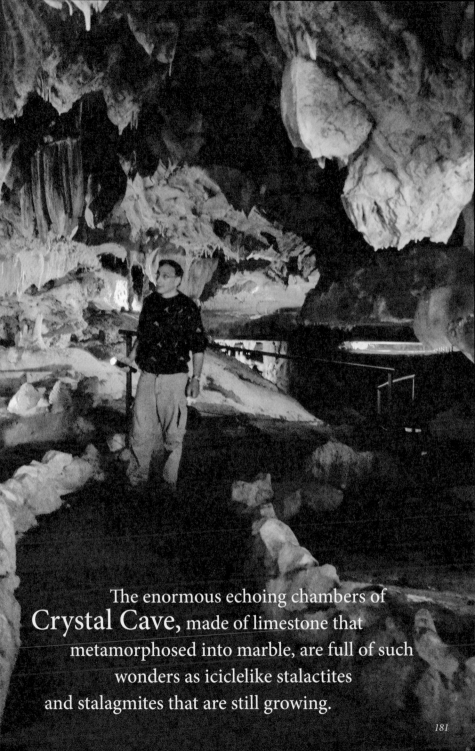

The enormous echoing chambers of
Crystal Cave, made of limestone that
metamorphosed into marble, are full of such
wonders as iciclelike stalactites
and stalagmites that are still growing.

But if all you can see from the highway is haze, blame that drastically reduced visibility on urban air pollution in the form of smog that drifts up from California's central valley. The number of "red alert" days, during which ozone air pollution levels in the park exceed federal environmental standards, is increasing. But when the smog is not as thick, you are well rewarded: The views from here can stretch for more than 100 miles.

CRYSTAL CAVE

Two miles before reaching the Giant Forest Museum, a winding side road (not accessible by RVs or trailers over 22 feet) leads northwest of the Generals Highway for 6 miles to reach the parking lot for ★CRYSTAL CAVE *(Crystal Cave Rd.; 559/565–4251 for information; www.sequoiaparksconservancy.org/crystalcave.html)*, which is generally open for public tours from mid-May through September. The best known of nearly 300 caves discovered so far in Sequoia and Kings Canyon Parks, this underground cavern is made of limestone that metamorphosed into marble (due to the uplift of the Sierra Nevada) annd then was polished by running water.

From the parking area, take a steep but pretty ½-mile walk along Cascade Creek down to the Spider Web Gate, where guides orient tour groups before leading them inside the enormous echoing chambers full of such wonders as iciclelike stalactites and stalagmites that are still growing, as well as hanging curtains and flowstone formations like the Pipe Organ, which looks just as its name suggests.

The cave is also interesting for its biological diversity. Some of the bats and creepy-crawly spiders and scorpions living here exist nowhere else in the world. This is important because the Sierra Nevada has been identified as one of the five "hot spots" for cave-animal diversity in the United States.

The lighted pathways inside Crystal Cave are paved, but they aren't wheelchair accessible; baby backpacks, strollers, and walking sticks are not allowed. Because the temperature inside is a chilly 48°F, bring a sweater or jacket.

You'll need to get tour tickets in advance *(www.recreation.gov)* for these explorations. The basic 50-minute tours are a short introduction to the cave's amazing ecosystem, ideal for families with kids and anyone short on time or not really all that keen on dark holes in the ground. The 1½-hour Discovery Tour is a more intimate experience that delves into the ecology of the cave environment. First-come, first-served and same-day tickets for these two tours are not sold at the cave; you can buy them in person at the Foothills or Lodgepole visitor centers or, for some dates, online. There are also longer, guided Wild Cave Tours for families and for adults 16 and over (advance registration only for both). These more adventurous and extensive tours let spelunkers scramble off-trail inside the cave for hours.

GIANT FOREST

Back on the Generals Highway, the forest canopy points skyward all around you, with encircling lodgepole and ponderosa pines, and white firs and giant sequoias towering above them all. After about an hour's drive uphill from the Foothills Visitor Center, the highway finally enters the ★GIANT FOREST (elevation 6,400 feet). This precious ecosystem harbors some of the world's largest groves of giant sequoia trees, which exist only on the western slope of the Sierra Nevada. In the late 19th century, timber loggers tried to turn a profit by cutting down giant sequoias, but their brittle aged wood proved too soft and fragile to be economically profitable for logging. These gentle giants fortunately came to be protected in a national park in 1890.

Nowhere in the world do giant sequoias grow in such abundance as they do in Sequoia National Park's Giant Forest.

Ironically, the national park's tourist development in turn stressed the natural ecosystem of the giant sequoia trees. Visitation rapidly increased after 1900, once tourist camps and cabins were constructed in the Giant Forest, with traffic jams and congestion after the Generals Highway opened in 1926. By the end of the 20th century, this development had damaged the giant trees' root systems resulting in a massive restoration project.

All commercial activity has been moved from the Giant Forest into the nearby Lodgepole and Wuksachi Village areas. Nearly 300 buildings that once stood cluttered among the trees have been demolished, and more than 200 acres of forested land are now being restored. One way in which this precious land has been restored further is via prescribed wildfire burns. Giant sequoia seeds can germinate only on bare mineral soil that has been scarred by fire. So after so many decades of total fire suppression, these deliberate fires are necessary to keep the trees reproducing.

Often visitors keep their voices hushed, as though the groves of giant sequoias were open-air cathedrals.

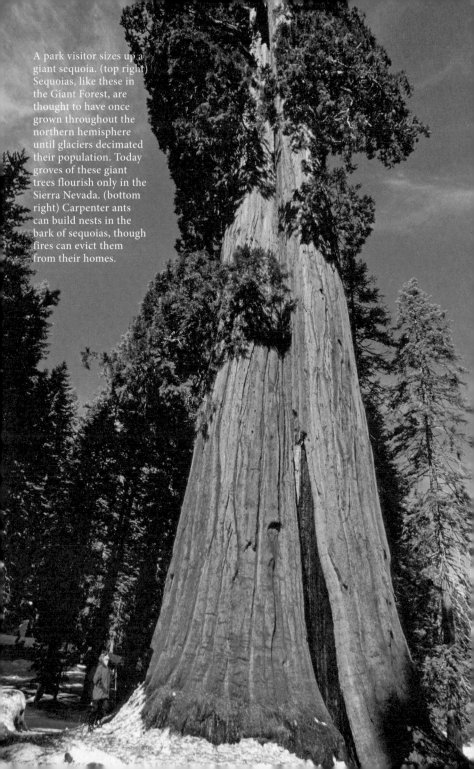

A park visitor sizes up a giant sequoia. (top right) Sequoias, like these in the Giant Forest, are thought to have once grown throughout the northern hemisphere until glaciers decimated their population. Today groves of these giant trees flourish only in the Sierra Nevada. (bottom right) Carpenter ants can build nests in the bark of sequoias, though fires can evict them from their homes.

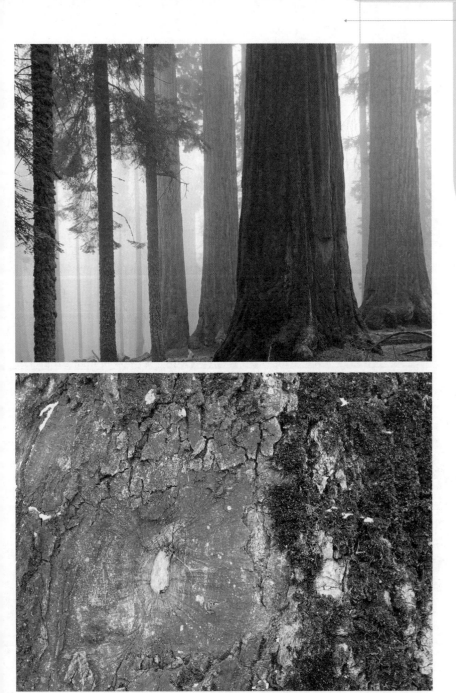

As it returns to robust health, the Giant Forest remains open to the public as a surprisingly tranquil day-use area. There is just something about these majestic living things, which can live to be more than 3,000 years old, that often inspires visitors to keep their voices hushed, as though the groves of giant sequoias were open-air cathedrals.

By the side of the highway, a historic wooden market building dating from the 1920s has been converted into the **Giant Forest Museum** *(Generals Hwy.; 559/565–4480)*, which is free and open year-round. Interactive exhibits here consider the human factor and the important role of wildfire in the natural history of the giant sequoias, while also illustrating the trees' size, age, and grandeur. Embedded in the pavement outside the museum, a tiled ruler demonstrates the enormous height and girth of the nearby **Sentinel Tree** as it runs alongside the building, outdistancing it by a noticeable measure.

On the opposite side of the road, a short walk from the main museum parking lot, **Beetle Rock** is a flat granite dome with great sunset views. The rock is named for the discovery of a new species of beetle here by amateur entomologist Edward Hopping in 1905.

The Giant Forest is strewn with a network of hiking trails *(see Best Day Hikes)*. If you're short on time, at least drive down the busy side road signposted for Moro Rock and Crescent Meadow on the south side of the museum so that you can see the **Auto Log**, which is less than a mile along this road. Until the log began to rot, park visitors were allowed to drive across the top of this fallen giant sequoia, which had a roadway notched into its top side. The side road is closed to vehicle traffic in winter, as well as on summer weekends, when free shuttles run from the Giant Forest Museum.

It's another mile farther along the same side road to iconic ★**MORO ROCK.** It's well worth the huff-and-puff ¼-mile ascent of nearly 400 stone steps from the parking lot to the top of the granite dome 300 feet up—don't attempt it when lightning is visible in the sky. The 360-degree vistas of the mighty peaks of the Great Western Divide, which separates the watersheds of the Kaweah River to the west and the Kern River to the east, are awe-inspiring. Even Mt. Whitney (elevation 14,505 feet), the tallest mountain in the contiguous United Sates, remains hidden from view behind these

★ Did You Know? ★

Giant sequoia trees are thought to have been named for Sequoyah, who invented a Cherokee syllabary in 1821.

A huff-and-puff ascent up nearly
400 steps takes you from the parking
lot to the top of Moro Rock,
a granite dome 300 feet up.

12,000-foot giants. Unfortunately, the spectacular view from the top is often diminished by pollution from the valley below.

Continue just over a mile along the road to **Crescent Meadow**, where black bears are often seen foraging for berries and acorns from spring through fall. Starting from the meadow's parking lot, a confusing number of trailheads call to day hikers and backpackers. The most popular trail leads 1.3 miles out to **Tharp's Log**, another fallen giant sequoia. This hollowed-out tree once served as a summer cabin for Hale Tharp, the first European resident of the Three Rivers area, who grazed his cattle in the meadow from 1861 until the area was established as a national park in 1890. Today, standing outside Tharp's Log, you can peer in at the cabin's restored furnishings, which include an unusual rock fireplace.

On the drive back toward the Generals Highway, you will come across the drive-through **Tunnel Log**, a giant sequoia that fell across the road here in 1937. Afterward, CCC workers cut a tunnel through it, but the opening measures only 8 feet high by 17 feet wide, so not all vehicles will fit through. Don't get stuck!

Nothing can compare with the ★**GENERAL SHERMAN TREE**, which is the biggest tree in the park. It's also the largest tree (by volume) in the world. Having survived not only the threat of the late-19th-century logging era, but also centuries of snowstorms and wildfires that have left its reddish-brown bark scarred, the General Sherman Tree today stands nearly 275 feet tall and measures more than 100 feet in circumference around its base—and it's still growing.

This estimated 2,000-year-old giant was named in 1879 by pioneer trapper and cattleman James Wolverton, who had served as a Civil War soldier under General William Tecumseh Sherman in the Union Army. Interestingly, the tree was briefly renamed the Karl Marx Tree in the late 1880s by the utopian Kaweah Colony that embarked on an experimental way of life in the Three Rivers area. As the colony labored to build roads and a timber-logging operation into the Giant Forest, conservationists who favored saving the giant sequoia trees from cutting only intensified their efforts, leading to the creation of the national park, which spelled the end of the colony's dreams. Visitors with limited mobility may park off the Generals Highway in front of the General Sherman Tree in the ADA-accessible lot. Everyone else should turn right off the Generals Highway onto the side road leading to the cool, forested **Wolverton Picnic Area** and park in the main lot instead, from where a paved trail visits the tree.

About 2 miles' drive north on the Generals Highway, during which you may be able to catch a glimpse of Marble Fork Canyon through the trees, you come to the busy Lodgepole Village (elevation 6,720 feet) area, complete with a market, deli, snack bar, campground, laundry and shower house. Step inside the **Lodgepole Visitor Center** (*63100 Lodgepole Rd.; 559/565-4436*) to find out more about the geology of the Sierra Nevada and its endemic wildlife, as well as the region's varied human history, which brims with stories of indigenous Monache peoples and early pioneers, as well as past and modern conservationists and tourists; video presentations are available upon request. The visitor center and all services in the Lodgepole Village area are usually open from May through October. Two miles farther north along the Generals Highway, a side road leads to **Wuksachi Lodge** (*64740 Wuksachi Way; 866/807-3598*), which has a hotel, restaurant, bar, and snack and gift shop that are open year-round.

Beyond Wuksachi, the Generals Highway passes by Halstead Meadow, another grassy, tree-shaded picnic area; the trailhead for hiking up Little Baldy (*see* Best Day Hikes); and the park's Dorst Creek Campground. The highway continues through the Giant Sequoia National Monument of the Sequoia National Forest north into Kings Canyon National Park.

MINERAL KING

It's an adventure just getting to **Mineral King** (elevation 7,500 feet), one of the oldest settled communities in the Sierra Nevada. Today, it's the least visited corner of Sequoia National Park. Before the arrival of Europeans, this pristine subalpine valley was a summer hunting camp for Native American tribes. By the 1860s, fur trappers and cattlemen began following the trails that Native Americans had trod up the Kaweah River canyon. The next decade brought hardscrabble miners looking to harvest the riches of the hills. They built a boomtown here called Beulah, and the name was later changed to Mineral King.

Although the mines turned out to be a bust, the road to Mineral King that the miners had built brought logging, hydroelectric development, and, later, tourists into the valley, which soon became a recreational summer resort made up of privately owned cabins, some of which still stand today. In the mid-20th century, the Walt Disney Company planned to build a ski resort here but was stopped by a political coalition that included the National Park Service, USDA Forest Service, and the Sierra Club. In 1978, Mineral King was controversially annexed to Sequoia National Park, ending a protracted battle

LODGEPOLE VISITOR CENTER

TELEPHONE:
559/565-4436

ADDRESS: 63100
Lodgepole Road

THE BIGGEST LIVING THING IN THE WORLD?

What's the largest living thing in the world? The verdict is still out, but here's a look at a few of nature's contenders.

Giant sequoia trees *(Sequoiadendron giganteum)* are members of the redwood family, which also includes coast redwoods *(Sequoia sempervirens)* growing on the Pacific Northwest coast and dawn redwoods *(Metasequoia glyptostroboides)* native to southwestern China. The coast redwoods are the tallest trees on Earth. The very tallest among them is a tree known as Hyperion, which stands 379 feet high in an undisclosed location in California's Redwood National Park.

While giant sequoia trees may not be taller than coast redwoods, they are more massive. The largest known giant sequoia is the General Sherman Tree, boasting an ever-increasing volume that is currently 52,500 cubic feet. This Giant Forest icon grows each year by a volume approximately equal in size to a 50-foot-high tree that is 1 foot in diameter.

But is this Sequoia National Park stalwart the world's largest living thing? Scientists say no. Also staking claims to that title are other gigantic spectacles of nature—from the 1,250-mile-long Great Barrier Reef off the east coast of Australia and an underground fungi that spreads across 2,200 acres in Oregon to an enormous grove of genetically identical quaking aspen trees in Utah whose roots are interconnected and together weigh 6,600 tons!

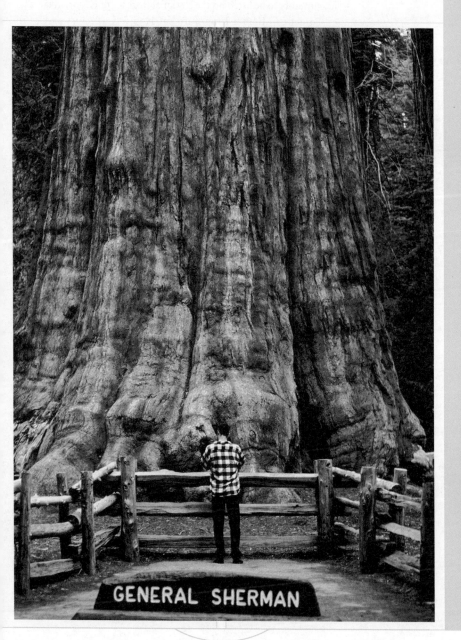

GENERAL SHERMAN

over private versus public land rights to this highly valued piece of Sierra Nevada wilderness. It took another 35 years for this historical community to be listed on the National Register of Historic Places.

To get to Mineral King, turn off Highway 198 just east of the town of Three Rivers and west of the national park's Ash Mountain Entrance Station. The 25-mile **Mineral King Road** is usually open only from late May through late October. It's an incredibly scenic road, with its sheer, head-spinning drop-offs into the dramatic river valley below and luxuriant mixed-conifer forests growing precipitously on the sides of granite mountains, but it's also a narrow and winding route requiring you to make almost 700 right-hand turns. In some places, the road is barely wide enough for two cars to pass each other safely (RVs and trailers are not recommended), so go slow. The drive takes at least 1½ hours each way.

If you're not going to stay overnight in a national-park campground at Mineral King or in a rustic cabin at Silver City Mountain Resort, before venturing up this road, do two things: one, get a very early start, and two, make sure your car's gas tank is full, because there is no place to fuel up after leaving Three Rivers.

The epic drive to Mineral King starts outside the national park boundary and follows the canyon of the East Fork of the Kaweah River. Don't rush the trip, because the scenic drive is the whole point—there aren't any major sights to see along the way, so just enjoy the views.

About 11 miles after leaving Highway 198, Mineral King Road passes an automated pay station, where you can use credit cards to pay entrance fees. The road continues to climb for another 7 miles onto the spectacular Hockett Plateau to reach some relics of 19th-century logging operations that remain for casual inspection. From Atwell Mill Campground, the Atwell-Hockett Trail leads a mile down to a small waterfall on the Kaweah River that usually appears in late spring and early summer. Although petite, the waterfall is surrounded by moss-covered rocks and thick vegetation, making it a surprisingly scenic spot.

Also from the campground, the steep but pleasant Paradise Ridge Trail leads up through Atwell Grove, the park's highest-elevation grove of giant sequoias, where, chances are, you'll finally have the forest all to yourself, and to lofty Paradise Ridge, where you'll enjoy fine views of the mighty Great Western Divide of the Sierra Nevada. Two miles farther east along Mineral King Road is **Silver City Mountain Resort** (*Mineral King Rd.; 559/242-3510; www.silvercityresort.com*), with rustic cabins and alpine chalets for rent, plus a store and restaurant famous for its homemade pie and

WARNING: MARMOTS AHEAD

A word of warning before you make the long drive to Mineral King: your car is in danger of becoming a snack for marmots.

Marmots, the largest members of the squirrel family, resemble groundhogs and prairie dogs and are the size of a small poodle. They live in the high mountainous regions of North America and Europe, typically at elevations above 6,000 feet. In most of the Sierra Nevada, you encounter them along high-elevation wilderness trails. The Mineral King Valley has an especially large population.

You'll usually hear marmots before you see them, as they communicate using high-pierced whistles. Don't be alarmed if a marmot runs right up to meet you; they're curious and fearless creatures. But these pesky rodents are known to chew on car hoses and wires. Why? Even though the antifreeze coolant found inside cars is poisonous to humans, it tastes addictively sweet to marmots.

If you leave your car parked for any length of time at Mineral King, you may return to find it seriously damaged, perhaps even undrivable. Occasionally, the determined critters get trapped inside engine compartments, so always check under the hood for stowaways before driving away. Locals recommend placing chicken wire around your vehicle to discourage marmots. You can buy some rolls of chicken wire in the town of Three Rivers before starting the journey up to Mineral King. Sometimes you can also find it at the Silver City Mountain Resort general store.

Backpackers need to pay attention to marmots, too, because your equipment just might be lunch. Marmots like to gnaw on hiking boots, pole grips, and backpack straps once they get a bit salty from sweat. Try to keep your gear safely with you at all times, and hope for the best.

THE BIG TREES

"Descending the precipitous divide between the King's River and Kaweah you enter the grand forests. . . . Advancing southward, the giants become more and more irrepressibly exuberant, heaving their massive crowns into the sky from every ridge and slope, and waving onward in graceful compliance with the complicated topography of the region . . . [which] extends from the granite headlands overlooking the hot plains to within a few miles of the cool glacial fountains of the summit peaks. . . . [H]ere for every old, storm-stricken giant there are many in all the glory of prime vigor, and for each of these a crowd of eager, hopeful young trees and saplings grows heartily on moraines, rocky ledges, along watercourses, and in the moist alluvium of meadows, seemingly in hot pursuit of eternal life."

–John Muir,
The Mountains of California, 1894

coffee. It's just 5 more miles to reach **Mineral King Ranger Station** (*Mineral King Rd.; 559/565–3768*), a small outpost providing essential visitor information and issuing wilderness permits. It's opposite Cold Springs Campground.

The road at last ends a couple of miles farther up the gorgeous but windswept and avalanche-prone **Mineral King Valley**. Reminiscent of the Rocky Mountains, the valley is most remarkable for its variety of rocks, including speckled granite, white marble, and black shale. Get out of the car to stretch your legs, and perhaps try out one of the valley's many hiking trails (*see* Best Day Hikes) to gain more spectacular views of the jagged mountains rising all around you.

The vistas from the valley floor are dominated by glacier-carved **Sawtooth Peak** (elevation 12,343 feet). Also scattered around the valley are a few cabins built in the late 19th and early 20th centuries, some of which have been painstakingly restored, and all of which may be of interest to history hounds. Although you can't enter them, walking around the outside of these small cabins lets you imagine what life was like for the early settlers of the valley, and the pleasure-seekers who made it their prized summer retreat in the late 1800s and early 1900s.

⊙► BEST DAY HIKES

For day hikers, plentiful paths inside Sequoia National Park range from easy nature walks to mountain goat–style climbs. Check the current schedules of ranger-guided hikes at the Giant Forest Museum and the Lodgepole and Foothills visitor centers, where you can buy hiking maps and interpretive trail brochures. The following sections are arranged geographically, with the easiest and most popular family-friendly trails listed first, followed by descriptions of more challenging and off-the-beaten-path trails for hiking enthusiasts.

GIANT FOREST

Many hikes in the Giant Forest area intersect, which means you could walk all day with hardly any backtracking. The 2-mile **Congress Trail** loop starts from the paved path leading to the General Sherman Tree, naturally making it one of the most heavily trodden trails in the park, then loses many of the crowds as it heads over wooden footbridges

> In Crescent Meadow, you may get a chance to spy on black bears foraging for berries or munching peacefully on wildflowers.

deeper into the serene forest. For even more solitude, the moderately difficult 6-mile **Trail of the Sequoias** loop, which starts along the Congress Trail, passes stately groves of giant sequoias before ascending a ridge, then continues out toward the High Sierra Trail for dizzying vistas, and returns via verdant **Crescent Meadow,** where you may get a chance to spy on black bears foraging for berries or munching peacefully on wildflowers.

Starting outside the Giant Forest Museum, the paved **Big Trees Trail**, which is graded for easy accessibility, loops for just over a mile around Round Meadow, with interesting interpretive signs illustrating giant-sequoia ecology all along the way. Also starting outside the museum, the gentle mile-long **Hazelwood Nature Trail** loop illustrates the importance of wildfire to the life cycle of the giant sequoias.

It's possible to walk about 1.5 miles from the museum along a signposted trail out to **Moro Rock**, or you can drive over for the brief, yet heart-pounding ascent via stone steps to the top of the granite dome, where the Great Western Divide stands spread out before

On following pages: (top left) Head into the woods on the Congress Trail, which passes by the General Sherman Tree. (bottom left) The walk to the summit and back on the Little Baldy Trail takes about four hours. (top right) Take in the High Sierra views from atop Moro Rock. (bottom right) Clamber across the Auto Log, over which vehicles used to drive.

201

A fawn pauses near the Little Baldy Trail.

Breathe in the scent of nature in Crescent Meadow, where wildflowers are in abundance come summertime.

you. Farther along the same road, Crescent Meadow has many inviting trailheads, but not all are signposted clearly. Take the fairly flat 2.2-mile **Crescent Meadow Loop**, which looks prettiest in the early morning or when wildflowers bloom in early summer. Along the way, you can detour to inspect historic Tharp's Log, a hollowed-out trunk that was converted to a rustic mountain cabin. Starting from the meadow, the first rolling stretch of the challenging **High Sierra Trail** takes you ¾ of a mile to head-spinning Eagle View, perched above the gorge of the Middle Fork of the Kaweah River, where an epic background shows off the peaks of the Great Western Divide.

From Wolverton Road, a short distance north along the Generals Highway, the difficult 13.4-mile roundtrip to **Alta Peak** is a serious proposition but rewards properly acclimatized hikers with deep views of the Kaweah River gorge and the craggy Great Western Divide jutting up in front of you. Some of the other lakes-and-meadows trails off Wolverton Road can be done as day hikes, though most hikers prefer to camp in the wilderness overnight (*see* the Foothills section, *below*).

Farther north along the Generals Highway, the Lodgepole Village turnoff leads to the trailhead for the moderate 3.4-mile round trip to **Tokopah Falls**, which Sierra Nevada snowmelt turns into a torrent in late spring and early summer. About 6 miles north of Lodgepole along the Generals Highway, a moderate 1.75-mile round-trip ascent of **Little Baldy**, a rounded granite dome once used as a fire lookout, provides 360-degree views from the summit. Starting from Dorst Creek Campground farther north along the highway, the easy 2.1-mile round-trip **Muir Grove Trail** out toward Pine Ridge is a walk through an almost undisturbed grove of giant sequoias. It's a small amount of effort to be rewarded with such peacefulness among the giant trees, something John Muir often wrote about in his journals during his early explorations of the Sierra Nevada.

FOOTHILLS

In the southern Foothills area of the park, the trails are usually much less traveled than those in the must-see Giant Forest. As you explore here, watch out for poison oak, ticks, and rattlesnakes. Also, don't venture too far off-trail, because if you do, there is a small chance that you just might find yourself in an illegal marijuana grow site, often guarded by potentially armed growers.

Although it's rare that a casual day hiker would run into a marijuana-growing operation, as they're usually well hidden in the wilderness of the park, it's always good to stay aware of the potential issue.

From Potwisha Campground, an easy ½-mile loop trail leads to summertime swimming holes along the Kaweah River. Off the same access road, it's a 3.9-mile moderate hike each way to **Marble Falls,** best visited in late spring when the waterfall is at its fullest, fed by melting mountain snows.

Starting from the Buckeye Flat Campground access road, a long and strenuously uphill 6-mile round-trip hike follows the **Middle Fork Trail** along the Kaweah River for excellent views of Moro Rock, Castle Rocks, and the Great Western Divide before ending with a short but steep climb to Panther Creek.

If it's too snowy to drive into the Giant Forest, you can hike in by setting out on one of the trails that begin in the remote South Fork Campground and lead you through the park's lowest-elevation giant sequoia groves. One such trail is a challenging (read: long and strenuous) 5-mile climb to Garfield Creek, past which you can wander through some of the park's most isolated and remote groves of giant sequoia trees.

MINERAL KING

During the adventurous side trip to Mineral King, even short hikes will help you absorb the singular beauty of this subalpine valley. Starting from Cold Springs Campground, the tame, 2.4-mile round-trip **Cold Springs Nature Trail** winds past historic cabins that predate the national park.

Before attempting longer day hikes that ascend to higher-altitude lakes and meadows, stop by the Mineral King Ranger Station for advice and to check on trail conditions. The most popular day hikes include the 6.8-mile round-trip to gorgeous **Eagle Lake** and the 7.5-mile round-trip trek to **White Chief Canyon**, which passes a wildflower meadow, historic miners' cabins, and marble caverns for expert spelunkers. The well-traveled 8.4-mile round-trip trail to **Monarch Lakes** also offers spectacular views back over the entire valley. Before leaving your car at the trailhead for any length of time (that is, longer than a short hike), protect it from those pesky marmots (*see* Warning: Marmots Ahead).

☻ OTHER ACTIVITIES

While most visitors to Sequoia National Park take time for a short day hike among the giant sequoia trees, there are plenty of other sports to try, all year round. Horseback rides are available nearby (*see* the Kings Canyon National Park chapter).

Besides what's described below, you may want to look into the **Sequoia Field Institute** (*47050 Generals Hwy. #10; 559/565–4251; www.sequoiaparksconservancy.org/adventures.html*), which offers educational programs and trips in the national park year-round. Options can range from family birding walks with a naturalist who can help identify Sierra songbirds to stargazing programs that feature ancient tales about the constellations or overnight backpacking trips led by entertaining local experts and focused on various natural- or cultural-history topics—anything from black-bear ecology to early pioneer-era experiences in the park. The in-depth knowledge shared by these trips' leaders makes them worth the extra effort of signing up weeks or even months in advance of your trip.

Backpacking—the greatest escape you can make in the park—lets you avoid the traffic noise and summer crowds that flood many day-hiking trails.

BACKPACKING AND MOUNTAINEERING

Wilderness trails beckon to backpackers and mountain climbers on both sides of the Great Western Divide. While you do need hiking experience and plenty of preparation to embark on any of these adventurous overnight trips, you'll be infinitely rewarded by the wilderness's amazing scenery—alpine lakes, profusely blooming wildflower meadows, dense forests where black bears and marmots freely roam, and high above it all, arid Sierra Nevada peaks down which cacophonous waterfalls rush in early summer. In short, backpacking is the greatest escape you can make in the park; you can avoid the traffic noise and the incessant summer crowds that flood many day-hiking trails.

The Giant Forest area, Lodgepole Village, and the Mineral King valley are the busiest gateways for backpacking trips into the Sierra Nevada high country. The most well-trammeled route is the epic ★**HIGH SIERRA TRAIL**, which starts from shady Crescent Meadow

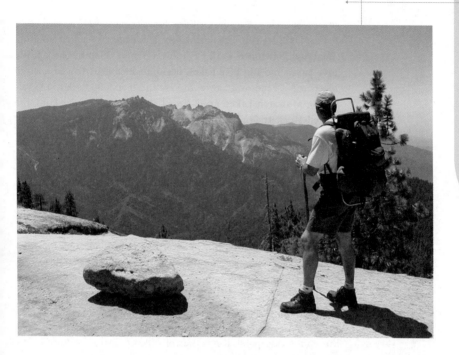

A backpacker drinks in the view on the High Sierra Trail.

and leads for more than 70 miles over the Great Western Divide to Mt. Whitney, at least a week's endeavor even for those in good physical shape. The first 11.5 miles to **Bearpaw Meadow** (elevation 7,800 feet) make an excellent two- or three-day backpacking trip, with time for detours to pretty alpine lakes above the meadow.

Prime scenery also rewards weekend trips to **Emerald and Pear Lakes**, a moderately challenging 6.1-mile hike each way on the heavily traveled Lakes Trail from the Wolverton Road trailhead. Also starting from Wolverton Road, a tougher 11.8-mile round-trip trail climbs steadily to **Alta Meadow**, where you can kick back among the wildflowers in early summer. From Lodgepole, a steep and difficult 14-mile round-trip trail to wildly contrasting **Twin Lakes** (the smaller one is completely surrounded by thick forest, while the larger of the pair backs up against granite talus and cliffs) passes fresh Cahoon Meadow.

Several rugged wilderness trails rise out of the Mineral King valley, testing the endurance of even experienced backpackers. Many of the day hikes to alpine lakes described in the previous section make great overnight backpacking destinations, too. The most well-traveled back-packing trail leads to **Franklin Lakes**, a difficult 10.8-mile roundtrip. The tough **Sawtooth Trail** passes over Timber Gap to reach **Little Five Lakes** and **Big Five Lakes**, beyond which experienced off-trail hikers can ascend over Sawtooth Pass and then loop back to the valley via **Monarch Lakes Trail**. From Atwell Mill Campground, the **Atwell-Hockett Trail** passes streams and verdant forests for 10 miles to reach lush Hockett Meadow.

PERMITS

Between late May and mid-September, all trails inside Sequoia and Kings Canyon national parks are subject to a daily quota. Check availability and make wilderness permit reservations ($15) up to six months in advance online at *www.recreation.gov,* which will send you a confirmation email that includes permit pick-up location information. To collect your permit, present a printout of this confirmation email and a photo ID to rangers at the trailhead desk as early as 1 pm the day before the start of your trek.

In the non-quota season, self-issue permits are available at Mineral King Ranger Station, Ash Mountain Wilderness Office, Giant Forest Museum (Lodgepole), Kings Canyon Visitor Center, or Road's End Permit Station (Cedar Grove). Note, however, that only the Ash Mountain office and Kings Canyon Visitor Center are open in the winter season.

Most of the staffed facilities rent food-storage containers, which are required in some areas. Containers cost $5–$12 for the first three days and $2–$3 per night after that.

Wilderness trips starting in nearby national forest lands are often subject to quotas, and reservations for wilderness permits are sometimes accepted.

Fishing

Fishing is more of a pleasurable pastime than a sport inside the park. The catch is almost guaranteed to be of the trout variety—rainbow, brown, golden, and eastern brook. The season is usually from late April until mid-November, except in the Kaweah River drainage, where anglers drop their lines year-round.

Many of the best fishing spots are accessible only via hiking trails—for example, from the Lodgepole Village area to Twin Lakes or from Mineral King to Big and Little Five Lakes. A few more-convenient

HIKING MT. WHITNEY

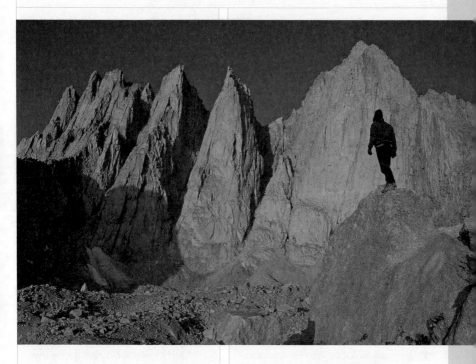

At an eye-watering 14,505 feet, **Mt. Whitney** is the highest peak in the contiguous United States. This soaring peak punctuates the eastern side of the Sierra Nevada, and it has the most popular backpacking trail in the entire region.

Though it's a popular challenge, it's definitely not something to be taken lightly. (If you finish it, you'll have serious bragging rights.) The 22-mile round-trip ascent is for fit, experienced alpinists.

Wilderness permits for both day use and overnight hiking are required year-round for the Mt. Whitney Zone, with specific trail quotas between May and October. Those starting from Whitney Portal on the east side of the Sierra Nevada must enter the competitive Mt. Whitney permit lottery, normally held February 1 to March 15 each year. Contact the **Inyo National Forest** (351 Pacu Lane, Suite 200, Bishop; 760/873-2483; www.fs.usda.gov/inyo) for info on trips beginning on the east side. Hikers approaching from the west (starting in Sequoia or Kings Canyon national parks) are subject only to the normal national park trailhead quotas.

SEQUOIA NATIONAL PARK IN THE WINTER

Snow usually blankets Sequoia National Park between November and April, which keeps away the crowds and adds an element of magical mystery to your experience, especially with the towering trees peacefully covered in white. If you do choose to visit in winter, you will be rewarded by peaceful snowshoe walks through groves of giant sequoias, while more adventurous types can lash on cross-country skis.

Although much of the park's wildlife takes a long winter's nap at this time, you may still glimpse birds flying overhead and mule deer bounding through the thick forests, especially in the warmer Sierra Nevada foothills, where a few stubborn black bears lumber about even during the coldest months. The fresh layers of snow also provide an excellent way to study animal tracks, which may go unnoticed or easily be trampled underfoot by hundreds of visitors during the summer months. For independent, self-sufficient tourists, the special effort it takes to visit Sequoia National Park during winter is well rewarded by both the scenery and the unusual opportunities for snow sports.

Only a few park roads remain open during winter, and even the Generals Highway typically closes for several months each year. The upper section of the highway through the Giant Forest and Sequoia National Forest leading to Kings Canyon National Park is especially subject to weather delays and closures after heavy storms. Always carry tire chains, which may be required at any time during winter. For current road conditions, call 559/565–3341.

Snowballs fly and children rush about in the **Wolverton** area. This spot off the Generals Highway, about 2 miles north of the General Sherman Tree, is where kids come to play in the snow and leap onto their sleds for a quick flight downhill.

If snowshoeing and cross-country skiing through silent groves of giant sequoias are more to your liking, head to the **Giant Forest** for ungroomed trails, including out to Moro Rock and Crescent Meadow on a side road that's sometimes closed to vehicle traffic in winter. Rent cross-country skis and snowshoes at the **Wuksachi Lodge** *(Generals Hwy.; 866/807-3598),* which also sells basic winter clothing and snow-play equipment like children's plastic sleds. Staff at the lodge groom cross-country skiing trails for beginner to experienced skiers.

If you'd like to join a ranger-guided snowshoe walk, call the **Giant Forest Museum** *(Generals Hwy.; 559/565-4480)* for reservations. The 2-mile, two-hour trek is usually scheduled on Saturdays and holidays. Equipment is provided for a small donation. For many visitors, this relatively short walk is certainly a lot of exercise (if you've ever tried snowshoeing before, you know it's more tiring than it might at first look), but it's also perhaps the most special experience you can have in the park during winter without venturing into the wilderness. The slow pace of the guided trek lets you savor the experience of the forest during the stillness of winter. The crisp, clear air means that the views are even more impressive than in summer. The **Sequoia Field Institute** *(559/565-4251; www.sequoiaparksconservancy.org/adventures.html)* also offer free snowshoe walks at Wakusachi Lodge.

Expert backcountry skiers well versed in survival skills can find rest at the end of a 6-mile, 2,000-foot ascent from Wolverton Meadow at the **Pear Lake Winter Hut** (elevation 9,200 feet). The hut, which sleeps 10 people, is usually open from mid-December through April. Allow all day to get there. It's heated by a wood-pellet stove, but bring your own bedding, which means subzero-rated winter-weight sleeping bags, to stay warm in the sleeping loft equipped only with basic bunk beds. For reservations, contact the **Sequoia Parks Conservancy** *(559/565-4251; www.sequoiaparksconservancy.org).*

For more winter recreation areas, including in the Giant Sequoia National Monument of the Sequoia National Forest, *see* the Kings Canyon National Park chapter.

You'll need to lace up your boots and hit a trail to reach some of the park's best fishing holes.

fishing holes, often requiring only a short walk along a well-trodden trail to reach, are found along the Kaweah River in the southern Sierra Nevada foothills area. Multiday wilderness pack trips undertaken with the aid of an outdoor outfitter that wrangles horses and mules explore the Golden Trout Wilderness of the **Sequoia National Forest** *(Western Divide Ranger District office: 32588 Hwy. 190, Springville; 559/539-2607; www.fs.usda.gov/sequoia)* south of the Sequoia National Park boundary.

LICENSES

Anglers ages 16 and older must carry a valid California fishing license, which you can buy online, at **Three Rivers Mercantile** *(41152 Sierra Dr.; 559/561-2378)* in Three Rivers, or at the general store at Hume Lake. The general limit is five trout per day, with 10 fish in possession. Additional restrictions apply inside the national park boundaries, so ask at one of the park's visitor centers for current regulations covering specific bait and hook types, daily limits, and catch-and-release requirements, which vary depending on your location and elevation within the park.

SWIMMING AND WHITE-WATER RAFTING

When thermometers in the foothills top 100°F during summer, a dip in the **Kaweah River** is enticing, as the water's chilly temperatures feel just right. Look for swimming holes in the river along the **Marble Fork**, accessed via a hiking trail north of Potwisha Campground, and on the **Middle Fork** east of Buckeye Flat Campground.

There's a secret swimming hole near the **Lodgepole Village Picnic Area**, too. To find it, ask any of the campground rangers or Lodgepole visitor center staff for directions. If it's a hot summer day, though, probably all you will have to do is follow the sounds of children's happy shouts.

Swimming anywhere in the park can be extremely dangerous in early summer, when mountain snowmelt can turn rivers into a torrent of rapids. As water levels drop later in the summer, sandy and rocky beaches appear. Ask rangers for advice about current conditions and the best swimming spots when you visit, and always exercise caution, as drowning is the number one cause of visitor fatalities in the park. Smooth rocks can be very slippery, and strong currents often run beneath calm surfaces. None of the swimming holes in the parks have any sort of lifeguard or posted ranger lookout, so it's important to look out for not only yourself but everyone else if you choose to swim here. If you see a swimmer get into trouble, immediately call a ranger or dial 911 from any pay phone to contact park dispatch for help with swift-water rescue.

All white-water rafting on the Kaweah River (with Class III–V rapids) happens outside the national park boundaries. The usual take-out point is Lake Kaweah reservoir, southwest of the town of Three Rivers. **Whitewater Voyages** (*11252 Kernville Rd., Kernville, 800/400–7238; www.whitewatervoyages.com*) and **Kaweah Whitewater Adventures** (*Three Rivers; 559/740–8251; kaweah-outdoors.com*) offer half- and full-day rafting adventures on the Kaweah River. The white-water-rafting season usually runs from late spring into early summer, but in recent years, drought conditions have curtailed trips. Call to check current offerings.

Spotlight on ✶
SUPERSIZED SIGHTS

Central California's trio of national parks—Yosemite, Sequoia, and Kings Canyon—is, simply put, a land of giants. Outdoor playgrounds on a monumental scale, the parks are marked by extraordinary sights: the world's biggest trees, massive granite monoliths, Sierra Nevada mountains soaring above 14,000 feet, and North America's highest waterfall and deepest canyon (yes, even deeper than the Grand Canyon). These tremendous natural wonders are packed into the alpine valleys, rocky river canyons, and jagged mountain passes of the 3,000 square miles of national parklands, including the Giant Sequoia National Monument. Wherever you wander here, you're sure to be awestruck.

◀◀ The sun sets and the moon rises over Yosemite Valley.

GIANT SEQUOIAS

The giant sequoia is the largest living tree on Earth. A rare species, it grows only in scattered groves in the western Sierra Nevada. Among the oldest living flora, these trees are remarkable survivors. Their tannin-rich bark and heartwood, resisting both insects and wildfires, ensures longevity in the forest. The wood is too brittle to be profitably used as lumber, so many trees survived logging attempts in the late 19th and early 20th centuries. Giant sequoias grow at an astounding rate—sometimes adding the equivalent of a 50-foot-tall tree to their own bulk in a single year—and they can live for centuries. Their Achilles heel is a shallow root system, which often topples mature giants in their golden age. The world's largest groves of giant sequoias are in Sequoia National Park's Giant Forest.

TIP

To find serenity among these gentle giants, come in late spring, when snow still blankets the forest floor and summer crowds are absent.

Yosemite's Mariposa Grove of giant sequoias

Giant Forest

Converse Basin

Grant Grove

KINGS CANYON AND SEQUOIA NATIONAL PARKS

200

175

150

125

100

75

50

25

Grizzly Giant
(209 ft.)

Ponderosa
Pine
(100 ft.)

Adult Man
(6 ft.)

Grizzly Bear
(9 ft.)

GROUND LEVEL
(0 ft.)

GIANT SEQUOIAS: WHO'S WHO

When measured by volume, the giant sequoia (*Sequoiadendron giganteum*) is the world's largest living tree. It belongs to the same family as the tallest living tree, the coast redwood (*Sequoia sempervirens*).

Giant sequoias themselves aren't exactly short: The tallest can grow 27 stories high. Despite their life span of over 3,000 years, they are outlived by the ancient bristlecone pine (*Pinus longaeva* and *P. aristata*), some of which are 4,000 or more years old.

(opposite page, clockwise from top left) Giant sequoia, coast redwoods, bristlecone pine tree.

HIDDEN GIANT: BOOLE TREE

An old-growth giant cloaked in moss, the Boole Tree in Sequoia National Forest's Converse Basin was spared by an early 1900s lumber-mill owner. It is now the world's sixth-largest giant sequoia. At the head of the trail leading to the Boole Tree is a field littered with the stumps of giant sequoias that did not share its fate.

Giant sequoias in Grant Grove.

Fallen Monarch log, Grant Grove.

GRIZZLY GIANT

LOCATION: Mariposa Grove, Yosemite National Park

HEIGHT: 209 feet

CIRCUMFERENCE: 96.5 feet

BIT OF TRIVIA: Thought to be the oldest giant sequoia in existence.

GENERAL SHERMAN TREE

LOCATION: Giant Forest, Sequoia National Park

HEIGHT: 274.9 feet

CIRCUMFERENCE: 102.6 feet

BIT OF TRIVIA: Named for Civil War general William Tecumseh Sherman.

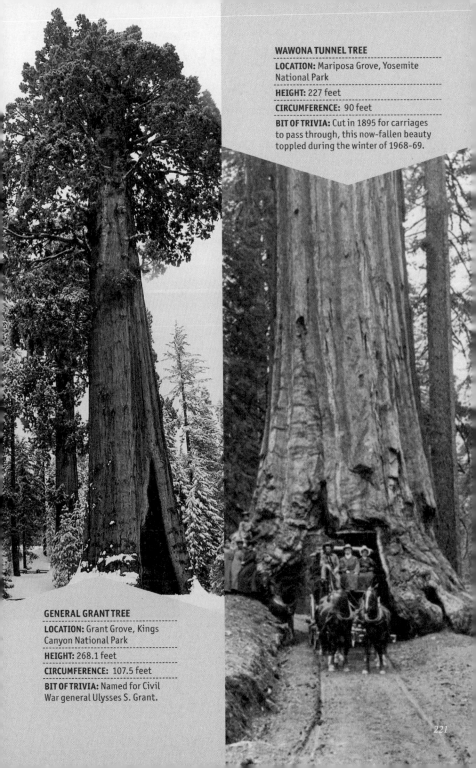

WAWONA TUNNEL TREE

LOCATION: Mariposa Grove, Yosemite National Park

HEIGHT: 227 feet

CIRCUMFERENCE: 90 feet

BIT OF TRIVIA: Cut in 1895 for carriages to pass through, this now-fallen beauty toppled during the winter of 1968-69.

GENERAL GRANT TREE

LOCATION: Grant Grove, Kings Canyon National Park

HEIGHT: 268.1 feet

CIRCUMFERENCE: 107.5 feet

BIT OF TRIVIA: Named for Civil War general Ulysses S. Grant.

HOW DID THEY GET SO BIG?

Yosemite, Kings Canyon, and Sequoia National Parks ride the Sierra Nevada, which reaches a heady elevation of 14,505 feet atop Mt. Whitney, the highest peak in the lower 48 states. The Sierra Nevada are made of granite, deposited underground by ancient volcanic activity, then tilted and uplifted along fault lines. Some of this subterranean rock has been dramatically exposed to form the parks' granite monoliths, most famously in the Yosemite Valley, with the curved tooth of Half Dome and the sheer wall of El Capitan. These granite icons are the result of weathering after glaciers polished the landscape and shaped the Yosemite Valley and the Kings Canyon thousands of years ago.

TIP

For the best views of Half Dome, drive up to Glacier Point. For a great view of El Capitan, sit beside the Merced River at Cathedral Beach.

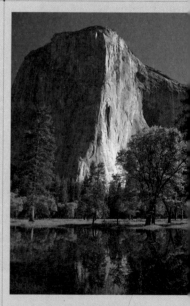

El Capitan.

Glacier Point

El Capitan

Half Dome

YOSEMITE NATIONAL PARK

SIZING UP THE MOUNTAINS

MT. LYELL (Yosemite):
13,114 feet

MT. WHITNEY (shown in photo):
14,505 feet

MATTERHORN (Switzerland):
14,693 feet

DENALI (Alaska):
20,320 feet

MT. EVEREST (Nepal):
29,029 feet

YOSEMITE FALLS

HIGHEST WATERFALL

Waterfalls in the Yosemite Valley are especially famous for their heart-stopping drops over sheer granite cliffs. The falls are at their fullest in spring, when snowmelt pours into the river valleys throughout the Sierra Nevada. When the falls' output peaks in May, clouds of mist billow from the base of the plunging chutes, making visitors at the bottom of the falls disappear from view. Stand there yourself and you'll hear the water's roar, as loud as a tornado. Don't forget to bring a rainproof jacket! Yosemite Falls, North America's highest waterfall at 2,425 feet, is especially impressive: At peak times, hydrologists estimate that almost 135,000 gallons of water tumble down its triple cascade every minute.

TIP

Hiking trails climb right up beside some of Yosemite's grandest falls. In spring, these slick footpaths let you feel the full force of nature's power.

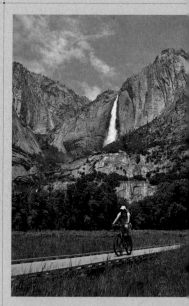

Biking past Yosemite Falls.

Yosemite Falls

YOSEMITE NATIONAL PARK

SIZING UP THE WATERFALLS

ANGEL FALLS (Venezuela):
3,212 feet tall

**YOSEMITE FALLS (shown
in photo):** 2,425 feet tall

**VICTORIA FALLS (Zambia/
Zimbabwe):** 354 feet tall

**IGUAZU FALLS (Brazil/
Argentina):** 269 feet tall

**NIAGARA FALLS (Ontario,
Canada/New York):** 176 feet tall

KINGS CANYON

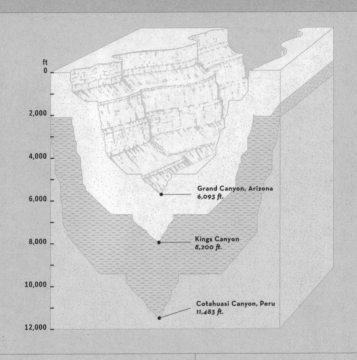

ft
0

2,000

4,000

Grand Canyon, Arizona
6,093 ft.

6,000

Kings Canyon
8,200 ft.

8,000

10,000

Cotahuasi Canyon, Peru
11,483 ft.

12,000

Kings Canyon

Junction View

Kings Canyon
Scenic Byway

**KINGS CANYON AND SEQUOIA
NATIONAL PARKS**

Reaching a depth of 8,200 feet when measured from Spanish Peak (10,051 feet) down to the confluence of the North and Middle Forks of the Kings River, Kings Canyon is one of the country's deepest canyons. The canyon bottom is easily accessible via a winding, scenic byway. Unlike the Grand Canyon, Kings Canyon was not cut only by a river. It's also the work of glaciers, those ancient rivers of ice, snow, and debris that flowed through during the last Ice Age. In 1965, controversial proposals aimed to dam the Kings River and flood the canyon in order to supply water to Los Angeles. Happily, those plans were blocked.

TIP

Drive the Kings Canyon Scenic Byway in early morning or late afternoon, when the pastel color palette is most varied. Stop at Junction View to be awed by the canyon's immensity.

Kings Canyon
National Park

The Kings Canyon Scenic Byway has stunning views at every one of its many turns.

The grandeur of Yosemite and the towering trees of Sequoia tend to overshadow the splendors of Kings Canyon, making it the least visited of the three Sierra Nevada national parks. But the secrets of Kings Canyon are fiercely guarded by its frequent visitors. It's known and loved best by those who have wandered all over the Sierra Nevada first, only to at last find in this remote canyon the serenity that John Muir sought—and then fought so hard for—in these lofty mountains.

230

GENERAL GRANT

A couple of aspiring explorers walk through the hollowed-out Fallen Monarch in Grant Grove. (left) The General Grant Tree is the largest tree in Grant Grove.

GENERAL GRANT TREE

HEIGHT: 268.1 feet

WIDTH: 40 feet (at base)

CIRCUMFERENCE: 107.5 feet

VOLUME: 46,608 cubic feet

The General Grant Tree was proclaimed a national shrine by President Dwight D. Eisenhower in 1956.

While not spotlighted in its name, Kings Canyon National Park has hidden delights. Among them are many imposing stands of the giant trees—including Redwood Mountain Grove, the largest known grove of giant sequoias in the world—along with the full spread of what the Sierra Nevada is famous for: treacherously beautiful alpine peaks, painterly wildflower meadows, cascading waterfalls, craggy granite formations, and icy-cool lakes.

What you'll remember best from your visit are the General Grant Tree, first protected on its own as a tiny national park in 1890; the mist-cloaked rocky beaches and gushing waterfalls alongside the Kings River, which rushes through the canyon's amazingly deep gorge; and blissful Zumwalt Meadow, where the strikingly colored western tanager makes its migratory stopover.

Because the park is seldom crowded, you can breathe a little more easily here as you enjoy a measure of solitude that's often absent in Sequoia and especially in Yosemite, which receives 4 million visitors each year.

Most tourists visit Kings Canyon between Memorial Day and Labor Day, when summer melts snow in the Sierra Nevada high country, opening up jaw-dropping wilderness trails; the chill is taken off the Kings River, which fills with swimmers, mostly shrieking children; and the Kings Canyon Scenic Byway is thrown open from

The giant sequoias in
Grant Grove are between
1,800 and 2,700 years old.

KINGS CANYON NATIONAL PARK

0 — 7.5 Miles
0 — 7.5 Kilometers

OWENS

To Bishop

INYO
NATIONAL
FOREST

To
Independence
& Lone Pine

JOHN MUIR
WILDERNESS

Pavilion Dome

Mount Goethe
13,264ft

McClure
Meadow

Mount Henry
12,196ft

LE CONTE DIVIDE

The Hermit
12,360ft

Mount Darwin
13,830ft

Mount Powell
13,361ft

Mount Goddard
13,568ft

Muir Pass

Bishop Pass
11,972ft

North Palisade
14,242ft

To
Big P

Charybdis

Le Conte
Canyon

Middle Palisade
14,040ft

John Muir Trail (JMT)

Mount Reinstein
12,604ft

Mather Pass
12,100ft

Split Mountain
14,058ft

Burnt Mountain
10,608ft

Windy Peak

SIMPSON MEADOW

Bench Lake

Striped Moun

SIERRA
NATIONAL
FOREST

CIRQUE CREST

IN
NATI
FO

Arrow Peak

MONARCH DIVIDE

MURO BLANCO

Pyramid Peak
12,777ft

Kennedy Pass
10,900ft

Granite Pass
10,673ft

Copper
Creek Trail

Woods Creek Trail

Mount Baxter
13,125ft

Converse Basin/
Boole Tree

Junction View

MONARCH
WILDERNESS

Cedar Grove
Overlook

Lewis Creek Trail

Mount
Clarence King
12,905ft

Diamond
13,126

Kings Canyon
Scenic Byway

Cedar Grove
Visitor Center
and Village

Mount
Gardiner

Rae Lake
Rae
Loo

General
Grant Tree

Hume Lake

Boyden
Cavern

Grizzly
Falls

Stables

Kings River

Mist Falls

McGee Overlook

KINGS

CANYON

Road's End Wilderness
Information Station/
Muir Rock

Charlotte Lake

Fallen Monarch/Gamlin Cabin
Stables

Sheep Creek

Zumwalt Meadow

Panoramic Point

Sentinel

Kings Canyon Visitor Center
and Grant Grove Village

Canyon View

Lookout Peak

Moraine

Knapp's
Cabin

Roaring River Falls

Bubbs Creek
Trail

University Peak
13,632ft

Kear
Pe
11,8

Kings Canyon
Overlook

Buck Rock

Mitchell
Peak

Canyon
Viewpoint

Roaring River

KINGS CANYON
NATIONAL
PARK

Mount Brad
13,289ft

Big
Stump

Quail Flat
Jct.

Montecito Sequoia
Lodge

Big Meadows Rd.

Big Meadows

KINGS-KERN DIVID

Junction Peak

Redwood
Mountain
Overlook

JENNIE LAKES
WILDERNESS

To
Fresno

Stony Creek Village

Generals Highway

JO PASS

Silliman Pass

Table Mountain
13,630ft

Mount Tgl
14,018

Lodgepole
Visitor Center
and Village

Centennial Peak
13,255ft

Tyndal
Creek

Crystal
Cave

Colby Pass

Elizabeth Pass

Triple Divide
Peak

Crabtree

General Sherman Tree

Generals Highway

Bearpaw Meadow

SEQUOIA
NATIONAL PARK

Moro Rock

Mount Kaweah
13,765ft

Potwisha

Buckeye Flat

Mount Guyot
12,300ft

To
Three Springs &
Visalia

Castle Rocks

Little Five Lakes

Rock Cree

Legend

- Ranger / Information
- Food Service
- Picnic Area
- Lodging
- Campground
- Gas Station
- **P** Parking Area
- ···· John Muir Trail /
  Pacific Crest Trail
- - - Other Trails

Grant Grove past the turn off to Hume Lake and Boyden Cavern all the way to Cedar Grove.

If you want to avoid the biggest crowds, plan your sojourn for early June or just after Labor Day, while the weather holds steady and hiking trails through the giant sequoia groves and the canyon remain open. You might even have some of those thickly forested trails to yourself—that is, unless you spot a galumphing black bear in search of berries.

More than half the size of Yosemite National Park to the north, Kings Canyon National Park covers more than 700 square miles, making it a little larger than its southern neighbor, Sequoia National Park. Although separated by geography, these two southern Sierra Nevada parks are administered together by the National Park Service, and most tourists usually don't visit one without getting at least a taste of the other.

The main tourist hub in Kings Canyon National Park isn't inside the canyon at all; it's Grant Grove, sitting near the top of the Generals Highway among tall stands of giant sequoia trees that compete with the Giant Forest of Sequoia National Park. Cedar Grove, the park's secondary tourist hub, is nestled deep inside the canyon that John Muir once called "a rival to the Yosemite."

You might even have some of those thickly forested trails to yourself—that is, unless you spot a galumphing black bear in search of berries.

Wrapped around the park and between Grant Grove and Cedar Grove is the Giant Sequoia National Monument of the Sequoia National Forest, which is loved for its hiking trails through primeval forests, idyllic lakes for summer recreation, and a fascinating marble cavern.

No matter which road you take into Kings Canyon—whether you choose to travel Highway 180, which twists up the mountain from the farmlands of California's central valley just outside Fresno, or the Generals Highway, an equally winding route connecting Kings Canyon National Park to Sequoia National Park—the journey here is at high elevation, so it quite literally takes your breath away. The Kings Canyon Scenic Byway, another twisted route with hairpin turns and heart-racing drop-offs, connects the park's tourist centers of Grant Grove and Cedar Grove. The latter is where Highway 180 finally rolls to a stop and the wilderness of the Sierra Nevadas begins.

The wilderness of Cedar Grove varies in its terrain, with rocky outcrops and cliffs, as well as forested areas and waterfalls.

PLANNING YOUR TIME

If your main intent is to hit the highlights, you could easily do Kings Canyon in a day. But if you want to soak in the serenity Muir encountered here, stay awhile. A stretch of even just a few days gives you time to take some short hikes around the tall trees of Grant Grove, to visit lesser-known wonders like the Boole Tree, and to try a ranger-guided activity such as a wildflower walk or a campfire talk under the stars.

If your time is limited and you'll be here just a day, then get an early start. Stop briefly in Grant Grove to see the famous tree and to get oriented to the park, and then head down to Road's End, about an hour's drive northeast along the canyon's byway. Try to arrive in Cedar Grove before lunchtime to get ahead of the worst day-tripper crowds. Time your return trip up the canyon to make photo-safari stops at scenic overlooks of the vast canyon, which look most idyllic around sunset.

If you've got two or more days to spend, take a day each in Grant Grove and Cedar Grove, then explore the Giant Sequoia National Monument and its thickly forested trails and alpine lakes. With a week or longer, make reservations well in advance for a backpacking or fishing and horseback-riding pack trip into the high-country wilderness.

⊙→ SIGHTS

See the Kings Canyon National Park map.

This section starts at the most popular spot in Kings Canyon National Park, which is Grant Grove. It then follows the Kings Canyon Scenic Byway, which links Grant Grove with Cedar Grove, the park's other tourist hub, via a stunning wilderness corridor through the Giant Sequoia National Monument of the Sequoia National Forest. Cedar Grove is located at the end of the road, where Highway 180 comes to an abrupt stop alongside the Kings River at the very bottom of the Kings Canyon. Finally, this section covers the Generals Highway, which connects Grant Grove with Sequoia National Park to the south, via even more forest lands now also protected as part of the Giant Sequoia National Monument.

GRANT GROVE

A few miles beyond the Big Stump Entrance Station, Highway 180 slows as it enters **Grant Grove Village** (elevation 6,589 feet). The busiest section of Kings Canyon National Park, the village offers the most visitor services in the park, including a post office, convenience market, gift shop, lodging, and an elegant restaurant. At the hopping **Kings Canyon Visitor Center** (*Hwy. 180; 559/565–4307*), a cooperative venture between the National Park Service, USDA Forest Service, and nonprofit Sequoia Parks Conservancy, you can peruse natural-history exhibits, then watch a 15-minute orientation film that gives you a bird's-eye view of the park, from its mellow groves of giant sequoias to the near-vertical high country of the Sierra Nevada. Also at the center you can learn about hiking options, including overnight backpacking, and horseback-riding trips up these mountains, which rank among California's highest (*see* Best Day Hikes).

Just north of the visitor center on Highway 180, a well-signposted turnoff leads downhill to the ★**GENERAL GRANT TREE**, a towering giant named after Civil War general and U.S. president Ulysses S. Grant. It's the second-largest tree in the world, measuring 268.1 feet high and more than 40 feet wide at the base of its gnarly, thick trunk. Designated a National Shrine, the historic landmark is also the United States' official Christmas tree (ordained so by President Calvin Coolidge in 1926). Because every park visitor is eager to see this famous sequoia, the parking lot here is usually overflowing. It's worth the wait and crowds, though. As you stand beside the

KINGS CANYON VISITOR CENTER

TELEPHONE: 559/565–4307

ADDRESS: Near the Big Stump Entrance, Highway 180

GENERAL GRANT
THE NATION'S CHRISTMAS TREE

GENERAL GRANT TREE
THE NATION'S CHRISTMAS TREE
A LIVING SHRINE

Dominating its forest neighbors, the General Grant Tree is considered by many to have the most beautiful "classic" giant sequoia form. The fossil record indicates this ancient species first appeared on the western U.S. about 50 million years ago. Changing climatic conditions reduced its range to isolated groves along the western slope of the Sierra Nevada. Congress created General Grant National Park in 1890, a 4 square mile area to protect the Big Trees from the lumberman's axe. In 1926, this tree was proclaimed the Nation's Christmas Tree, and annual celebrations are held at its base each December. More recently the Tree was dedicated as America's only living National shrine in memory of those who died defending this country.

Estimated Age
Height Above Base
Circumference at Base
Maximum Basal Diameter

GENERAL GRANT
1800-2000 years
267 ft. (81.5m)
107.6 ft. (32.8m)
40.3 ft. (12.3m)

GENERAL SHERMAN
2300-2700 years
274.9 ft. (83.8m)
102.6 ft. (31.1m)
36.5 ft. (11.1m)

General Grant Tree, peering up at its lofty green branches that climb like a ladder toward the sky, it's impossible not to feel awed, especially if you visit early on a peaceful summer morning when dew droplets shine in the sun, or if you snowshoe around the imperial grove after a winter storm blankets it in a mantle of silence.

Surrounding this star attraction are multiple sequoias, some scarred by fire and others numbering among the loftiest, greenest, and most impressive of their kind still standing. Inside the enormous grove is the historic **Gamlin Cabin**, built by a 19th-century homesteader; it eventually became the national park's first ranger station. Also amid the grove you can scramble inside the impressive **Fallen Monarch**, a hoary, hollowed-out remnant of a giant sequoia carved by fire. During the late 19th century, this natural treehouse variously served as a hotel, saloon, and U.S. cavalry stables.

On the opposite side of Highway 180 and just before the John Muir Lodge, a side road (which is often closed to traffic during winter) leads steeply for more than 2.5 miles to truthfully named **Panoramic Point**. An easy paved trail leads from the parking lot to the lookout itself, where a sign identifies noteworthy peaks in the Sierra Crest, a hugging-the-clouds ridge that parallels the Great Western Divide, where water on the west flows to the Pacific Ocean and water on the east runs into the Great Basin Desert. The peaks visible here are so enormous that they hide from view even Mt. Whitney, the highest point in the contiguous United States, which sits behind them at an elevation of 14,505 feet.

A GRANDER CANYON

"In the vast Sierra wilderness far to the southward of the famous Yosemite Valley, there is a yet grander valley of the same kind. It is situated on the south fork of Kings River, above the most extensive groves and forests of the giant sequoia, and beneath the shadows [of] the highest mountains in the range, where the cañons [sic] are deepest . . . .

"From this long, flowery, forested, well-watered park the walls rise abruptly in plain precipices or richly sculptured masses . . . . The so-called war of the elements has done them no harm. There is no unsightly defacement as yet; deep in the sky, inviting the onset of storms through unnumbered centuries, they still stand firm and seemingly as fresh and unworn as new-born flowers.

"I fancy the time is not distant when...a road will be built up the South Fork of Kings River through the sequoia groves, into the great cañon . . . . Let our lawgivers then make haste before it is too late to set apart this surpassingly glorious region for the recreation and well-being of humanity, and all the world will rise up and call them blessed."

−John Muir, "A Rival of the Yosemite: The Cañon of the South Fork of the Kings River, California," *The Century Illustrated Monthly Magazine*, November 1891.

KINGS CANYON SCENIC BYWAY

To get from Grant Grove to Cedar Grove, the one and only route to take is the ★KINGS CANYON SCENIC BYWAY (Highway 180), which passes through the Giant Sequoia National Monument inside the Sequoia National Forest. This remarkably scenic highway, with its series of heart-in-your-throat twists and turns, is the only road leading down from any direction into Cedar Grove. This means that after you've successfully made the white-knuckle trip deep into the canyon and you're ready to explore elsewhere, backtracking is your only option. But the Kings Canyon Scenic Byway has such memorably scenic Sierra Nevada views that most people don't mind driving it twice.

Highway 180 is open year-round from Grant Grove to the Hume Lake turn-off, in Sequoia National Forest, but beyond the turn-off the road is usually open only from mid-April until early November. Both portions are equally scenic, though the sheer canyon drop-offs appear only past the Hume Lake turn-off. This section covers the highway all through Giant Sequoia National Monument between the Kings Canyon National Park boundaries near Grant Grove and near Cedar Grove.

Kings Canyon's maximum depth of 8,200 feet makes the Grand Canyon's vertical drop of 6,000 feet look small in comparison.

The road pierces the glacially carved **Kings Canyon**, one of North America's deepest canyons when measured from Spanish Peak (elevation 10,051 feet), located just west of the national park in the Sequoia National Forest, down to the confluence of the North and Middle forks of the Kings River. Its maximum depth of 8,200 feet makes the Grand Canyon's vertical drop of 6,000 feet seem minor in comparison.

For much of the 20th century, this canyon was under threat, first from the timber industry, which cut down hundreds of sequoias, then from developers, who wanted to dam the Kings River to supplement the water supply to the city of Los Angeles, just as the damming of Yosemite's Hetch Hetchy Valley had attempted to slake San Francisco's thirst. The timber industry shut down when the national park expanded in 1940, but even before this, logging of the sequoias was proving unprofitable. As these giants age, their wood becomes

You'll get to see Kings Canyon Scenic Byway in both directions, since it's the only road to Cedar Grove.

softer and more brittle, and they often splintered apart upon impact after being felled. As for the dam plan, after much political wrangling, it was scrapped in 1965.

A few miles north of Grant Grove, beyond the **McGee Overlook** (which is a great place to pull over for vistas of the pastoral San Joaquin Valley), a signposted dirt road leads off to the north through shadowy forest into **Converse Basin**, one of the strangest and perhaps saddest places in the national monument. Here a thriving meadow lies starkly littered with the stumps of giant sequoias cut down by 19th-century loggers, and the naked sight can be a shock to those who have come to the park seeking pristine wilderness. The only old-growth survivor still standing is the magnificent **Boole Tree**, named after the lumber mill owner who spared it. Cloaked by deep and buggy forest, you can discover the giant for yourself via a relatively short hiking trail.

Back on Highway 180 and east of Princess Campground, another detour, this time to the south, off Highway 180, leads 3 miles to ★HUME LAKE, found in one of the most handsome parts of the Giant Sequoia National Monument. Formed in 1908 by a multiple-arch dam, this lake once supplied water for the world's longest lumber flume, which reached the mill town of Sanger, almost 75 miles away. Shrouded by evergreen trees, this sparklingly clear, chilly lake is fed by Tenmile Creek, which flows into the Kings River. The lake is popular with campers and swimmers (*see* Other Activities). Open year-round, a lakeshore **Christian family camp** (*64144 Hume Lake Rd.; 559/305-7770; www.hume.org*) offers limited group accommodations, a takeout burger shop, a small market, and a gas station.

Beyond Hume Lake, Highway 180 tackles more challenging switchbacks as it drops into the canyon proper. Although there are more than a few viewpoints to choose from, be sure to pull off at **Junction View**, where jagged peaks rub shoulders at the confluence of the Middle and South forks of the Kings River. The highway levels a few miles later, then plunges downward again as it twists and turns by Yucca Point and Convict Flat, named for the prisoners who hazardously labored to build this road during the 1930s.

Finally, Highway 180 plunges downhill to meet the rushing Kings River. You'll come to several bridges before you hit Road's End, but only one before you've crossed over into the national park boundaries.

★ Prime Pumps ★

In July 2015, a lightning strike ignited the Rough Fire, burning over 150,000 acres along Kings Canyon Scenic Byway. Some damage remains visible to visitors descending into the still-lovely canyon, but due in part to prescribed burns, the giant sequoias and the Grant Grove and Cedar Grove villages were spared.

Just beside that first bridge lies **Boyden Cavern** (*Hwy. 180; 888/965–8243; boyden cavern.com*), which finally reopened in 2020 after closing due to damage from the 2015 Rough Fire. Not as large as Crystal Cave (*see* the Sequoia National Park chapter), the marble-and-volcanic-rock cave is still impressive, with intriguing ribbon draperies nicknamed "cave bacon" for their rusty color, the translucency of the minerals, and the spaghetti-like helictites that appear to defy gravity.

Purchase tickets online or at the gift shop for the family-friendly tours, which last about 45 minutes and are available hourly throughout the day from mid-May to November. It's only 55°F inside the cave, so bring a jacket, and wear sturdy shoes to grip the paved lighted pathways.

TOO BIG TO BE TRUE?

In Sequoia National Monument's Converse Basin you just might be stumped. That is to say, you'll see before you a field of stumps, with the largest of them named the Chicago Stump. The tree itself, a giant sequoia, was shipped east by train to Chicago and reassembled for the 1893 World's Columbian Exposition, where skeptical crowds derided it as the "California Hoax" because they found it hard to believe a real tree could grow this big.

After Boyden Cavern, Highway 180 gently curves alongside the Kings River for 5 more miles to the **Grizzly Falls Picnic Area**, another good place to stop and stretch your legs. It's only a short walk from the car to glimpse the 75-foot-high waterfall, which often mists over the footpath in late spring and early summer.

CEDAR GROVE

The least-visited area of Kings Canyon, **Cedar Grove** (elevation 4,600 feet) is named after its scattered stands of fragrant incense-cedar trees, the aroma of which can be detected only if you stand close enough to practically embrace them. More than 30 miles and about an hour's drive from Grant Grove, this secluded area of the park feels wonderfully remote. The canyon walls here comfortably widen beside the Kings River, which, in early spring, blasts with such force that white water sprays onto the highway.

You could spend many a long summer's afternoon swimming in the river, walking in the woods past waterfalls and around lush meadows, or tackling hiking trails that ascend to scenic overlooks of the canyon. However you choose to spend your time here, it's well worth the detour. Note, though, that from late fall through early spring, the public can't get to Cedar Grove at all (not even by hiking or snowshoeing).

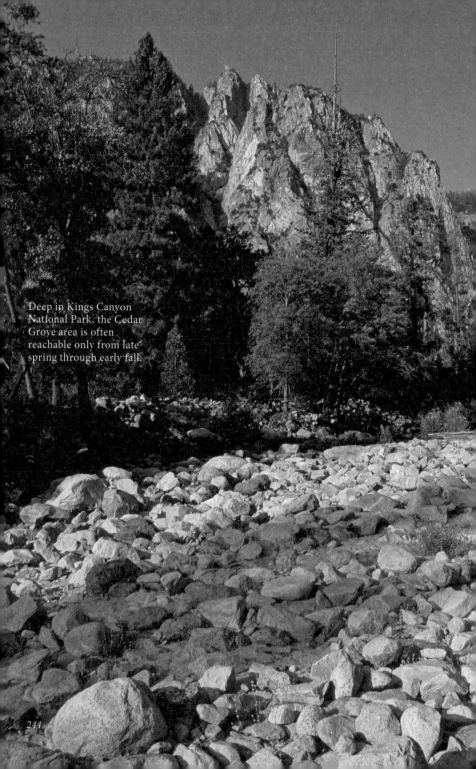

Deep in Kings Canyon National Park, the Cedar Grove area is often reachable only from late spring through early fall.

The only way to get into and out of Cedar Grove by car is via the Kings Canyon Scenic Byway (Highway 180). After crossing over the park boundary from the Sequoia National Forest on Highway 180, a series of bridges hovering beside summer-only beaches brings you into the main **Cedar Grove Village** (elevation 4,635 feet) area. Here, you can step inside a rustic log cabin, home to the **Cedar Grove Visitor Center** (*Hwy. 180; 559/565–3793*), closed in winter. Browse its book collection, and ask about ranger programs at the adjacent amphitheater. On the opposite side of the bridge is a motel-style lodge, which has a small market, a public shower house for beachgoers, and a small grill with picnic tables on a balcony overlooking the Kings River.

Beyond the village turn-off, Highway 180 pushes another 6 miles deeper into the canyon. About a mile east of the village, look for the small roadside pull-out for **Canyon Viewpoint**. The mighty work of glaciers that carved this canyon, now filled by grassy meadows with groves of trees climbing the cliff sides, is evidenced by the distinct U-shaped sides of the valley. Unlike the sharper V-shaped valleys cut by rivers, the glacially carved canyons of the Sierra Nevada have a softer U-shape: a flat valley floor with gently curving talus slopes on both sides leading upward to sheer vertical walls of granite.

Another mile farther east along the highway, **Knapp's Cabin** is just a short scramble from the roadside pull-off. During the 1920s, wealthy Santa Barbara outdoorsman George Knapp used this scenically set cabin to store supplies for deluxe fishing and camping expeditions with family and friends. The cabin is one of the few places in Cedar Grove to enjoy a long vista of the canyon floor spreading westward, best viewed around sunset.

**CEDAR GROVE
VISITOR CENTER**

TELEPHONE:
559/565–3793

ADDRESS:
Highway 180

Halfway between the village and Road's End, leave your car behind to take the short walk to **Roaring River Falls**. This pint-size cataract plunges into a deep pool, which roils turbulently in early spring. Although it's tempting to jump into the pool below the waterfall later in summer when things calm down, that's still a downright dangerous idea, and rangers don't advise it.

From the waterfall pull-off, it's less than 2 miles east along Highway 180 to idyllic ★ZUMWALT MEADOW, named after early preservationist D. K. Zumwalt. In early spring, this lush meadow backed by high granite cliffs is often flooded, appearing more like a swamp. Later in spring and early summer, as the waters recede to small streams running off from beside the river, a profusion of wildflowers blooms, including purple lupines and pinkish pussy paws.

For wildlife-watchers, the chance to observe birds and black bears with their cubs lumbering alongside the river is a huge draw. Walk out to the wooden suspension bridge for a grand view of the river, then continue east toward the boardwalk, which has the best views of the meadow, including of mule deer that frequently graze here.

After passing North Dome (elevation 8,717 feet), where adventurous rock climbers can occasionally be spotted, Highway 180 rolls to a halt at **Road's End**. Due to a land deal with the Zumwalt family, a proposed trans-Sierra highway was never built here. Road's End today is the gateway to the dramatic high country of the Sierra Nevada (*see* Backpacking and Climbing). For an idea of the sheer size of the peaks encountered up there, just crane your neck upward from the parking lot at the Grand Sentinel, which rises a dizzying 3,500 feet above the canyon floor on the south side of the river.

The chance to observe birds and black bears with their cubs lumbering alongside the river is a huge draw.

A short walk toward the river from the parking lot along a dirt footpath brings you to **Muir Rock**, a flat elevated slab that served as an informal pulpit for conservationist John Muir when he would escort groups of friends here on pleasure outings to talk about environmental ethics—only natural in such an inspiring setting.

From the **Road's End Permit Station** (*Hwy. 180*), rangers dispense permits, rent bear cannisters, and provide information on a variety of guided hikes and walks in the Cedar Grove area in summer. For more information visit the park website, *www.nps.gov/seki*.

An alternative return route to Cedar Grove from Road's End leaves Highway 180, just east of Roaring River Falls. The pavement quickly turns to gravel along the one-way, 3-mile-long River Road, also known as the "Motor Nature Trail," which heads westward past prime fishing holes to the horse corrals.

Black-chinned hummingbird and black bear.

Opposite: Roaring River Falls, midway between Cedar Grove Village and Road's End.

ALONG THE GENERALS HIGHWAY

Connecting the Grant Grove area of Kings Canyon National Park to Sequoia National Park, the high-elevation Generals Highway winds through a less heavily touristed section of the Giant Sequoia National Monument of the Sequoia National Forest. Escaping the crowds here is thankfully not much more difficult than turning off the

Kings River was possibly named by explorers in 1805 who reached the river on the Feast of Epiphany, a day noting the three kings' arrival to the birthplace of Christ.

Those looking to
see wildlife, such
as black bears and
birds, are drawn to
Zumwalt Meadow.

A 1.5-mile trail winds through Zumwalt Meadow in Kings Canyon National Park's Cedar Grove.

highway onto a roughshod dirt forest-service road, which is normally open from late spring until early fall. The Generals Highway itself is subject to road closures after snowstorms (*see* Kings Canyon National Park in Winter).

About 3.5 miles south of the busy junction with Highway 180, the Generals Highway passes **Redwood Mountain Overlook**. Here a breathtaking sweep of Sierra crags frame a sea of trees hiding one of the world's largest old-growth groves of giant sequoias, where hiking trails lead deeper into the forest (*see* Best Day Hikes). A bit farther south along the highway, past the Quail Flat junction (where you can pick up the scenic back road to Hume Lake), is the **Kings Canyon Overlook**, which offers a broad view of the canyon partially blocked by tall trees in the foreground.

The next signposted turnoff is at **Big Meadows Road**, which leads off-road to trailheads for trips into the pretty Jennie Lakes Wilderness (*see* Backpacking and Climbing). If you're feeling adventurous, follow Forest Route (FR) 14S11 for about 15 miles (a high-clearance 4WD vehicle is recommended) northeast to Summit Meadow, where energetic hikers can tackle the 0.5-mile trail up **Lookout Peak**, which offers even more all-encompassing canyon vistas.

En route back to the highway along the same road, turn right at Horse Camp to uncover **Buck Rock Lookout** (elevation 8,500 feet), a 1920s-era fire observation station with unmatched views of the Great Western Divide of the Sierra Nevada. The lookout is open to the public and is staffed in summer; access is via steep flights of nerve-racking metal stairs suspended from the side of the rock.

Back on the Generals Highway, you will pass old-fashioned **Montecito Sequoia Lodge**, which stays open year-round for family fun, from swimming and crafts and outdoor activity camps in summer to sledding, ice-skating, and skiing in winter. About 4 miles after the lodge is **Stony Creek Village**, a pit stop with a small motel, restaurant, market, and gas station that are usually open from May through October. The Generals Highway continues southward into Sequoia National Park.

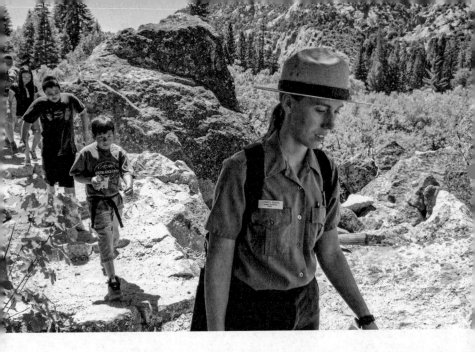

Youngsters enjoy
a ranger-led hike
through the park.

⟜ BEST DAY HIKES

For day hikers, plentiful paths inside Kings Canyon National Park
and the Sequoia National Forest next door range from easy nature
walks to mountain goat–style climbs. You can get information about
ranger-guided hikes and purchase hiking maps and interpretive trail
guides at the visitor centers in Grant Grove (year-round) and Cedar
Grove (closed in winter).

GRANT GROVE

Many hiking trails in the Grant Grove Village area interconnect, so
you can walk almost all day without backtracking. Everyone walks the
easy 0.35-mile paved interpretive **General Grant Tree Trail** to touch
the giant sequoias and stand beneath their mighty branches. You can
escape some of the crowds and still walk among the giant sequoias
on the moderate 1.5-mile **North Grove Loop**, which heads downhill
through the forest, then scrambles back uphill to the parking lot.

Hikers with more energy and time take the challenging 6-mile
Sunset Loop Trail toward pretty Sequoia Lake, starting from the
Grant Grove Visitor Center and passing springtime waterfalls. Back
near the park entrance station at the Big Stump Picnic Area, it's a

A splashy finale awaits hikers and horseback riders on the Mist Falls trail.

relaxing 0.5-mile stroll past the stumps of giant sequoias that were logged in the 19th century down to stream-fed **Hitchcock Meadow**, where wildflowers bloom.

North of Grant Grove, off the Kings Canyon Scenic Byway, you can visit the gigantic old-growth **Boole Tree** on a moderate, rolling 2-mile round-trip hike through shady Converse Basin. A shorter, easier nature trail that shows off some of the region's most distinctive flora and fauna begins at Princess Campground, near the level 3-mile recreational loop trail around **Hume Lake**.

CEDAR GROVE

The Cedar Grove area offers a variety of day hikes. Start with the easy 1.5-mile interpretive loop around **Zumwalt Meadow**, which is particularly lovely in late spring and early summer. Mule deer and black bears often forage here. Self-guiding interpretive-trail brochures may be available at the trailhead for a small donation; if not, you can pick them up at the visitor center.

A short trail off the Kings Canyon Scenic Byway leads to Roaring River Falls in Cedar Grove.

The moderate 3-mile **River Trail** along the South Fork of the Kings River is a peaceful way to trek from Roaring River Falls to Road's End via Zumwalt Meadow, and even walking along it for a short way will take you through forests shared with black bears and along small granite staircases that climb a short way up the canyon's wall. Starting from Road's End, it's a moderately challenging 3.8 miles across the forested floor of the canyon and up a series of granite staircases, which grant panoramic views of the canyon and glimpses of the Sierra Nevada high country, to ★**MIST FALLS**, which pour thunderously in late spring and early summer. An alternative 4.3-mile return route from the falls crosses the Bailey Bridge to the shadier south side of the river. That bridge also lets you access the difficult **Bubbs Creek Trail**, where a steep set of switchbacks leads approximately 3.5 miles each way from Road's End to views of The Sphinx rock formation.

For seasoned hikers, the challenging 8-mile **Hotel Creek–Lewis Creek Loop**, which reaches head-spinning views of the Sierra Nevada and wanders through meadows flush with birdlife, ascends laboriously from the trailhead near the pack station turnoff from the Cedar Grove Village area. After the first 2 miles, be sure to take the side trail to windy **Cedar Grove Overlook** (elevation 6,000 feet) for the best scenic view of the canyon that you can access without an overnight backcountry permit.

Along the Generals Highway

Along the Generals Highway south of Grant Grove, you can uncover less-trampled trailheads. Inside the national park boundaries, loop trails of varying lengths lead deep into peaceful and solitary **Redwood Mountain Grove**, where black bears can often be spotted ripping up giant sequoia tree logs to feed on the insects swarming around inside.

Farther south along the Generals Highway are two trailheads offering 360-degree views of the Central Valley and the Sierra Nevada crest. The moderate 1-mile ascent of **Buena Vista Peak**, which begins just south of the unmissable Kings Canyon Scenic Overlook, is often crowded but leads to a 360-degree view overlooking Redwood Canyon and gazing out past the Buck Rock fire lookout toward the crest of the Sierra Nevada divide.

More energetic trails of varying lengths lead into the **Jennie Lakes Wilderness**. Starting mostly off Big Meadows Road, they all climb challengingly through mixed forests of pine and fir trees and amble alongside alpine lakes. For mountaintop views and more solitude, it's a difficult 6.5-mile round trip up **Mitchell Peak**, where the sky-piercing mountains of the Monarch and Great Western Divides will spread out before you.

⊶ OTHER ACTIVITIES

Although day hiking is the most popular activity for visitors to Kings Canyon National Park, backpacking trips into the Sierra high country are also favorite journeys for those with more time and energy. Swimming and fishing are great ways to spend a lazy summer afternoon, or horseback rides into the mountains can be arranged. During winter, snowshoeing and cross-country skiing engage park visitors.

Backpacking and Climbing

Kings Canyon is a major gateway for wilderness treks into the Sierra Nevada high country, including in the northern section of Kings Canyon National Park, usually visited only by hard-core backpackers on their way to or from Yosemite National Park. The busiest departure point for backpackers of all abilities, from beginner Boy Scouts to accomplished alpine mountaineers, is Road's End, where Highway 180 finishes in Cedar Grove.

★ Black Bear Stats ★

Average weight for males: 300–600 pounds

Active times: dawn and dusk

On their menu: berries, nuts, grasses, insects

For the ultimate taste of the wilderness, the amazing four-day, 45-mile ★**RAE LAKES LOOP** climbs beyond Mist Falls to the north of Road's End and the stream-fed Paradise Valley past the skyscraping Castle Domes, then follows the epic **John Muir Trail (JMT)**, which travels from Yosemite all the way to Mt. Whitney, into the Rae Lakes basin, before toppling over Glen Pass (elevation 11,978 feet). The loop returns to Road's End via Junction Meadow, a favorite haunt of black bears and where you can detour to East Lake and Lake Reflection. Then it follows along the Bubbs Creek Trail, which passes Charlotte Dome, offering multipitch hauls for rock climbers.

A tougher trail, **Copper Creek**, steeply ascends from Road's End into the rocky wonderland of Granite Basin, where experienced back-packers can venture to alpine lakes. More trails lead over the Sierra Nevada crest, including from the JMT crossing near Charlotte Lake to Onion Valley outside the town of Independence, off U.S. Highway 395, on the east side of the Sierra Nevada mountains. Off the Generals Highway, the Jennie Lakes Wilderness is also prime backpacking territory and offers endless overnight trip destinations; ask at the Kings Canyon Visitor Center in Grant Grove for recommendations.

PERMITS

Between late May and mid-September, all trails inside Kings Canyon and Sequoia national parks are subject to a daily quota. Check availability and make wilderness permit reservations ($15) up to six months in advance online at *www.recreation.gov*, which will send you a confirmation email that includes permit pick-up location information. To collect your permit, present a printout of this confirmation email and a photo ID to rangers at the trailhead desk as early as 1 pm the day before the start of your trek. In the non-quota season, self-issue permits are available at Mineral King Ranger Station, Ash Mountain Wilderness Office, Giant Forest Museum (Lodgepole), Kings Canyon Visitor Center, or Road's End Permit Station (Cedar Grove). Note, however, that only the Ash Mountain office and Kings Canyon Visitor Center are open in the winter season. Most stations rent bear-proof food-storage containers ($5–$6), which may be required for wilderness travel.

Most wilderness trips within national forest boundaries do not require wilderness permits, although a free campfire/campstove permit is required. Pick one up at the **Kings Canyon Visitor Center** or at the **Hume Lake Ranger District Office** (*35860 E. Kings Canyon Rd./ Hwy. 180, Dunlap; 559/338–2251; www.fs.usda.gov/sequoia*).

Exploring the park like Theodore Roosevelt and John Muir once did—on horseback—these riders head toward Mist Falls.

Kings Canyon National Park has one stable (in Grant Grove) and one pack station (in Cedar Grove). At either place, in season, you can get outfitted to see the park by horseback.

FISHING

Although you're unlikely to catch anything big enough to boast about, the South Fork of the Kings River in the Cedar Grove area of the park offers wonderfully lazy and, more important, shady fishing holes, especially near Road's End and along the one-way River Road heading back west toward the main village area. It's easy to catch fish here, and the fishing holes are easy to find. Fishing is allowed in both the national park and the Sequoia National Forest, including at Hume Lake, which is stocked with trout periodically throughout the summer by the California Department of Fish and Game. **Sierra Fly Fishing** (*P.O. Box 631, Bass Lake; 559/683–7664; www.sierraflyfisher.com*) offers half- and full-day fly-fishing trips, gear included, at prime spots along the Kings River.

LICENSES AND RULES

Anglers ages 16 and older must carry a valid California fishing license, sold at Hume Lake and at **Three Rivers Mercantile** (*41152 Sierra Dr.; 559/561–2378*) in Three Rivers. The fishing season for rainbow, brown, golden, and eastern brook trout is from late April through mid-November. The general limit is five trout per day, with a maximum of 10 fish in possession at any one time. Additional restrictions apply inside the national park boundaries; ask at visitor centers for current fishing regulations covering specific bait and hook types, daily limits, and catch-and-release requirements, which vary depending on your location and elevation inside the park.

Horseback Riding

Both of the national park's horse-riding outfits are owned by the Loverin family, who are longtime area residents. **Grant Grove Stables** (*off Hwy. 180; 559/335–9292 in summer*) offers short trail rides into the sequoia groves daily in summer. The **Cedar Grove Pack Station** (*off Hwy. 180; 559/565–3464 in summer, 559/802–7626 in the off-season*) offers hour-long rides to longer trips into the Sierra Nevada high country during summer, including multiday guided trail rides for fishing enthusiasts.

In the Sequoia National Forest, **Horse Corral Pack Station** (*Big Meadows Rd.; 559/565–3000 in summer, 559/365–0008 in the off-season; thehorsecorralpacker.com*) has one- and two-hour rides appropriate for beginners, as well as all-inclusive multiday guided rides into the wilderness for experienced riders.

Swimming, Boating, Kayaking, and White-water Rafting

The most popular place for swimming, and one of the safest places to swim in early summer, is easily accessible **Hume Lake** in Sequoia National Forest, not far from Grant Grove and just off the Kings Canyon Scenic Byway leading to Cedar Grove. Rowboats, canoes, and kayaks can be rented from a Christian family camp. Families flock to Hume Lake, not only for its friendly atmosphere but also because lakes are calmer places to swim than mountain streams or the Kings River, which rush with thunderous snowmelt in early spring. Even so, note that lifeguards are not always on duty here.

Although the **Kings River** can be chilly—water temperatures climb only to about 62°F in summer—that can feel refreshing during the dog days of August. And when water levels drop later in the summer, sandy and rocky beaches appear beside the Kings River as it often runs closely alongside Highway 180 between Boyden Cavern and Road's End. Among the prettiest beaches on the river are the busy **Lewis Creek** and **Muir Rock**, both in the Cedar Grove area. For more privacy, the **Red Bridge** beach is a 10-minute walk from the Road's End parking lot up the trail signposted for Bubbs Creek and Zumwalt Meadow. Flotation devices (e.g., inner tubes) and watercraft are prohibited on the South Fork of the Kings River in the Cedar Grove area.

Ask rangers for advice about current conditions and the best swimming spots when you visit, **and always exercise caution when swimming—especially in the river, where swift currents**

The South Fork of the Kings River teems with brown and rainbow trout and is considered one of the best trout fisheries in the Sierras.

naturally occur and are not always visible from the surface—because drowning is the number one cause of visitor fatalities in the park. Swimming can be extremely dangerous in early summer, when mountain snowmelt turns the river into a torrent of rapids. Almost none of these swimming holes in the park or national forest have any sort of lifeguard, so it's important to look out for not only yourself but everyone else if you choose to swim here. If you see a swimmer get into trouble, immediately call a ranger or dial 911 from any pay phone to contact park dispatch for help with swift-water rescue.

If you want to brave some of those violent rapids outside the park, don a life jacket and hop in a raft for a guided excursion. The white-water-rafting season usually runs from late spring into early summer when water levels are high enough. **Kings River Expeditions** (*4015 N. Madera Ave.; Kerman; 559/233–4881, 800/846–3674; www.kingsriver.com*) typically offers one- and two-day white-water rafting trips on Class III rapids along the Middle Fork of the Kings River near Pine Flat reservoir, west of Kings Canyon National Park. **Whitewater Voyages** (*11252 Kernville Rd., Kernville; 800/400–7238; www.whitewatervoyages.com*) also offers Kings River rafting trips outside Fresno. Although no previous experience is generally required, and the trips are open to both adults and children who meet the minimum-age requirements, they're not trips to be taken lightly. Come prepared for a fun workout in the hot summer sun.

KINGS CANYON NATIONAL PARK IN THE WINTER

When Kings Canyon National Park is blanketed by snow from November through April, it attracts experienced winter-sports enthusiasts as well as beginners. Winter is not a common season to visit the park, which makes it the least crowded time of year to experience the magic of the giant sequoia groves.

Wherever you go in the park once it's covered in snow, you'll hear the excited shouts of children fresh up from California's parched Central Valley, who are eager to get their first taste of the cool, white stuff. Sledding and snow play are popular in Grant Grove, especially around the Big Stump and Columbine picnic areas. The Columbine area, near the General Grant Tree, is also where carolers sing a few Christmas favorites the second Sunday of December for the annual Trek to the Tree (*see* Festivals and Seasonal Events in the Practical Information chapter).

Though closed to vehicle traffic in the winter, Panoramic Point is among the ungroomed trails leading through the giant sequoia groves that are open to cross-country skis and snowshoes. You can rent cross-country skis and snowshoes at the Grant Grove gift shop (*Hwy. 180; 559/335-5500*). If you want to trek through the snow with others, call the Kings Canyon Visitor Center (*559/565-4307*) to reserve a spot on a ranger-guided snowshoe walk (all equipment is provided for a small donation). This 1-mile, two-hour tour is often scheduled on Saturdays and holidays. The **Sequoia Parks Conservancy Field Institute** (*559/565-4251; www.sequoiaparksconservancy.org/adventures.html*) also offers free snowshoe walks from John Muir Lodge.

Four more winter recreation areas are located on national forest land inside the Giant Sequoia National Monument: Cherry Gap, north of Grant Grove along Highway 180; and three areas off the Generals Highway near Quail Flat and Big Meadow. Farther south along the Generals Highway, the **Montecito Sequoia Lodge** (*63410 Generals Hwy.; 800/227-9900; www.mslodge.com*) grooms up to 50 kilometers of cross-country ski trails, weather permitting. The lodge particularly draws families thanks to fun winter activities like daytime and nighttime downhill tubing with a handle tow, ice-skating on a lighted rink, snowboarding, and snowshoeing. Equipment rentals and lessons are available.

Come winter, only a few roads remain open in Kings Canyon National Park and the Sequoia National Forest: Highway 180 to Grant Grove and Hume Lake and the Generals Highway to Sequoia National Park. The latter especially is subject to weather delays and snowplow closures after heavy storms. Always carry tire chains, which may be required at any time from late fall through early spring. For road conditions, call 559/565-3341.

(opposite) In winter, inner tubes get put to work on the slopes instead of the river.

Where to Stay and Eat

Sunset over Tuolumne River

Up high in the mountains, in the Vogelsang High Sierra Camp, you'll be surrounded by peaks and lakes.

⊙⊶ THE LOWDOWN ON LODGING

The camaraderie of outdoor adventurers sparks over a campfire, shown here at Tuolumne Meadows Lodge.

After dark, when day-trippers have gone home and serenity settles over the national parks, the sights and sounds of the outdoors take on new wonder. Staying overnight inside the parks is a trip highlight for many. The choices vary, from sleeping alfresco, where you can watch the moonrise and stargaze into the wee hours, to hiding away inside a romantic, rustic pioneer-style cabin or a historic hotel room with nature stretched out before you courtesy of panoramic windows. Whichever option you go with, you'll wake up the next morning with no worries of dealing with traffic. You're already right in the park, primed to beat the crowds to the next trailhead or viewpoint.

Lodgings in and around the national parks have higher rates during the peak summer months of June, July, and August. Almost all accommodations drop their rates during the off-season (October through March in Yosemite, early September through late May in Sequoia and Kings Canyon). Sometimes the rates dip by more than 30%. If budget saving is a priority, accommodations outside the park still put you near the action and can be less expensive. To make sure you get a room or site in the park, or as close by as possible, **book your lodgings as far in advance as you can.**

National park lodges are all entirely **no-smoking**. **Air-conditioning is a rare commodity** at in-park accommodations, which are typically either fan-cooled or have windows to let in the breezes.

If the following recommended lodgings are fully booked, you can try one of the many chain motels and hotels found in gateway towns just outside the parks. In California, these accommodations are also no-smoking. Lodgings outside the park usually offer more perks, such as telephones, satellite TV, and Wi-Fi access. These properties sometimes allow pets, which are usually not welcome at in-park accommodations, unless they're on a short leash and accompanied by their owner inside the national parks' campgrounds. Inquire at each property individually about whether there are any restrictions on children as guests. It's not always the case that children can stay for free in the same room as their parents. Policies vary by property.

All properties are open year-round unless stated otherwise.

Credit cards are accepted at most accommodations inside the parks (except for some campgrounds, as described in the next section) and at most motels, hotels, and lodges outside the parks. Ask when booking about any and all payment policies.

⟜ THE LOWDOWN ON CAMPING

Use *www.recreation.gov* to make reservations for national park and national forest campgrounds. Book well ahead of your visit, as campgrounds fill up almost as quickly as hotels and lodges—particularly in the parks and especially on summer weekends and holidays. **Do not arrive in Yosemite National Park without a reservation as there are no longer any first-come, first-served sites, and last-minute reservations probably won't be an option.**

With the exception of South Fork, campgrounds in Sequoia and Kings Canyon national parks also require reservations. If you arrive without one, check to see if there is last-minute availability (the best time to try is between 10 am and noon, when the previous night's campers are vacating their sites). Alternatively, look into campgrounds in the nearby Sequoia National Forest (*www.fs.usda.gov/activity/sequoia/ recreation/camping-cabins*), which don't fill up as quickly and which accept, but don't necessarily require, reservations.

★ Shutterbug's Tip ★

If you're a keen photographer, there's extra incentive to stay inside the parks: catching the best light at dawn and sunset.

Many campgrounds in the park accommodate both tents and RVs, although RV dump stations are rare and there are usually no electricity or other hookups for RVs at any public (e.g., national park or national forest) campgrounds. Limited pull-through sites are available, and restrictions on the length of RVs allowed vary from place to place within the parks. Private campgrounds located far outside the park boundaries may offer sites with full hookups and amenities including swimming pools and internet access. Permits are required for wilderness camping.

When national park campgrounds are full, check national forests for sites. Information for national forest campgrounds near the parks is listed in the camping chart later in this chapter.

"More, please." These young campers enjoy dinner alfresco.

While camping in the Sierra Nevada, **proper storage of all food and scented items is essential**. Feeding any wildlife is prohibited by law. Habituation to human food causes black bears and other animals to become aggressive, and eventually they must be destroyed. Avoid incidents by removing all food and scented items from your vehicle at night and placing them in the food-storage lockers provided at national park campgrounds and at many parking lots, or at least lock everything out of sight in the trunk.

Campfires are normally allowed in the parks, but only at designated picnic areas and developed campsites that have preexisting fire pits and grills. Occasionally during summer, when fire conditions in the parks are dangerously high and the forests are like dry tinder, additional restrictions may be imposed; ask at visitor centers.

Depending on where your backpacking trip takes you, campfires may not be allowed in the wilderness areas you camp in; ask the wilderness ranger issuing your backcountry permit about current fire restrictions. Camping in national forest lands may require a special campfire permit, available at visitor centers. It's more convenient to carry a camp stove instead of relying on building campfires in the wilderness, which can be a risky proposition, especially in years when low rainfall results in high fire risk.

Credit cards are accepted only to guarantee campground reservations, not for on-the-spot payments. If you're grabbing a first-come, first-served site, be sure to pay for it within 30 minutes of arrival at the campground by depositing the nightly fee in an envelope provided at the campground entrance, where you'll also find a locked "iron ranger" to deposit the fee envelopes into. Change is normally not available, so **bring lots of $5 and $1 bills**—or consider any small overpayment for your campsite a donation to the national parks, which can always use the extra funds.

⊕ THE LOWDOWN ON PLACES TO EAT

Food served by park concessionaire services at cafeterias, snack bars, and most lodge restaurants ranges from standard burgers and chips to poke bowls and healthful Mediterranean fare. Most dining options are geared to convenience rather than culinary fireworks. There are, however, exceptions. **Select park lodges, like The Ahwahnee in Yosemite, have restaurants that consistently stand out,** not only for their seasonal menus and fine-dining atmosphere but also for their historical surroundings and gorgeous views.

Outside the national parks, the cuisine varies a lot; the only reliable rule of thumb is that the farther from the parks you go, the more affordable the food becomes.

Are you thinking about brown-bagging it? Compared with many of the parks' vistas and other spots capturing the surrounding beauty, designated picnic areas in Yosemite, Kings Canyon, and Sequoia can be unexciting. There's often not much to distinguish them, and they're usually situated along busy park roads that endure heavy traffic noise, tucked into a shady spot without much of a view. Also, because so many visitors illegally feed the parks' wildlife, you may be hounded to death for food by noisy Steller's jays or encounter a curious black bear, patiently waiting for you to forgetfully turn your back on your picnic cooler for just a few seconds.

The best places to picnic in the parks are often at scenic vistas, such as Glacier Point in Yosemite. The Yosemite Valley and Tuolumne Meadows areas are also memorable places for a picnic. Almost any place in the park is fair game, save one: **picnicking inside a national-park campground that you aren't staying at is a no-no.**

In addition to the restaurants recommended in this chapter, many casual places to eat, such as grills, delis, cafeterias, markets, and snack bars, are briefly mentioned in each of the individual national park chapters earlier in the book. For dining and lodging price categories, *see* How to Use This Book.

Picnicking at Glacier Point in
Yosemite National Park.

278

⊕ YOSEMITE NATIONAL PARK

Although places in the valley are far from quiet in summer, there's nothing like rolling out of bed to see the early-morning sun lighting up the steep granite walls rising all around you, or to hear the babbling Merced River running right by your campsite and to watch the moon rise over Glacier Point.

If you'll be spending more than a day at Yosemite, then, ideally, you'll want to stay right in the park. Park lodging is operated by Yosemite Hospitality, a subsidiary of the Aramark park concessionaire. If cost is your main concern, **gateway town accommodations are often a better value than surprisingly expensive in-park lodgings, but they're not nearly as convenient** and the headache of commuting to and from the park is usually not worth it for first-time visitors. In fact, if you stay in Yosemite Valley, you can opt not to drive at all once you're ensconced in your in-park accommodations. Just walk or take the shuttle from your nightly resting place.

There's no one particular gateway city for Yosemite that's preferred, just certain recommended properties in various towns; these places are reviewed below. Also, if you're willing to make the drive, the town of Mariposa, about an hour west of the park via Highway 140, has a pleasant collection of short-term rentals and bed-and-breakfast inns.

Whether you're staying in the park or just outside it, **it's essential for you to make reservations—and make them well in advance**—for any stays May through September and on weekends and holidays year-round. For reservations with Yosemite Hospitality, which can be made up to a year or more in advance, call *888/413–8869* or reserve online at *www.travelyosemite.com*. Individual property contact information is also given with each review below.

HOTELS AND LODGES INSIDE YOSEMITE

See the price chart on p. 16.

★**The Ahwahnee.** In the grand tradition of the historic national park lodges, The Ahwahnee offers an unexpected dose of refinement in the midst of Yosemite Valley, starting from when you pull up to the valet parking stand to when you hear the tinkling of ivories issuing out of the grand dining room. As you amble through the hotel's impressive public areas, inspect the gorgeous architectural detail—from Native American–inspired motifs to art-deco mosaic

Following page: The Ahwahnee is acclaimed for its architecture, which blends with nature, as seen by its floor-to-ceiling windows in its Great Lodge and Solarium Room. Its dining options include the dining hall, where food is artfully presented.

murals to California-style Arts and Crafts woodworking and stained glass. Converse in one of the fireside lounges, or sip a cocktail as you view Half Dome from the back patio, especially impressive just before sunset. The swanky-meets-rustic theme continues into the 99 guest rooms inside the six-story hotel. Top-floor parlors and suites have floor-to-ceiling windows overlooking the valley. Much plainer are the 24 air-conditioned cottages tucked away from the hotel in shady groves of dogwoods and pines. Each cottage room has a patio, some with postcard views over the valley. Hotel guests can swim year-round in The Ahwahnee's heated outdoor pool, which is slightly removed from the hubbub of the lobby. *1 Ahwahnee Rd., Yosemite Village; 209/372–1407, reservations 808/413–8869; www. travelyosemite.com.* $$$$

★**Curry Village & Housekeeping Camp.** Opened in 1899, this historic tourist camp and the similarly rustic camp just down the road, beside the river, combine to form a beloved Yosemite Valley institution. Some people return here every summer, and even newcomers will feel swept up in the infectiously rambunctious atmosphere, where adults can act like kids at summer camp again, playing flashlight games late into the night and parking bicycles right outside their own front door. Generations of families have slept in these canvas tents and rustic wooden cabins near Happy Isles, where a bubbling brook darts around granite rocks that make perfect sunbathing perches. Curry Village is tent camping without having to pitch your own tent and with a real bed to sleep in. You can choose unheated or heated canvas tents with cot-style beds and a shared bathhouse nearby or studio cabins with solid walls (and therefore more privacy) and shared or private baths. Larger, en-suite cabins also have electrical wall heaters and outlets. None of the cabins have campfire or kitchen facilities. With room for more than 1,000 guests, Curry Village can get very crowded, especially on summer weekends. The nearby Housekeeping Camp rents more basic, semi-enclosed sleeping platforms—essentially three concrete walls with canvas forming the fourth wall and the roof—that have one double bed and two single bunks. Units, which have Merced River beach access, come with picnic tables and fire rings, making this the only lodging option in the valley where you can enjoy cooking your own dinner and roasting marshmallows over an open fire after a day of hiking. Curry Village is usually closed for a few weeks in early December, then closed weekdays from mid-January to mid-March, and the Housekeeping Camp is open only from mid-April

There's nothing like rolling out of bed
to see the **early morning sun**
            lighting up the steep granite walls
rising all around you.

Perfecting a putt on the grounds
of the Wawona Hotel.

or May to early October. *Southside Dr., Curry Village; 209/372-8333, reservations 888/413-8869; www.travelyosemite.com.* **$$**

Tuolumne Meadows Lodge & White Wolf Lodge. During the brief summer of the Sierra Nevada high country, these seasonal canvas tents are your only overnight option in Tuolumne Meadows other than pitching your own tent. Less rambunctious than Curry Village in Yosemite Valley, the Tuolumne Meadows Lodge and the White Wolf Lodge are both pleasant places to bed down and to do some stargazing after the day-trippers leave. The metal-framed canvas platform tents have beds but are not equipped with electricity. Instead, you must rely on the LED lantern they provide and an old-fashioned wood-burning stove (for heat only; no cooking), with shared bathhouses. Tuolumne Meadows has 69 of these tent cabins that come with bedding for up to four. In addition to 24 soft-sided cabins, White Wolf Lodge also rents four simple wooden cabins with a few more creature comforts, including limited electricity and heat. All these cabins are usually open from mid-June through mid-September, weather permitting. Rustic breakfasts and dinners (the latter by advance reservation only) are served at both lodges. Guests can also order boxed lunches from the lodges the night before to take on the trail with them. *Tioga Rd.; reservations 888/413-8869; www.travelyosemite.com.* **$**

Wawona Hotel. With its shady verandas, antique light fixtures, and old-style concrete swimming tank outside, the Wawona Hotel transports guests to another time—the Victorian era, to be precise. This National Historic Landmark near Yosemite's south entrance was built in 1879 using a wood-frame construction. It is the largest Victorian-era hotel inside a national park. Stop in the hotel's piano parlor to view the historical photographs of pioneers and early tourists in the park. The parlor is also a good place to relax, thanks to its cozy overstuffed sofas, a fireplace, and a piano that's frequently played by a local performer. Given that the lodgings come with a heaping dose of yesteryear, don't expect anything too fancy, although a 2020 renovation freshened up the rooms and lobby. About half of the 104 guest rooms, both in the main hotel and in nearby cottages, have private baths; others share public bathhouses (bring a warm robe and shower sandals). There are no phones or TVs, the lack of which enhances the hotel's restful, unhurried atmosphere (which is possibly disturbed only by noise penetrating the thin walls). Rooms may be furnished too elementally for some, but others appreciate them precisely for their back-to-basics, time-

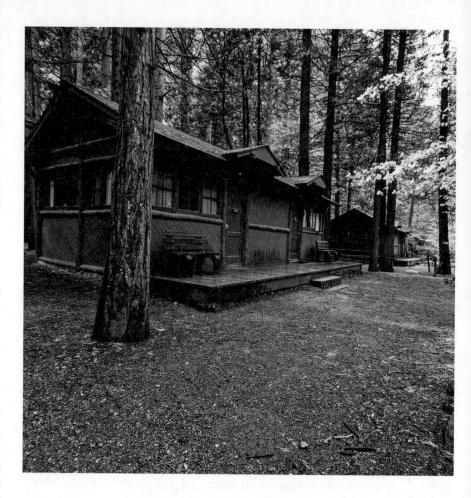

Hard-sided cabins come with solid walls, a step up from the canvas cabins.

warped appeal. *Forest Dr., off Wawona Rd.; 209/375–6556, reservations 808/413–8869; www.travelyosemite.com.* $$

Yosemite Valley Lodge. When Yosemite Valley's waterfalls peak in May, there is no place closer to the action than this lodge with comfortable, well-equipped rooms. It's a short walk from here to the heart of Yosemite Village, too. Another perk is the lodge's tours and activities desk, which can arrange everything from bicycle rentals to guided bus tours. Staying here also lets you beat the crowds that line up nightly outside the extraordinary Mountain Room restaurant (*see* Restaurants in Yosemite). The 245 rooms incorporate eco-friendly elements and are decorated in soothing earth tones. Some rooms have French doors opening onto a small balcony with views of the falls. Family rooms sleep six comfortably. There's no air-conditioning, but fans are provided, and you can cool off in an outdoor swimming pool, which is open from Memorial Day through Labor Day, weather permitting. *Northside Dr., Yosemite Village; 209/372–1274, reservations 888/413–8869; www.travelyosemite.com.* $$$

Generations of families have slept in these canvas tents and rustic wooden cabins near Happy Isles, where a bubbling brook darts around granite rocks that make perfect sunbathing perches.

HOTELS AND LODGES OUTSIDE YOSEMITE
See the price chart on p. 16.

Château du Sureau. Incredible personalized attention from the staff sets this polished property apart from other lodging options near

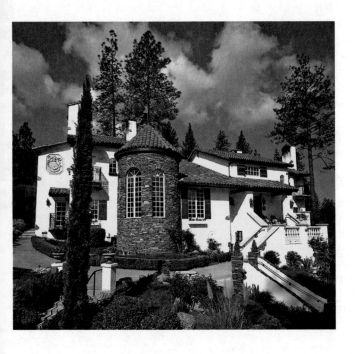

THE LURE OF THE LODGES

"If you build it, they will come" could apply easily to the railroad companies who laid track in the early 1900s to draw wealthy Easterners westward. These shrewd businesses took the idea an inspired step further when many of them thought to also build luxury hotels at the end of the line to accommodate weary riders. When these top-notch properties were set in the beautiful natural surroundings of a national park, travelers had the best of both worlds.

The railroads were not the only ones who profited. NPS director Stephen Mather believed that attracting wealthy, influential visitors to the national parks would lend support and congressional funding to the national parks system. He wanted Yosemite to have a grand lodge and so he persuaded the concessionaire Yosemite Park & Curry Company to undertake the building of the park's stunning masterpiece, The Ahwahnee.

Architect Gilbert Stanley Underwood won the commission for the project in 1925. He had previously designed lodges at the Grand Canyon and in Bryce and Zion national parks. For Yosemite, Underwood was asked to build a first-class hotel that was fireproof (a necessity in a forested area), that blended in with the granite cliff landscape of the site, and that showcased the park's iconic Half Dome.

Constructing the hotel was a tough undertaking. The roads to and from the remote site were challenging, making the trucking of materials difficult. In order to make the structure fire resistant, Underwood used hidden steel framing and concrete. To make it seem more natural, concrete was made to resemble redwood by being poured into timber shells, giving it a grained texture, and then getting a dye job.

The valley's indigenous heritage is captured in some of the hotel's architectural detail: the motifs and patterns found in the basketry of the local Indian tribes were used on ceiling beams, stained-glass windows, and concrete floors. Other elements, like mosaics, reflect the 1920s art-deco style.

In its early days, the elegant Ahwahnee saw many a wealthy patron, as well as the U.S. Navy, which seized the hotel in the early 1940s for a hospital for wounded soldiers. Four decades later, Queen Elizabeth II rested her royal head here. Other noteworthy visitors have included the Shah of Iran; Walt Disney; Will Rogers; Lucille Ball; and presidents Dwight D. Eisenhower, Herbert Hoover, John F. Kennedy, and Ronald Reagan. Luxury cars and even limousines are still frequently seen today in front of the National Historic Landmark. They built it, and they still come.

—*Debbie Harmsen and Marge Peterson*

In the 1920s, architect Gilbert Stanley Underwood (left) designed lodges in several national parks, including the beautiful Ahwahnee (above) in Yosemite.

Yosemite. A 10-room inn and a two-bedroom villa decorated in exquisite Provençal style, with canopied bedchambers, wall tapestries, and butter-yellow and sky-blue schemes as well as authentic 19th-century artwork, make up this small, self-styled estate. Canopied beds, antique soaking tubs, and wood-burning fireplaces are among the amenities in many of the château's rooms. Guests have access to an intimate spa and an outdoor swimming pool. Little touches like tea and snacks upon arrival add to the romantic nature of the place, with its cozy nooks and very private bedroom retreats. Other amenities include a small spa and a standout restaurant (*See* The Elderberry House in Restaurants Outside Yosemite). The inn is farther from the park than many other places to stay—it's about 15 miles south of Yosemite's South Entrance Station, off Highway 41—but if a luxurious hideaway is what you're after, it's worth the drive. Just don't expect to drive up to the grand porte cochere out front and then step into the gracious lobby in your muddy hiking boots. *48688 Victoria La., Oakhurst; 559/683–6860; chateaudusureau.com.* $$$$

Evergreen Lodge. A short drive from the Big Oak Flat Entrance Station and Hetch Hetchy, this classic 1920s mountain resort amid tall pine trees provides a rejuvenating stay for romantic couples or active families. Beautifully kept duplex cabins and private stand-alone cottages with private baths and decks come in a variety of sizes and configurations, some sleeping up to six. The woodsy decor makes it look a lot like a ski resort, with plush beds and kitchenettes in some units. Relax in the family-friendly recreation hall, equipped with board games, tourist information, and free Wi-Fi access. Other amenities include a swimming pool, an indoor-outdoor dining room serving excellent food and cocktails, a general store, and a cozy tavern that occasionally hosts live music. A diverse recreation program offers everything from mountain bike rental to whitewater rafting and flight tours over Yosemite Valley. *33160 Evergreen Rd., Groveland; 209/379–2606, 800/935–6343; www.evergreenlodge.com.* $$$

Hotel Charlotte. Run by a convivial couple, this hotel listed on the National Register of Historic Places can give you a taste of pioneer life during the California Gold Rush era. The helter-skelter architecture of the place, with its snug rooms and creaky narrow hallways, along with historic photographs hanging in the public spaces, let you imagine the speculative scene in the mid-19th century. The air-conditioned rooms all have satellite TV and private bathrooms (some with antique claw-foot tubs), and three of them are pet-friendly. Most of the 13 rooms come with shabby-chic country furnishings and are on the upper story. *18736 Main St. (Hwy. 120), Groveland; 209/962–6455; www.hotelcharlotte.com.* $$

Rush Creek Lodge & Spa. Just half a mile from Yosemite's Big Oak Flat Entrance on Highway 120, this new property is as close to the park as you can get without being inside it. The rooms in the villas scattered around the 20-acre property offer the most privacy, but those in the Guest Lodge are closest to the action: two hot tubs, a saltwater swimming pool, restaurant, tavern, fire pit, rec room, lounge, and general store. The 143 spacious contemporary/rustic rooms come equipped with board games rather than televisions, but activities like table tennis, kid-friendly craft opportunities, and nightly s'mores around the campfire keep the little ones entertained. Sign up for guided hikes and snowshoe tours, or schedule a massage. *34001 Hwy. 120, Groveland; 209/379–2373; www.rushcreeklodge.com.* $$$$

Sierra Sky Ranch. Off Highway 41 just 10 miles south of the park, this inn located near a hidden grove of giant sequoia trees provides a restful, rustic retreat. Built in 1875, and formerly a working cattle ranch, it has been an inn since 1946. Expect to find tidy rooms with simple country-style decor and French doors that open out onto airy porches for unwinding on a summer's evening. Stay connected to the modern world with cable TV and free Wi-Fi access. A swimming pool in summer and a steak house are on-site. Heating and air-conditioning in the 28 rooms make the ranch a four-season getaway, while the stone fireplaces in the great room are a wintertime bonus. *50552 Road 632, Oakhurst; 559/683–8040; www.sierraskyranch.com.* $$$

Tenaya Lodge at Yosemite. With its perfect-for-cold-weather perks, this might be the place you want to stay when the snow is falling. A short drive south of the park on Highway 41, the upscale Tenaya Lodge offers more hotel-style amenities than most in-park lodgings, including indoor and outdoor heated swimming pools, a seasonal ice-skating rink, indoor and outdoor hot tubs, a fitness center, and a well-equipped spa. The 294 hotel rooms and adjacent cottages have fairly bland earth-toned decor, but with a grand lobby, multiple dining options on-site, and daily activities like guided hikes and archery lessons, it's easy to stay busy all day. Pet-friendly and ADA-accessible accommodations are available. Fifty two-bedroom cabins located a 10-minute walk from the main lodge are perfect for families and small groups who want to gather at the communal fire pits to make s'mores. *1122 Hwy. 41, Fish Camp; 559/683–6555, reservations 866/771–9629; www.tenayalodge.com.* $$$$

Yosemite Bug Rustic Mountain Resort. An alternative-minded, overgrown youth hostel in the woods with a great diversity of accommodation options, the sociable "Bug" is a Yosemite institution. With raucous dormitory lodge rooms, peaceful but basic wood-framed tent cabins with beds, private rooms in wooden duplexes with private or shared baths, and two houses suitable for small groups, the rustic Bug's got something for everyone traveling on a budget. All guests have access to a common kitchen for cooking meals, where you can share any leftover backpacking supplies with other travelers, who are often happy to pitch in and make budget feasts together. There's also a sociable café serving lots of local and organically grown foods on-site, as well as a health spa with a hot tub and sauna and yoga classes. Thanks to its wandering hiking trails and seasonal summer swimming holes, the Bug's thickly forested property feels almost like being in Yosemite, even though it's a 30-minute drive west of the park along Highway 140. The YARTS bus (*see* the Getting Around section of the Practical Information chapter) stops here, too. *6979 Hwy. 140, Midpines; 209/966–6666, 866/826–7108; www.yosemitebug.com.* $$

Yosemite Lodging at Big Creek Inn Bed & Breakfast. Popping out along the roadside like a fairy-tale cabin in the woods, this intimate bed-and-breakfast inn 2 miles south of the park, off Highway 41, offers an array of perks that put it ahead of the competition. Extremely hospitable innkeepers? Check. Private balconies with meadow views as well as a shared sundeck? Check, check. Guest rooms equipped with satellite TV, DVD player, and Wi-Fi access? Check, check, check. The inn has three rooms; if you're visiting on a snowy winter's night, pick one with a gas fireplace. A continental breakfast, sometimes with warm pastries or hot country-style oatmeal, is served in the homey dining room. *1221 Hwy. 41, Fish Camp; 559/641–2828; www.yosemiteinn.com.* $$$

Yosemite's Scenic Wonders Vacation Rentals. For location, variety, and size, these rental units about half an hour from Yosemite Valley are hard to beat. Sitting just outside the national park boundary, off Wawona Road and south of Glacier Point Road, the Yosemite West private housing development is an ideal base for exploring the park. More than 30 rental units are available. Types of rentals range from log cabins and chalets to apartments and condominiums. Generous floor plans can accommodate groups, sometimes up to 10 or more people, making these rentals an excellent choice for families. Compared with other vacation rentals in or near the park, most of these units have more modern furnishings as well as more amenities, such as full kitchens, satellite TV, and heating. *7403 Yosemite Park Way; 888/967–3648; www.scenicwonders.com.* **$$–$$$$**

Campgrounds in and Around Yosemite National Park

See the camping chart on pp. 296–297.

Yosemite National Park has 13 campgrounds with a combined total of more than 1,400 campsites. Most campgrounds are seasonal, and all of them require reservations via *www.recreation.gov.* In addition, there are campgrounds available in nearby national forest lands. Again, many are seasonal, with opening and closing dates that vary from year to year. Reservations are a good idea but aren't usually required.

If you'd rather not pitch your own tent or carry a camp stove and food into the wilderness, the ★**HIGH SIERRA CAMPS** (*www. travelyosemite.com*) are a popular circuit of wilderness canvas-tent dormitories in the beautiful Sierra Nevada high country off Tioga Road. Each camp—Merced Lake, Vogelsang, Glen Aulin, May Lake, and Sunrise Camp—is located within a day's hike of another. All camps have restrooms; three have hot showers. All you need to carry on the trail are your own sheets or sleep sack and towels. These camps are usually open from mid-June until mid-September, weather permitting. For reservations, submit an online application to the lottery between early October and November 1 for the following season; to see about last-minute availability, check online at *www.travelyosemite. com* and submit a request. The rates are about $150 for one night's accommodation, which includes breakfast and dinner. A sack lunch can be ordered separately.

At Yosemite Valley campgrounds, such as Lower Pines, North Pines, and Upper Pines, don't expect much privacy; the sites are small and crowded close together. Nevertheless these campgrounds are always the most sought after, mostly for their prime positions near the park's main attractions and for their proximity to perks like hot showers at Half Dome Village and nearby grocery and laundry facilities.

Tuolumne Meadows is another desirable campground, with its easy access to its namesake area; it offers many of the same amenities as Yosemite Valley. For more peace and (possibly) quiet—and stunning stargazing opportunities—pick lesser-known, more remote campgrounds off Tioga Road or Glacier Point Road. Or choose to camp outside the park entirely in less developed national forest campgrounds that surround Yosemite.

Restaurants in Yosemite

See the price chart on p. 16.

In addition to the places recommended here, the Yosemite Valley has snack bars, a grocery market, a food court, delis, and grills for fast, easy meals. Along Tioga Road, which is open only in summer, a small market at Tuolumne Meadows supplies picnickers and campers, while the Tuolumne Meadows Lodge and White Wolf Lodge serve family-style breakfasts and dinners. There are small convenience stores in Wawona and Crane Flat for buying snacks and drinks. All of these are open year-round unless otherwise noted.

The Ahwahnee Dining Room. With its beautifully arranged tables, formally outfitted waitstaff, and ambient piano music, this restaurant set in Yosemite Valley's landmark Ahwahnee presents itself as a sumptuous affair. But looks can be deceiving; sometimes the menu does not consistently deliver the artfully balanced seasonal tastes it promises. For some people, however, main courses such as free-range chicken and grass-fed prime rib *are* a big draw. Others are pulled in by the 34-foot-high beamed ceilings and rustic beauty of the dining room. Rather than dinner or the Sunday brunch (when a sumptuous—if expensive—buffet is a tradition for many), come for lunch instead and order a market-fresh salad or turkey sandwich on multigrain ciabatta. Truly outstanding are special holiday dinners and other seasonal food-and-wine celebrations (*see* Festivals and Seasonal Events in the Practical Information chapter). The wine list offers several wines by the glass and a wide selection of bottles, most from Napa and Sonoma but a handful from lesser-known California regions. At dinner, a collared shirt and slacks are preferred for men, and the dress code for women is upscale (no hiking boots, outdoor wear, jeans, etc.). Make dinner reservations as far in advance as possible—to be on the safe side, aim for at least a month ahead of time during summer; during less busy times of year, a couple of weeks prior is probably sufficient. *1 Ahwahnee Rd., Yosemite Village; 209/372-1489; www.travelyosemite.com.* **$$$$**

Curry Village. At this historic tents-and-cabins camp in Yosemite Valley, families and outdoor athletes can fuel up for a full day's worth of adventures. If you're in a hurry in the morning, grab an icing-rich cinnamon roll or oversize lemon-poppyseed muffin from the Coffee Corner. Later in the day, dig into a pizza and a salad on the tree-shaded deck, the prettiest of the dining locations in Curry Village, or order a hot sandwich or burger combo at the Meadow Grill. The bustling dining pavilion serves cafeteria-style

While away the time with a cocktail in the Mountain Room's rough-hewn bar, where rock climbers down a beer as they brag about the day's accomplishments.

Campgrounds in and Around Yosemite National Park

CAMPGROUND NAME	LOCATION	OPEN	RESERVATIONS	# OF SITES	FEE	RVs	FACILITIES
Bridalveil Creek	South of Yosemite Valley	July–mid-Sept.	Yes	110	$36	Yes	Potable water, restrooms. Group and horse campsites.
Camp 4	Yosemite Valley	Year-round	Yes	36	$10 per person	No	Potable water, restrooms
Crane Flat	North of Yosemite Valley	July–mid-Oct.	Yes	166	$36	Yes	Potable water, restrooms
Curry Village	Yosemite Valley	Year-round	Yes	403 canvas tent cabins	About $150	No	Potable water, restrooms, camp store, restaurants, laundry
High Sierra Camps	North of Yosemite Valley	Mid-June–mid-Sept.	Yes	55 canvas tent cabins	$150 (with meals)	No	Potable water, restrooms, laundry, catered food
Hodgdon Meadow	North of Yosemite Valley	Year-round	Yes; Mid-Apr.–mid-Oct.	105	$36	Yes	Potable water, restrooms. Group campsites.
Housekeeping Camp	Yosemite Valley	Mid Apr.–mid-Oct.	Yes	266 three-wall cabins	About $110	No	Potable water, restrooms, campfire rings, camp store, laundry
Lower Pines	Yosemite Valley	Mid-Apr.–mid-Oct.	Yes	60	$36	Yes	Potable water, restrooms
North Pines	Yosemite Valley	Mid April–mid-Oct.	Yes	81	$36	Yes	Potable water, restrooms

Campground	Location	Open	Reservations	Sites	Fee	Pets	Notes
Porcupine Flat	North of Yosemite Valley	June–mid-Oct.	Yes	52	$24	No	Boil drinking water at creek, vault toilets
Tamarack Flat	North of Yosemite Valley	June–Oct. 15	Yes	52	$24	No	Boil drinking water at creek, vault toilets
Tuolumne Meadows	North of Yosemite Valley	June–Sept.	Yes	304	$36	Yes	Potable water, restrooms. Group and horse campsites. Dump station nearby.
Upper Pines	Yosemite Valley	Year-round	Yes	238	$36	Yes	Potable water, restrooms. Dump station available.
Wawona	South of Yosemite Valley	Year-round	Yes; Mid-Apr.–early Oct.	93	$36	Yes	Potable water, restrooms. Group and horse. Dump station nearby.
White Wolf	North of Yosemite Valley	July–mid-Sept.	Yes	74	$36	Yes	Potable water, restrooms
Yosemite Creek	North of Yosemite Valley	July–mid-Sept.	Yes	75	$24	No	Boil drinking water at creek, vault toilets

NOTE: Backcountry campgrounds at Little Yosemite Valley and near the High Sierra Camps (Glen Aulin, May Lake, Sunrise, Merced Lake, and Vogelsang) are not part of the campground reservation system. A wilderness permit is required to stay at these campgrounds.

breakfast and dinner options; although filling, they tend to be bland. *Southside Dr., Half Dome Village; 209/372–8333; www.travel-yosemite.com.* $

★**Mountain Room Restaurant.** If you're commemorating a wedding anniversary or high-fiving a successful summit of Half Dome, you can celebrate in style in this room with a view inside the Yosemite Valley Lodge. From the welcoming smile of the host at the front desk to the attentiveness of your server, this classic national-park lodge restaurant always feels like a special occasion. Open only for dinner, the Mountain Room serves dishes of hearty fare like charbroiled steaks, rainbow trout, and pork chops that are expertly executed, with locally sourced ingredients. And then there are the dessert options, which might include cherry cobbler, apple pie, or bourbon pecan pie. Reservations are accepted only for large groups; otherwise, seating is first-come, first-served. This policy usually means there's a wait in peak season—30 minutes is common, but it can stretch even longer on summer weekends—but you can pleasantly while away the time with a cocktail in the adjacent bar, where windows on three sides and a few outdoor tables provide verdant views. Request a window table, from which you can see the famous Yosemite Falls. The view is a powerful enhancement to what is already the finest cooking you'll find in the entire park. *Yosemite Valley Lodge, Northside Dr., Yosemite Village; 209/372–1281; www.travelyosemite.com.* $$$

Wawona Hotel Dining Room. The Victorian-era Wawona Hotel is a civilized retreat from the hurly-burly of Yosemite Valley. Its genteel dining room is cheered by picture windows and unique hand-painted lights displaying images of giant sequoia trees. It's deservedly popular for its hearty, pioneer-style breakfasts of bacon, eggs, sausage, eggs Benedict, buttermilk pancakes, and the like. Also drawing in crowds are the Western barbecue cookouts on summer Saturday evenings. Expect standard American fare at lunch, but more creative, often seasonally inspired cuisine for dinner, such as beef pot roast in a red wine demi-glaze or cedar-plank roasted salmon. Be sure to set aside some time to sip a pre-dinner cocktail in the cozy hotel lounge or on the old-fashioned veranda. Reservations are accepted only for groups of six or more. *Forest Dr., off Wawona Rd.; 209/375–1425; www.travelyosemite.com.* $$

★ Veg Alert! ★

The June Bug Cafe in Midpines is particularly vegetarian- and vegan-friendly, with several veg choices on the menu for each meal, from veggie burgers to pasta with pesto.

Restaurants Outside Yosemite

See the price chart on p. 16.

★**The Elderberry House Restaurant.** This sumptuous restaurant at the Château du Sureau inn off Highway 41 south of the park evokes a dramatic French provincial ambience with its candelabras, fine-art oil paintings, and gorgeous garden terraces. Even more unforgettable is the polished service, from the attentive waitstaff to the hard-to-find vintages in the standout wine cellar. The chef's prix-fixe dinner menu (from $125) changes nightly but includes semi-modern dishes with a farm-to-table emphasis. On Sundays a sumptuous brunch is offered, while an afternoon high tea is served on the first and third Sundays of the month. *48688 Victoria La., Oakhurst; 559/683–6800; www.chateausureau.com. $$$$*

Evergreen Lodge Restaurant. West of the park's Big Oak Flat Entrance Station, off Highway 120 near Hetch Hetchy, this old-fashioned mountain resort has a cozy restaurant that offers much more than the usual roadside fare. Breakfast includes hearty French toast with fresh fruit and eggs Benedict. If you're in a hurry, order up coffee, pastries, or a deli lunch to go from the general store. Once the sun sets, the restaurant, which has a spacious heated back patio, serves hungry hikers filling entrées such as steak, pan-seared salmon, or creative burgers, along with microbrews and specialty cocktails. It's the resort's restful ambience—so far from the highway traffic and the nonstop crowding of Yosemite Valley—plus a stellar Californian wine list that put it over the top. *33160 Evergreen Rd., Groveland; 209/379–2606; www.evergreenlodge.com. $$$*

Iron Door Saloon. A locals' hangout that's nonetheless welcoming to visitors who stream through Groveland on their way to Yosemite's Big Oak Flat entrance, this restaurant and bar claims to be the oldest continually operating saloon in California, opening in 1896. The menu is mostly your usual roadside bar fare—burgers (including a buffalo burger), chicken strips, fish-and-chips, and a handful of other entrees—but the charmingly rustic vibe, from the big game trophies on the walls to the memorabilia, including historic photos of Yosemite, plastered on every surface, make it worth a stop. Hearty breakfasts are served in the attached dining room. *18761 Main St., Groveland; 209/962–8904; www.irondoorsaloon.com. $$*

June Bug Cafe. Although it's a 25-mile drive west of Yosemite Valley, this café at the Yosemite Bug, a funky, hippie-flavored hostel and cabin complex, is one of the best bargains in the Yosemite region. The cozy wooden dining room dishes up hearty hikers' dinners such as honey-mustard roasted salmon or grilled pork chops with mashed potatoes as well as sandwiches, salads, pizza, and quesadillas for lunch. The choices for vegans and vegetarians are plentiful, too, and some of the produce comes from their own organic garden. Drop by in the morning for muesli, omelets, and buckwheat pancakes, and to pick up sack lunches before hitting the trail later. *Yosemite Bug Rustic Mountain Resort, 6979 Hwy. 140, Midpines; 209/966–6666; www.yosemitebug.com.* **$$**

★**Whoa Nellie Deli.** A more unlikely roadside spot there never was: this regular gas station on the east side of the Sierra Nevada has a chef-run deli serving sophisticated meals. It's open only during summer, usually from the last weekend in April through late October, but it's worth the drive (a stunning 30 minutes from Tioga Lodge) for hearty burgers, baby back ribs, and barbecue chicken sandwiches, as well as specialties like buffalo meat loaf, grilled pork chops, and fish tacos. Some of the outdoor picnic tables have views of Mono Lake. *Tioga Gas Mart, 22 Vista Point Rd., Lee Vining; 760/647–1088; www.whoanelliedeli.com.* **$$**

☯ SEQUOIA AND KINGS CANYON NATIONAL PARKS

Except for Wuksachi Lodge in Sequoia, in-park accommodations are no frills. You'll nonetheless pay a premium to stay in the parks, but it is well worth it to spare yourself the long, often winding drive from even the closest towns. Besides, the chance to sleep near the forests of giant sequoia trees or in the belly of the Kings Canyon beside a roaring river is exactly what you've come to the parks for.

This section covers lodgings inside Sequoia and Kings Canyon National Parks, in the Giant Sequoia National Monument of the Sequoia National Forest, and in gateway towns outside the parks. Reservations are essential from Memorial Day through Labor Day. Because these parks are so close together, you could overnight in one park and day-trip to the other. This may not work if you base yourself in a more remote area, however, such as Mineral King or Cedar Grove.

HOTELS AND LODGES IN SEQUOIA AND KINGS CANYON

See the price chart on p. 16.

The rustic yet elegant restaurant at the Wuksachi Lodge offers dining with a view.

These places are not renowned for their luxury, but they're perfectly serviceable, and, as the only places in the park, they put you close to all the action.

Cedar Grove Lodge. Near where Highway 180 ends in the Kings Canyon beside the Kings River, this basic three-story lodge has 18 bare-bones motel-style rooms with queen beds, phones, and air-conditioning, plus three more lodge rooms with patios overlooking the river. While you won't want to spend much time in these thin-walled, somewhat cramped accommodations, they are your only choice in this beautifully remote area of Kings Canyon. The lodge is usually open from late May through early October. *Hwy. 180, Cedar Grove; 559/335–5500, 877/436–9615; www.visitsequoia.com.* $$

John Muir Lodge & Grant Grove Cabins. Named after the famous Sierra Nevada conservationist, this rustic place offers the

The chance to sleep
near the forests of
giant sequoia trees or in the
belly of the Kings Canyon
is exactly what you've come
to the parks for.

only accommodations in busy Grant Grove Village. The lodge has 36 nicely updated rooms with rough-hewn furnishings, flat-screen TVs, phones, and bathtubs ideal for a posthike soak. You can also stay in one of the 49 cabins on the property and be surrounded by trees. The most popular cabins are the eight duplex wooden cabins with private baths and "Cabin 9" (also called the Honeymoon Cabin), all of which have electricity, heating, carpeting, and Mission-style furnishings. Forty of the cabins share public bathhouses; hard-sided wooden cabins have heating and electricity, but soft-sided tent versions do not. Rooms in the lodge are available year-round, but the cabins are closed in winter. *Hwy. 180, Grant Grove; 559/335–5500, 877/436–9615; www.visitsequoia.com.* **$$–$$$**

Silver City Mountain Resort. Near the end of the treacherously winding road into the Mineral King Valley in southern Sequoia National Park, this privately owned collection of 13 rustic cabins and Swiss chalets that sleep up to eight people and two rooms puts hiking enthusiasts near spectacular mountain trails. While far from luxurious, they are usually restful places to lay your head, with knotty pine walls and tin roofs befitting this historical mining settlement. Some of the comfier cabins are equipped with full kitchens, stone fireplaces, decks, and free-standing bathtubs. Most of them have electricity and private baths, and those that don't instead come equipped with kerosene lamps and have access to a well-maintained shower house. The food at the restaurant is quite good—the pie is legendary. The on-site market offers limited options, so bring any supplies you may need with you. The resort is usually open late May through mid-October. *Mineral King Rd.; 559/242–3510; www.silvercityresort.com.* **$$$–$$$$**

Wuksachi Lodge. North of Lodgepole Village and the Giant Forest, the Wuksachi Lodge is the most deluxe hotel in Sequoia National Park. The tall-ceilinged lobby of this wood-and-stone hotel is impressive, and you can sink into a plush chair by the fireplace or sip an Irish coffee from the small bar in its inviting common areas. The lodge's 102 spacious hotel rooms with private baths, telephones, and TVs are actually located in three three-story satellite buildings a five-minute walk from the front desk, snack and gift shop, and restaurant; some are bright and modern, while others could use an update. Wi-Fi is available throughout but can be spotty in the rooms. For dining with views, the lodge dining room (*see* Restaurants in

Sequoia and Kings Canyon) serves breakfast, lunch, and dinner. *64740 Wuksachi Way, off Generals Hwy.; 559/565–4070, 866/807–3598; www.visitsequoia.com.* **$$$**

HOTELS AND LODGES OUTSIDE SEQUOIA AND KINGS CANYON

See the price chart on p. 16.

Buckeye Tree Lodge. The rushing Kaweah River sings guests to sleep at this family-run lodge just outside the southern entrance to Sequoia National Park. The 11 riverfront rooms, plus an eight-person standalone house, are basic but light-filled and comfortable, with showers, air-conditioning, Wi-Fi, and HDTV, plus access to picnic tables, grills, and a small pool. The front desk also handles check-in for the larger but darker units across the highway at the Sequoia Village Inn. *46000 Sierra Dr. (Hwy. 198), Three Rivers; 559/561–5900; www.buckeyetreelodge.com.* **$$$$**

The Darling Hotel. Developers meticulously restored a dilapidated, three-story, 1930s, art-deco building, transforming it into this hotel, which opened in 2020 and is a good option if you'd like to stay in the heart of a town, near restaurants, pubs, and shops. All 32 rooms and suites reflect a modern take on art-deco style, with plush furnishings, 12-foot ceilings, and spacious bathrooms with 1930s-era accents. The rooftop restaurant and lounge, Elderwood, offers panoramic city and mountain views. *210 N. Court St., Visalia; 559/713–2113; thedarlingvisalia.com.* **$$–$$$**

Montecito Sequoia Lodge. Off a tree-lined side road in the Sequoia National Forest between Sequoia and Kings Canyon National Parks, this family-oriented summer camp offers lakeside lodgings year-round. Established in 1946, the resort today operates on the old-fashioned "all inclusive" plan, where accommodation rates include three buffet meals a day (but not always family-camp activities, which can be separate and optional). Choose from 37 upscale motel-style rooms (scattered in lodges around the property); eight rustic cabins with wood-burning stoves, electric heating, and shared bathhouses with showers; or four light-filled family cabins with private bath. During the summer, the resort puts on different themed family camps each week, with outdoor activities, open-mike and variety-show nights, arts-and-crafts workshops for kids, and theme parties. Most people who stay here in summer come for the family camps, so you may feel like an outsider if you stay here independently during that time. In winter, the resort is the best place near either park for snow sports. Enjoy family-style buffet dinners in the resort's dining room (*see* Restaurants Outside Sequoia and Kings Canyon). *63410 Generals Hwy; 559/565–3388, 800/227–9900; www. mslodge.com.* $$–$$$

Rio Sierra Riverhouse. Step through the bright blue gate of this stylish B&B in Three Rivers, catch sight of the sandy beach fronting the Kaweah River, and suddenly your vacation has begun. Three units, including a master suite that spans the entire top floor, feature private baths, Wi-Fi, and whimsical decor, from shabby-chic chandeliers to vintage film projectors. A two-bedroom cottage up the road has a full kitchen and sun deck. Breakfast (not included) is a continental affair, and on many nights there are complimentary s'mores around the beach campfire. *41997 Sierra Dr. (Hwy. 198), Three Rivers; 833/239–7450; www.rio-sierra.com.* $$$

CAMPGROUNDS IN AND AROUND SEQUOIA AND KINGS CANYON

See the camping chart on pp. 310–311.

Sequoia and Kings Canyon national parks have 14 campgrounds. Three are open year-round, and most require reservations, which you can make via *www.recreation.gov.* There are also campgrounds in the surrounding Sequoia National Forest (*www.fs.usda.gov/activity/ sequoia/recreation/camping-cabins*). Many are seasonal, with opening and closing dates that vary from year to year. Reservations are a good idea but aren't generally required. *See also* the Campgrounds in and Around Sequoia and Kings Canyon National Parks chart later in this chapter.

If you arrive without a reservation during peak times, your best chances of finding a first-come, first-served site still available are in more remote areas of the parks (for example, Cedar Grove in Kings Canyon or Mineral King in Sequoia). To avoid frustration, stop in at one of the main visitor centers to check availability before making the long drive out to these spots. Pay showers are available at Grant Grove and Cedar Grove in Kings Canyon, at Stony Creek Village between the national parks, and at Lodgepole Village and Silver City Mountain Resort near Mineral King in Sequoia National Park.

If you'd rather not pitch your own tent nor carry a camp stove and food into the wilderness, the **Bearpaw High Sierra Camp** (*www. visitsequoia.com*) is an 11.5-mile hike along the High Sierra Trail starting from Crescent Meadow in Sequoia National Park. Open from mid-June until mid-September, it offers private canvas tents, flush toilets, hot showers, and a catered breakfast and dinner starting at $385 per night. Box lunches are available for an additional fee. For reservations or to check last-minute availability, call *877/436–9726* up to one year before your trip.

In the Giant Sequoia National Monument, the **Sequoia High Sierra Camp** (*www.sequoiahighsierracamp.com*) is less than a 1-mile hike from the Marvin Pass trailhead off Big Meadows Road. It offers 32 deluxe canvas-tent cabins with hand-carved furnishings, high-thread-count linens, and feather-down pillows, as well as flush toilets and hot showers in a shared bathhouse. Overnight rates of $250 per person include a chef-prepared dinner and breakfast and a packable picnic lunch. The camp is typically open from mid-June through mid-September; make reservations by calling *866/654–2877*.

Also in the Giant Sequoia National Monument off Big Meadows Road, the **Big Meadows Guard Station** built by the Civilian Conservation Corps in the 1930s is available for rent between mid-June and mid-October. The 900-square-foot cabin has a fully equipped kitchen; guests must supply their own bedding and toiletries. For more information, contact the **Hume Lake Ranger District** *(35860 E. Kings Canyon Rd. [Hwy. 180], Dunlap; 559/338–2251; www. fs.usda.gov/sequoia)*. The cabin costs $125; make reservations online at *www.recreation.gov* or by calling *877/444–6777*.

The campgrounds in Sequoia and Kings Canyon offer pretty settings for a relaxing getaway, though none have bells and whistles (or even RV hookups). Those around Lodgepole, Grant Grove, and Dorst Creek get quite busy in summer with vacationing families, as do Cedar Grove, deep inside Kings Canyon, and the hotter, drier Sequoia foothills campgrounds near Ash Mountain. Mineral King is even more remote and has less-developed campsites that attract a more hard-core set of outdoor adventurers (watch out for those marmots!). Campgrounds in the national forest lands between Kings Canyon and Sequoia national parks can be just as popular, although they generally fill up after the national park campgrounds do. The exception to this is at Hume Lake, where easy access to water sports and summer vacation-friendly amenities such as a convenience store and takeout burger and ice-cream shop make car camping more fun for families, especially if you have young kids.

Restaurants in Sequoia and Kings Canyon

See the price chart on p. 16.

The main tourist areas of Sequoia and Kings Canyon National Parks—Lodgepole, Grant Grove, and Cedar Grove Villages—all have snack bars, delis, grills, or basic restaurants for convenient meals on the run and grocery markets for stocking up before picnics and campfire cookouts.

Grant Grove Restaurant. The ecofriendly restaurant at Grant Grove offers hearty American fare in an elegant, lodgelike setting across from the Kings Canyon Visitor Center. Whether indoors around the stone fireplace under high wooden beams or on the outdoor deck, diners have expansive views overlooking Bradley Meadow and the surrounding giant trees. Local, sustainably sourced ingredients star on a menu featuring sandwiches, juicy burgers, salads, and pizza. Breakfast features hearty omelets, pancakes, and fresh-baked muffins. *Hwy 180; 559/335–5500; www.visitsequoia.com. $*

The Peaks Restaurant at Wuksachi Lodge. Walk through the tall-ceilinged hotel lobby to find this rustic-looking restaurant, a short drive north of Lodgepole Village. Open year-round, it has a stone fireplace and panoramic windows looking onto groves of lodgepole pine and fir trees. The dinner menu features dishes made with seasonal local ingredients. Lunch is more casual (mostly just sandwiches and salads), and breakfast is an all-you-can-eat buffet. There's full cocktail service from the small hotel bar. *64740 Wuksachi Way, off Generals Hwy.; 559/565–4070. $$–$$$*

Restaurants Outside Sequoia and Kings Canyon

See the price chart on p. 16.

Fugazzi's California Bistro. In downtown Visalia, less than an hour's drive west of Sequoia National Park, Fugazzi's is an urbane eatery with colorfully painted walls and sofas that are divinely comfortable. Perch at the bar with a martini, or nab a table and nosh on fresh, oversize salads or satisfying bowls of pasta. There are some inventive thin-crust pizzas, too, like one topped with Thai chicken and another with local vegetables. The list of California wines and domestic microbrews is especially welcome after a long day's hike. *127 W. Main St., Visalia; 559/625–0496; www.fugazzisbistro.com. $$–$$$*

Montecito Sequoia Lodge. In the Giant Sequoia National Monument, between Sequoia and Kings Canyon national parks, this resort puts on a spread of above-par buffet meals that are usually

available to nonguests (call ahead to check). The log cabin-style dining room is often full of ravenous families sharing meals that might
feature grilled fresh tilapia, corn salad, and homemade ice cream and
berry pies. If there's a wait, kick back on the outdoor deck, which has
beautiful sunset views. *63410 Generals Hwy.; 800/227–9900; www.
mslodge.com.* **$$–$$$**

Ol' Buckaroo. A hip roadside stop with outdoor tables overlooking the river, the Ol' Buckaroo brought California's food truck craze
to tiny Three Rivers, just outside Sequoia National Park. The formula
proved so popular that the full-service Buckaroo Diner now serves
the same small dinner menu, highlighting produce from local organic
farms in exceptionally well-prepared choices such as seasonal salads,
grass-fed burgers, and sweet tea chicken. Brunch is served Sundays
only, with park-bound drivers fueling up on brown butter waffles and
French press coffee. *41695 Sierra Dr. (Hwy. 198); 559/465–5088; www.
olbuckaroo.com.* **$$–$$$**

Sierra Subs & Salads. The town of Three Rivers is just a short drive
to the south entrance of Sequoia National Park. This small deli makes
creative, fresh sandwiches and salads, healthy wraps, and grilled panini
like the Black Bear Grill, with roast beef and Ortega chilies, or the
Hollywood Tremor, with turkey, bacon, sundried tomato, and chi-
potle cream cheese grilled on ciabatta. Enjoy your meal at one of the
picnic tables overlooking the Kaweah River, or get a sandwich and a
fresh-squeezed frozen lemonade to go. *651 Sierra Dr. (Hwy. 198), Three
Rivers; 559/561–4810; www.sierrasubsandsalads.com.* **$**

Camping in and Around Sequoia and Kings Canyon National Parks

All of the following campgrounds have drinking water available, unless otherwise noted.
Those marked with an asterisk (*) are located outside the national park boundaries,
and are not operated by the NPS. There are no hookups for RVs in these campgrounds.
The RV column on the chart indicates if road access is acceptable and sites are large
enough for RVs; some have pull-through sites, while others are back-in only. Dates in
the following chart are general: because weather in the Sierras can be unpredictable,
campgrounds can open as many as four weeks late or may close earlier than expected.

CAMPGROUNDS IN AND AROUND SEQUOIA AND KINGS CANYON NATIONAL PARKS

CAMPGROUND NAME	AREA/PARK	OPEN	RESERVATIONS	# OF SITES	FEE	RVs	FACILITIES
Atwell Mill	Mineral King/Sequoia	Late May–late Oct.	Yes	21	$22	No	ADA site, vault toilets (no potable water after 2018)
Azalea	Grant Grove/Kings Canyon	Year-round	Yes, during peak season	110	$22	Yes	ADA site, flush toilets
* Big Meadows	Off Generals Hwy.	June–Sept.	Yes	44	$32–$64	Yes	Vault toilets (no potable water)
* Buck Rock	Off Generals Hwy.	May–Oct.	No	9	Free	Yes	Vault toilets (no potable water)
Buckeye Flat	Foothills/Sequoia	Mid-March–late Sept.	Yes	28	$22	No	ADA site, flush toilets
Canyon View	Cedar Grove/Kings Canyon	Varies May–Oct.	Yes	16	$50–$60	No	ADA site, large- and midsize-group sites, flush toilets
Cold Springs	Mineral King/Sequoia	Late May–late Oct.	Yes	40	$22	No	Vault toilets, Potable water through mid-Oct.
* Convict Flat	Hwy. 180	May–Oct.	No	5	Free	Yes	Vault toilets (no potable water)
Crystal Springs	Grant Grove/Kings Canyon	Late May–early Sept.	Yes	50	$22–$50	Yes	ADA site, midsize-group sites, flush toilets
Dorst Creek	Giant Forest/Sequoia	Late June–early Sept.	Yes	222	$22–$70	Yes	ADA sites, RV dump station, flush toilets, large-group sites, free Sequoia Shuttle
* Horse Camp	Off Generals Hwy.	June–Oct.	No	5	Free	Yes	Equestrian sites, vault toilets (no potable water)

Name	Location	Season	Reservations	Sites	Fee		Facilities
*Hume Lake	Hume Lake	Mid-May–early Sept.	Yes	74	$32–$64	Yes	Flush toilets, Wi-Fi Internet access
*Landslide	Hume Lake	May–Oct.	No	9	$32	No	Vault toilets
Lodgepole	Giant Forest/Sequoia	Mid-April–Nov.	Yes	214	$22	Yes	ADA sites, RV dump station, flush toilets, free Sequoia Shuttle
Moraine	Cedar Grove/Kings Canyon	Late May–early Sept.	Yes	121	$22	Yes	ADA sites, flush toilets
Potwisha	Foothills/Sequoia	Year-round	Yes	42	$22	Yes	ADA site, RV dump station, flush toilets
*Princess	Hume Lake	Late May–mid-Sept.	Yes	88	$32–$64	Yes	RV dump station, vault toilets
Sentinel	Cedar Grove/Kings Canyon	Late Apr.–mid-Nov.	Yes	82	$22	Yes	ADA site, flush toilets
Sheep Creek	Cedar Grove/Kings Canyon	Late May–mid-Sept.	Yes	111	$22	Yes	Flush toilets
South Fork	Foothills/Sequoia	Year-round (fee in summer)	No	10	$22	No	Vault toilets (no potable water)
*Stony Creek	Off Generals Hwy.	May–late Sept.	Yes	48	$32–$64	Yes	Vault toilets
Sunset	Grant Grove/Kings Canyon	Late May–early Sept.	Yes	159	$22–$50	Yes	ADA sites, flush toilets; large-group sites
*Tenmile	Hume Lake	May–Oct.	Yes	11	$32–$64	Yes	Vault toilets (no potable water)

Geology, Flora, and Fauna

The sun rises above Mt. Whitney and its needles.

The incredible biodiversity of the Sierra Nevada and its parks is as intriguing as its geological history: not for nothing was Yosemite declared a World Heritage Site in 1984. There's so much of it to see and fortunately there's still time.

Environmental pollution, harmful introduced species, and loss of habitat can't keep the parks down. The extraordinary and once-endangered peregrine falcon is among the creatures making a comeback, and the giant sequoia forests are healthier than they've been since the arrival of the first European pioneers and immigrants in the 19th century. Yosemite, Sequoia, and Kings Canyon today protect more than 250 native species of vertebrates (possessing backbones, for the most part) and 1,200 kinds of vascular plants (those with conductive tissue that allows them to breathe and move water and food throughout their bodies).

The parks' wildflowers include
purple owl's clover.

World-famous climber Peter Croft treks up the north ridge of Mt. Conness in the Sierra Nevada mountains, on the eastern edge of Yosemite National Park.

Mesmerized by the Merced River
in Yosemite Valley.

⊕ GEOLOGY

The Sierra Nevada is the highest mountain range in California, and its Mt. Whitney is the highest peak (14,505 feet) in the contiguous United States. The Sierra Nevada range, the crest of which easily rises above 13,000 feet as it passes through Yosemite National Park, divides the Central Valley of California lying to the west from the lowlands of the Great Basin Desert spreading to the east. In Sequoia National Park, the Great Western Divide parallels the Sierra crest, while in Kings Canyon National Park, the monumental Monarch and Goddard Divides are massive ridges pointing west from the Sierra crest.

This entire region once lay at the bottom of an ancient sea, where layers of sediment were compacted into sedimentary rock. Then, as the oceanic plate started to slide beneath the North American continent, in a process called subduction, it provoked an intense period of volcanic activity along the West Coast. Magma from this molten oceanic plate either pushed above the surface in volcanic explosions or cooled underground and became granite. These granite reserves, called plutons, are aggregated into even larger masses of rock called batholiths, which tilted and rose along fault lines to form the Sierra Nevada. This same gigantic process of shifting rock continues today, but it won't make them taller, because the mountains are being weathered down by erosion at the same rate that they're growing. Erosion is also exposing underground granite and exfoliating the granite you can already see, creating such unforgettable formations as Yosemite's Half Dome.

As the Sierra Nevada is uplifted and tilted over time, rivers including the Tuolumne, Merced, Kings, and Kern have cut deep canyons into the west side of the range. Ice Age glaciers formed along the crest of the Sierra Nevada, from where they slipped and slid over the exposed granite rock domes and cliffs, leaving evidence of glacial polish (usually smoothed or grooved surfaces where pebbles scraped as they were carried along by the glaciers) such as you can see from Yosemite's Glacier Point. Most important, these glaciers softened the sharp V-shaped valleys of the mountain range into wider U-shaped valleys, most famously in Yosemite Valley but also at Cedar Grove in Kings Canyon National Park.

When the glaciers retreated, they left behind moraines (fields of glacial debris, ranging from small silt to large rocks) and lake basins, many of which are increasingly filled in with sediment, as is the case with the Yosemite Valley's famous Mirror Lake.

(opposite) The light playing off Half Dome at different times of the day.

319

FLORA

GIANT SEQUOIA

Easily identified by its massive girth and towering height, the giant sequoia grows only on the western slopes of the Sierra Nevada at elevations of 4,500 to 7,000 feet. Its seed-bearing cones are surprisingly small, measuring just a few inches long. Its bark, softer than that of other conifers, also reveals dark wine-red stains; far from nefarious, these discolorations stem from the tannin inside, which helps these long-lived giants survive wildfires, an important process without which new sequoias would never sprout nor grow. The biggest known giant sequoia is the General Sherman Tree, which is growing in Sequoia National Park's Giant Forest.

WILDFIRES: A FRIEND OF THE FOREST

Not all wildfires are disasters. In many cases they're essential to a forest's health. This was not a popular view in the 1930s, when the National Park Service and the U.S. Forest Service began what would be three decades of aggressively suppressing fires. The federal government partly reversed its position in the '60s, reasoning that the financial burden of stanching many of these fires outweighed saving natural and cultural resources from destruction. Also changing the government's tune was scientific research showing that wildfires were essential to the natural life cycle of woodland forests, findings that ultimately led to a new national environmental policy.

Nowhere was this new policy of permitting wildfires to burn with minimal containment more critical than in Sequoia and Kings Canyon National Parks, where the policy was first tested. These areas were key due to a finicky seed cone. The giant sequoia tree cones can release their seeds only in very hot and dry conditions and can germinate successfully only on bare mineral soil that has been cleared of competing plant growth. Both conditions usually occur after a wildfire.

Today, technical fire crews in the national parks identify forested areas that have not burned in a long time and regularly initiate prescribed burns to clear out underbrush, which reduces the potential for disastrously large-scale fires that could wipe out an entire ecosystem for decades. As you travel in the parks, especially in summer, keep an eye out for prescribed fires. Firefighters are often on hand to answer questions.

CALIFORNIA POPPY

In the Sierra foothills early in spring, California poppies yield their silky, fan-shaped petals, which vary in hue from deep orange to pale yellow. You might spot them on roadsides throughout the parks, from lower-elevation valleys to mixed conifer forests, where hillsides and grassy meadows may appear carpeted in gold. California's state flower is tolerant of drought and grows well in poor soil. An extract from this showy flower was once used medicinally by Native Americans as an extremely mild sedative, as the California poppy is only a distant relative of the opium poppy, from which more potent narcotics are derived. The California poppy's medicinal uses by indigenous tribes included relieving toothaches and sleeplessness and ridding children's scalps of lice.

BRISTLECONE PINE

If you thought the giant sequoia was long-lived, well, you'd be correct, but the title for oldest tree on Earth goes to the bristlecone pine. This gnarled tree can live to be more than 4,000 years old and grows on the east side of the Sierra Nevada, among other places in the western United States. Hiding out in remote groves just below the timber line, the bristlecone pines are twisted and often have dead wood exposed. Blame both characteristics on the rough winds that batter these thin-air dwellers, which grow incredibly slowly through short summer and deep-freeze winters in dry, almost desertlike soil. The pine owes its name to its cones with claw-like bristles and scrub-brush branches densely filled with needles.

327

LODGEPOLE PINE

In the mixed-conifer forests of the Sierra, telling the many types of pines apart can pose a challenge if you don't know the trick, which is sizing up the different cones and examining the branches to count the number of needles in discrete clusters on the branches. If the needles are paired, you're likely looking at a lodgepole pine, which, as its name suggests, grows remarkably straight and tall. The name derives from the Native Americans' use of the thin trunks to construct tepee frames. Lodgepole cones are relatively small, only a few inches long in most cases. As with giant sequoias, lodgepole cones need wildfirelike heat before they'll release their precious seeds to sprout in the newly scarred, bare mineral soil of a partly denuded forest floor.

PONDEROSA PINE

If the long needles come in threes and the exteriors of the cones are prickly to the touch, chances are you've come upon a ponderosa pine. Another telltale sign is that the flaky and pale bark of older ponderosa pine trees, which are also known as yellow pines, takes on the appearance of pieces of a jigsaw puzzle all fitted together. If you get up close to any specimens, you may find that the bark has a faint scent of vanilla. Perhaps the most common trees on the western side of the Sierra Nevada, ponderosas have served as an abundant source of lumber in forests throughout California that are not protected as they are in the national parks.

SNOW PLANT

The stalky, short snow plant, which is red all over from stalk to fleshy, flowering stem, is one of the most unique plants in the Sierra Nevada region. It is impossible not to notice it poking above forest floors carpeted by pine needles, especially when it pops up at the edge of melting patches of snow starting in May. The contrast between its bright reddish color and the deep greens of the forest or stark white snow can be startling. This beautiful specimen is like a vulture of the plant world, preying on other decomposing plant matter in the surrounding soil.

SUGAR PINE

When it comes to pines, the sugar is king. The largest known of the species, sugar pines are capable of stretching upward of 200 feet above the forest floor. Their cones are proportionally enormous, growing up to 18 inches long and so heavily laden by scales that their posture tends to take on an accordionlike droop. Sugar pines yield clusters of needles that grow in groups of five, another way to help distinguish them from other pines. Native Americans and early pioneers in the Sierra Nevada would carve the sugar pine's bark to encourage the release of a slightly sweet tree resin that could then be chewed like gum.

FOXTAIL PINE

The foxtail pine is an irregular, jagged tree that exists on granite outcroppings and slopes at elevations above 8,000 feet. A native of California, the foxtail pine is found in very few places outside Sequoia and Kings Canyon national parks, where it is one of the most common subalpine trees. Foxtails grow surprisingly low to the ground, with bushy branches filled with needles in groups of five that curl around like its namesake animal's tail. Its reddish-brown bark is remarkably thick, acting as insulation during the long winters. Foxtail pines adapt to harsh conditions by growing slowly; with luck, one may live to be 2,000 years old.

LUPINE

Low-lying lupine plants are common throughout the Sierra Nevada, especially alongside hiking trails and in the valleys. Although there are many lupine varieties, most display vertical rows of blueish-purple flowers that resemble small pods when closed. Some of the several dozen species in the region have proved to be poisonous if ingested. Other common lavender-colored wildflowers in the region include larkspur, which grows several feet (yes feet, not inches) tall at elevations above 5,000 feet, and the sweet-scented sky pilot, a rare specimen that grows only at elevations above 10,000 feet.

FAUNA

BIGHORN SHEEP

In the high country of the Sierra crest, muscular bighorn sheep can be seen scrambling on granite outcroppings and along mountainsides. In winter they descend to lower elevations on the east side of the range, where green grazing lands are more plentiful during the colder months. However, loss of habitat, hunting (which is now prohibited), and increased predation by mountain lions have driven down the numbers of bighorn sheep, currently the only federally endangered mammal in Yosemite, Sequoia, and Kings Canyon. In 2000, there were about 100 of these sheep in the Sierra Nevada, but thanks to recovery efforts—including the relocation of some herds to the parks in 2015—their number is up to more than 600. Like their fellow park residents, the mule deer, bighorns rut in autumn, when antlered males fight each other dramatically over mates. Rams have heavy, curled horns, while ewes' horns are short and slightly bent. From afar, it's easy to spot both sexes' white rumps, which stand out brightly against their furry brown coats.

BLACK BEAR

The region's most celebrated mega-fauna is the black bear. Some have black fur, though a golden-tan or cinnamon color is more common. Unlike grizzlies, which were wiped out in California in 1922, black bears don't have a shoulder hump. They're much smaller than grizzlies, measuring about the same height as a human adult but weighing more (averaging about 300 pounds), depending on their age and sex. They also have larger ears than their formerly endangered grizzly cousins. Although they naturally forage most often for acorns and berries, black bears are omnivores. They hibernate lightly for up to seven months during the winter, and at lower elevations that see more moderate winters they may not sleep much at all. Their populations are spread equally throughout the Sierra Nevada. You've got a good chance of seeing one by visiting from late spring through early autumn, when the bears are most active. They're also prevalent in the Sierra Nevada wilderness.

OUR BEAR BRETHREN

"Bears are made of the same dust as we, and breathe the same winds and drink of the same waters. A bear's days are warmed by the same sun, his dwellings are overdomed by the same blue sky, and his life turns and ebbs with heart-pulsings like ours, and was poured from the same First Fountain. And whether he at last goes to our stingy heaven or no, he has terrestrial immortality. His life not long, not short, knows no beginning, no ending. To him life unstinted, unplanned, is above the accidents of time, and his years, markless and boundless, equal Eternity.

God bless Yosemite bears!"

—John Muir, *John of the Mountains: The Unpublished Journals of John Muir*, 1938.

STELLER'S JAY

Bright blue Steller's jays are a ubiquitous annoyance in all three parks due to their relentless attempts to steal food from picnickers and campers. Of course, it's not really their fault, as these intelligent birds have quickly become accustomed to humans who have invaded their natural habitat. If you can get past their most irritating habit, try to admire their tenacity for survival; they range freely across the western half of the North American continent, all the way from Alaska to Mexico. They will eat almost anything and naturally feed on all types of fruits and berries, as well as nuts, which they can hold with their feet as they pound the hard shell open with their beaks. Not to be confused with the blue jay, the Steller's jay has a darker upper body with a jet-black head and prominently peaked crown.

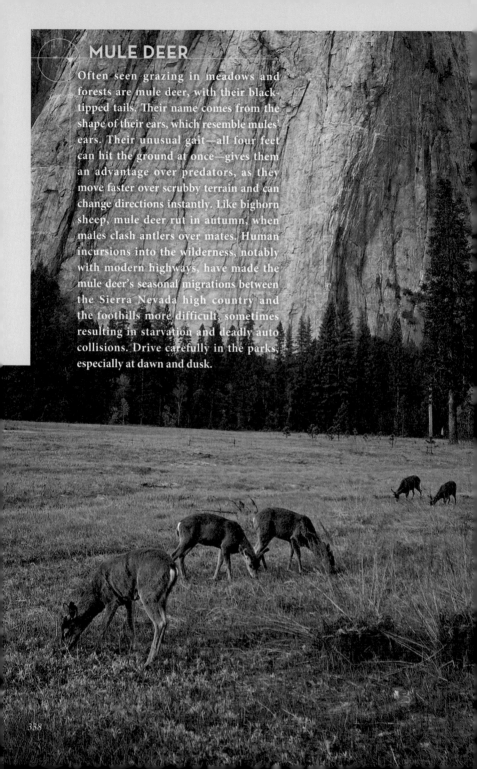

MULE DEER

Often seen grazing in meadows and forests are mule deer, with their black-tipped tails. Their name comes from the shape of their ears, which resemble mules' ears. Their unusual gait—all four feet can hit the ground at once—gives them an advantage over predators, as they move faster over scrubby terrain and can change directions instantly. Like bighorn sheep, mule deer rut in autumn, when males clash antlers over mates. Human incursions into the wilderness, notably with modern highways, have made the mule deer's seasonal migrations between the Sierra Nevada high country and the foothills more difficult, sometimes resulting in starvation and deadly auto collisions. Drive carefully in the parks, especially at dawn and dusk.

PEREGRINE FALCON

A predatory bird once faced with extinction, peregrines now may be spotted with binoculars as they nest from March through July in the granite walls and domes of Yosemite National Park. In summer, mature birds migrate into the Sierra Nevada high country. Similar in size to a crow, these "duck hawks" are slate-blue or brownish-black with prominent white throats and black markings on their cheeks that resemble mustaches or sideburns. Thanks to their excellent eyesight and the world-record-breaking speed of their dives, peregrine falcons are able to hunt and feed on other birds also in flight. Their impressive wingspan may extend almost 4 feet.

CALIFORNIA MOUNTAIN KINGSNAKE

With black, red, and white stripes along its entire lengthy body, this snake is often confused with the venomous coral snake. But no worries here: the coral snake doesn't live in these parts, and the mountain kingsnake isn't venomous. Instead, it kills its victims—mostly lizards, mice, and other small rodents—by constriction. While humans don't interest them in the slightest, these mighty powerful predators infamously prey on other snakes (thus giving them the royal title of "kingsnake"), everything from harmless gopher snakes to the most venomous rattlers.

GREAT GRAY OWL

Yosemite is home to about two-thirds of the 200 to 300 great gray owls living in California. The largest owl in North America, *Strix nebulosa yosemitensis,* a California State Endangered Species, reaches about 2 feet tall. Their ears, unlike the tufted ears common to many other species of owls in this region, are smaller and asymmetrical, which together with their enormous disc-shape faces permit them to focus on the sounds of their prey. Although you're unlikely to spy one, you might hear its deep-throated voice echoing through the trees in spring.

MARMOT

Yellow-bellied marmots live high up in the Sierra Nevada, where they make their homes among the granite-rock piles of talus slopes and along riverbanks. These rocky strongholds help protect the furry ground squirrels (and one of the largest rodents in North America) from such natural predators as eagles and hawks. Marmots are among the most curious and disarmingly fearless animals you'll meet in the parks, most often along high-country hiking trails and also in the Mineral King Valley of Sequoia. Marmots have an unusual addiction: They've developed a taste for antifreeze coolant, and they'll go to great lengths to get it.

MOUNTAIN LION

Although the mountain lion is an occasional predator, chances are you won't see one of these solitary, stealthy cats at any of the three parks. That doesn't mean they're not out there, closely watching and wondering if you'll notice them. Also called cougars, these enormous carnivores live throughout the Sierra Nevada, from the foothills up through the forests and into the mountains. They're tawny colored, can be 8 feet long, and weigh up to 200 pounds. They're capable of taking down a mule deer or elk, though not a black bear, the only creature in the region that outsizes them. Attacks on humans are not unheard of but are rare.

FLORA

CALIFORNIA BUCKEYE

A deciduous tree, the California buckeye—aka California horse chestnut—is common in the western Sierra Nevada foothills, where it blooms with very long and fragrant clusters of white and pale-pink flowers, usually in late spring or early summer. But you have to hurry to see them: to conserve water, they drop their flowers as soon as summer heats up.

INCENSE CEDAR

With its scent of earthy incense and cinnamon-colored bark, the cedar can reach almost 200 feet tall. At Kings Canyon's Cedar Grove, the sheer number of incense cedars growing in a narrow canyon is thought to intensify their fragrance, especially when strong winds are blowing. The cedar's durable wood is often lurking beneath the yellow coat of the everyday No. 2 pencil.

MANZANITA

The manzanita, noted for its crooked branches, is the most common shrub at lower elevations in the Sierra Nevada foothills, where to the delight of rabbits, squirrels, and other small house-hunting mammals, it grows 3 to 6 feet high in dense thickets on hillsides. Hikers are less pleased by the plant, given its obstructionist tendency to sprawl through the tangled undergrowth of the native chaparral.

POISON OAK

If you see tripartite leaves on that low-lying shrub along the trail, recall the summer-camp mantra, "leaves of three, let them be." You're looking at poison oak, which can also manifest itself as a leafless, twiggy plant. If you've been exposed to its toxic oil, you'll generally develop a fiercely itchy red rash anywhere from a few hours to three days after you touch it. The sooner you wash the affected skin, the better. (*See* the Practical Information chapter for more steps to take.)

FAUNA

BAT

The caves within Yosemite, Sequoia, and Kings Canyon teem with bats. More than half the bat species here are rare enough to be listed on endangered species lists. Although not threatening to humans, bats do carry and can transmit dangerous diseases such as rabies, so caution is advised while caving. Enormous bat colonies can be observed whirling and flying out of caves en masse at dusk for feeding time, returning around sunrise. You can also observe bats when they roost in snags—dead, hollowed-out trees still standing in the forest after lightning strikes and wildfires.

MOUNTAIN YELLOW-LEGGED FROG

These critically endangered relatives of the western toad are among the amphibians you may spot croaking alongside higher-altitude mountain lakes and streams, especially on the west side of the Sierra at an elevation of more than 10,000 feet. The frogs lay their eggs in lakes and streams so cold that the larvae must survive in the icy waters throughout the long winter. When they emerge onto land, their bellies and the underside of their back legs are colored a pale yellow. The now-forbidden practice of stocking alpine lakes with trout, which feed on the frogs' eggs and larvae, was responsible for the frogs' alarming decline.

WESTERN FENCE LIZARD

Moving fast as a gathering thunderstorm atop rocks and along the forest floor, the western fence lizard is instantly recognizable by the iridescent blue patches on the belly and throat of adult males, who proudly display these blue-colored parts to intimidate rivals. The "push-ups" you'll probably see them do—moving their front limbs up and down quickly—is a defensive move that also attracts mates. Generally about 6 to 8 inches long, these lizards feed on insects and spiders, and in turn become food for snakes and predatory birds.

Practical
Information

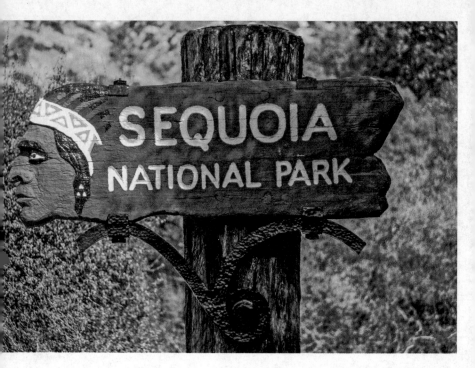

⊙ BEST TIMES TO VISIT

The national parks covered in this book are open year-round.

Spring is a busy time in Yosemite National Park (though not as busy as summer). Everyone comes to see waterfalls at their fullest, when they're fed by snowmelt, usually in May. Wildflowers bloom over a period of several months, starting in March or April in the Sierra Nevada foothills region, then moving upward in elevation through the parks, with high-country meadows not peaking until July.

Summer—basically from Memorial Day through Labor Day—is when tourism peaks. The busiest months are July and August, when the high country of the Sierra Nevada is relatively snow-free. If you're looking to escape the worst crowds, avoid the parks on a holiday weekend.

The quietest times when you can still take advantage of warmer weather are the week before Memorial Day and the week after Labor Day. The first half of June is also a good time to visit, because all the park roads are typically open, but the biggest crowds haven't arrived yet. It's also well before the late-summer thunderstorms.

Autumn is a much quieter period in the parks because fall foliage is not very brilliant in evergreen forests. In September and October, many visitor services start shutting down for the season. On the plus side, the solitude in the parks is refreshing, and you may have hiking trails all to yourself, especially if you visit Tuolumne Meadows in Yosemite National Park, Mineral King in Sequoia National Park, or Cedar Grove in Kings Canyon National Park just before their respective roads close for the winter.

Winter is an unusual time to visit the parks, but it can be very rewarding. Although many park roads are either closed for the season or subject to winter-storm closures, some areas of each park stay open even when snow falls, usually between November and April. Yosemite has the most wintertime attractions, ranging from special celebrations in Yosemite Valley to a family-friendly ski school at Badger Pass Ski Area. The few weeks after Thanksgiving are the slowest in Yosemite. If you don't mind dealing with limited open hours, you'll be rewarded with the lowest lodging prices of the year and a quiet, uncrowded park experience that few ever get to enjoy. In Sequoia and Kings Canyon national parks, you can go snowshoeing or cross-country skiing among the groves of giant sequoias in winter. For more winter-specific info, *see* the feature boxes at the end of each national park chapter.

AVERAGE TEMPERATURE HIGHS AND LOWS BY MONTH

FESTIVALS AND SEASONAL EVENTS

SPRING

Earth Day, all three parks. The activities vary from year to year, but the festivities for Earth Day, April 22, generally include guided hikes, family-friendly eco-activities, music, games, and volunteer cleanup and restoration of the great outdoors. *209/ 372-0200; www.nps.gov/yose. 559/565-3341; www.nps.gov/seki.*

National Park Week, all three parks. Held annually around Earth Day, this week invites people to explore the nation's national parks with free admission across the system. Yosemite, Sequoia, and Kings Canyon each honor the celebration with different events. *209/372-0200; www.nps. gov/yose. 559/565-3341; www.nps.gov/ seki.*

SUMMER

National Park Day, all national parks. This nationwide festival on August 25 honors all of the country's national parks. It's celebrated with a week of special ranger-led walks, talks, and campfire programs, as well as with movies and other activities geared to families. *209/372-0200; www. nps.gov/yose. 559/565-3341; www.nps. gov/seki.*

Perseid meteor shower, all three parks. Caused by particles of comet dust crashing into Earth's atmosphere, this natural fireworks show peaks in the night sky between midnight and sunrise (the timing varies each year) on August 11 and 12. In Yosemite, visitors gather at Glacier Point, high above the valley. *209/372-0200; www.nps. gov/yose. 559/565-3341; www.nps.gov/ seki.*

Tuolumne Meadows Poetry Festival, Yosemite. This free festival featuring morning writing workshops and afternoon readings and spoken word performances takes place one weekend in mid-August at the Parsons Memorial Lodge. *209/372- 0200; www.nps.gov/yose.*

Dark Sky Festival, Sequoia & Kings Canyon. In early August, this three-day celestial celebration showcases the Sierra Nevada's night sky, undiminished by light pollution. Highlights include telescope viewings, constellation tours, astronaut talks, nighttime-photography workshops, and special appearances by the Milky Way. *559/565-3759; www.sequoiaparksconservancy.org/darkskyfestival.html*

FALL

Vintners' Holidays, Yosemite. From early November to the beginning of December, The Ahwahnee hosts this oenophilic extravaganza, with wine tastings galore, meet-and-greets with California winemakers, and gala dinners. Advance reservations are essential. *888/413-8869; www. travelyosemite.com.*

WINTER

Bracebridge Dinners, Yosemite. While the food is wonderful, come for the dazzling setting and performances. In mid-December, The Ahwahnee hotel dining room is transformed to look like a 17th-century English manor's great hall for a series of holiday feasts. The gourmet fare might include pheasant pie and roast-beef tenderloin, as well as hot mulled wine and plum pudding in honor of the holiday. The meals are accompanied by Renaissance-style performances with music, singing, and dancing. Advance reservations are essential. *888/413-8869; www.travelyosemite.com.*

Chef's Holidays, Yosemite. The Ahwahnee brings gourmet food to the forefront during this event held mid-to-late January. Meet the star chefs of famous kitchens from San Francisco to New York City, along with California winemakers, then learn their secrets at cooking classes and demonstrations, followed by gala dinners. Advance reservations are essential. *888/413-8869; www.travelyosemite.com.*

Trek to the Tree, Kings Canyon. On the second Sunday of December, up to 100 Christmas carolers gather at the base of the General Grant Tree, where park rangers lay a wreath of greenery in honor of the nation's military veterans. *559/565-3341; www.nps.gov/seki.*

New Year's Eve, Yosemite. Live music and festive meals help ring in the New Year at Yosemite's three hotels. The grandest celebration is at The Ahwahnee, where there is dancing in the grand dining room, while a lower-key family-friendly celebration takes place at the Yosemite Valley Lodge. *209/372-1403; www.travelyosemite.com.*

COMMUNICATIONS

INTERNET

High-speed wireless internet access is limited inside the parks. In Yosemite, Wi-Fi is available to guests only at The Ahwahnee and the Wawona Hotel. At Yosemite Valley Lodge and Curry Village Lounge, Wi-Fi is free for guests and available to visitors for a modest fee. For free Wi-Fi, head to Degnan's Kitchen, the casual restaurant in Yosemite Valley. In Sequoia and Kings Canyon, free Wi-Fi is available in the Wuksachi Lodge lobby, the John Muir Lodge lobby, and Grant Grove Village.

PHONES

Cell-phone coverage is very limited in the parks. Some networks and some types of mobile phones will work in certain areas, while others won't, but none is very reliable. In Yosemite National Park, places in the Yosemite Valley and along Tioga Road have spotty coverage. The best service tends to be in Yosemite Village and Curry Village. In Sequoia and Kings Canyon parks, you may get minimal reception in the Foothills and Grant Grove areas. Instead of relying on your cell phone, consider buying a prepaid phone card that you can use with the pay phones scattered throughout the parks at visitor centers, campgrounds, lodges, markets, and gas stations.

ENTRY FEES AND PASSES

A seven-day pass at Yosemite, Sequoia, and Kings Canyon costs $35 per car, $30 per motorcycle, and $20 per person for those on foot, bike, or a noncommercial bus. An annual pass for Yosemite National Park or Sequoia and Kings Canyon national parks costs $70. The annual "America the Beautiful" National Parks and Federal Recreation Lands Pass costs $80 and can be purchased at any park entrance station or online at *store.usgs.gov/pass*. For U.S. citizens and permanent residents, seniors ages 62 and older pay $80 for a lifetime pass valid for entry to all national parks and federal recreation lands, while those with a permanent disability receive a free lifetime pass.

Special permits are required for backpacking in the wilderness. You should reserve these permits as far in advance as possible, especially for weekend trips and during the peak summer season.

Wilderness regulations vary for each park; *see* the individual park chapters for helpful details, including costs and how to apply for permits.

⊕ GETTING TO THE PARKS

AIR TRAVEL

Rental cars are available with advance reservations at each of these airports.

Fresno Yosemite International Airport (FAT) is the closest airport to all three national parks. Connecting flights from gateway hubs to this regional airport are infrequent. The airport is 7 miles northeast of downtown Fresno, off Peach Avenue, north of Highway 180, and it is 65 miles from the south entrance of Yosemite National Park and 50 miles to the west entrance of Sequoia and Kings Canyon. *559/621–4500; 559/454–2052; www.flyfresno.com.*

San Francisco International Airport (SFO) is northern California's busiest airport. It is served by most domestic and many international airlines. The airport is 13 miles south of San Francisco, off Highway 101, and it is 190 miles from the Arch Rock entrance of Yosemite National Park and 200 miles to the west entrance of Sequoia and Kings Canyon. *650/821–8211 or 800/435–9736; www.flysfo.com.*

Oakland International Airport (OAK), in the East Bay area, is served by some domestic and international airlines. The airport is 10 miles south of downtown Oakland via I–880, off Hegenberger Road and 98th Avenue, and it is 170 miles from the Arch Rock entrance of Yosemite National Park and 225 miles to the west entrance of Sequoia and Kings Canyon. *510/563–3300; www.oaklandairport.com.*

Mineta San José International Airport (SJC), in the South Bay area, is served by many domestic and some international airlines. It's as close to all three parks as the other Bay Area airports: 180 miles from the Arch Rock entrance of Yosemite National Park and 205 miles to the west entrance of Sequoia and Kings Canyon. The airport is 4 miles northwest of downtown San Jose, off Highway 101. *408/392–3600; www.flysanjose.com.*

Sacramento International Airport (SMF), served by some domestic and international airlines, is handy for Yosemite National Park, just 150 miles from the park's Big Oak Flat Entrance Station; it is 235 miles from the west entrance of Sequoia and Kings Canyon National Parks. The airport is 12 miles northwest of downtown

(opposite)
Generals High-
way connects
Sequoia and
Kings Canyon
National Parks.

Sacramento, off I–15 via Airport Boulevard. *916/929–5411; www. sacramento.aero/smf.*

Los Angeles International Airport (LAX) is southern California's busiest airport. It is served by most domestic and many international airlines. It's convenient for southern Sequoia National Park, just 225 miles from the park's Foothills Entrance Station. It is 250 miles from the Big Stump Entrance Station to Kings Canyon and 280 miles from the south entrance of Yosemite National Park. The airport is 18 miles southwest of downtown L.A., off Sepulveda Boulevard, west of I–405 (San Diego Freeway) and north of I–105 (Century Freeway). *310/ 646–5252 and 855/463–5252; www.flylax.com.*

Reno-Tahoe International Airport (RNO) in western Nevada is served by many domestic and some international airlines. It's a good choice for entering Yosemite National Park from the east side when Tioga Road is open (usually June until October). The airport is 4 miles southeast of downtown Reno, east of South Virginia Street at Plumb Lane, off U.S. Highway 395, and it is 150 miles from the east entrance of Yosemite National Park. There is no automobile entrance on the eastern side of Sequoia and Kings Canyon National Parks. *775/328–6400; www.renoairport.com.*

Car Travel

The following routes are generally the best highways to get you quickly to the parks from major urban areas nearby. For California road conditions, call 800/427–7623.

Yosemite Valley is about a 2 hour drive from Fresno, 3½ hours from Sacramento, 4 hours from San Francisco, and more than 5 hours from Los Angeles. It's 3 or more hours to the park from Reno, Nevada, which is usually only an option between June and October, depending on whether or not the road is snow-free.

The Foothills Entrance Station of Sequoia National Park is a 1½-hour drive from Fresno, 4 hours from Sacramento, and 4½ hours from either San Francisco or Los Angeles. Kings Canyon National Park's Grant Grove area is a 1½-hour drive from Fresno, 4 hours from Sacramento, 4½ hours from San Francisco, and 5 hours from Los Angeles.

From Fresno: To reach Yosemite, take Highway 41 north, continue north on Wawona Road, and take Highway 140 east into the valley. To reach Sequoia, travel via Highway 99 south, then drive east on Highway 198 past Visalia for about an hour to the Foothills Entrance Station near Three Rivers. To reach Sequoia or Kings

(opposite)
Mountain biking
can be a great
way to explore
the area around
the parks.

Canyon, take Highway 180 east to the Big Stump Entrance Station, past which you can turn north toward Kings Canyon or south toward the Giant Forest area of Sequoia.

From Sacramento: To reach Yosemite, take Highway 99 south to Stockton, then Highway 4 east to Copperopolis, detour onto County Road E–15 southeast to Yosemite Junction, and join Highway 120 east, continue on Big Oak Road, then turn left onto Highway 140 east. To reach Sequoia or Kings Canyon, take Highway 99 south to Fresno, then Highway 180 east to the Big Stump Entrance Station, past which you can turn north toward Kings Canyon or south toward the Giant Forest area of Sequoia.

From San Francisco: To reach Yosemite, cross the Bay Bridge on I–80 into Oakland, then take I–580 east toward Stockton, detour onto I–205 past Tracy, jog north onto I–5, drive east on Highway 120, continue on Big Oak Road, and finally take Highway 140 east into the valley. To reach Sequoia or Kings Canyon, cross the Bay Bridge on I–80 into Oakland, then take I–580 east toward Stockton, detour onto I–205 past Tracy, jog north onto I–5, drive east on Highway 120, take Highway 99 south to Fresno, and finally Highway 180 east to the Big Stump Entrance Station, past which you can turn north toward Kings Canyon or south toward the Giant Forest area of Sequoia.

From Los Angeles: To reach Yosemite, take I–5 north to Highway 99 north to Fresno, then continue as above. In winter, the drive along Highway 140 east of Merced on Highway 99 is a much easier approach route to Yosemite Valley. To reach the Foothills Entrance Station of Sequoia National Park, take I–5 north and connect to Highway 99 north, then drive east on Highway 198 past Visalia for about an hour to the Foothills Entrance Station near Three Rivers. To reach Kings Canyon, take I–5 north and connect to Highway 99 north, then drive east on Highway 198 to Visalia, take Highway 63 north past Orange Cove, then Highway 180 east through Squaw Valley and Dunlap to the Big Stump Entrance Station.

From Reno: When the Tioga Road is open (usually from June until October), it's possible to enter Yosemite National Park from the east side of the Sierra Nevada on Highway 120, which branches off U.S. Highway 395 outside the town of Lee Vining. There is no eastern entrance for vehicles for Sequoia and Kings Canyon National Parks.

From Yosemite to Kings Canyon and Sequoia: From Yosemite Valley it's a 2½-hour trip south on Highway 41, then east along Highway 180 to the Generals Highway, which connects Sequoia and Kings Canyon parks. If you turn left at the junction of Highway 180

and the Generals Highway, it's a 15-minute drive north to Grant Grove, from where it's another hour's drive to Cedar Grove, both in Kings Canyon National Park. If you turn right at the junction, it's a 45-minute drive southeast to Lodgepole and one hour's drive to the Giant Forest Museum, both in Sequoia National Park.

Bus Travel

The **Yosemite Area Regional Transportation System** (*209/388–9589 or 877/989–2787; www.yarts.com*) operates several buses daily from various towns along Highway 140, including Merced, Mariposa, Midpines, and El Portal, into Yosemite. From mid-May to mid-September, a bus travels from Sonora through Groveland along Highway 120 and enters the park at Big Oak Flat, and another bus travels from Fresno along Highway 41 to the south entrance and continues north along Wawona Road to Yosemite Valley. In July and August, when the Tioga Pass is open, YART buses travel once daily from Mammoth Lakes through Lee Vining and Tuolumne Meadows before arriving at Yosemite Valley. In June and September, the bus runs on weekends only. Bus riders are exempt from paying the park entrance fee charged to drivers.

GETTING AROUND

Bicycle Travel

In Yosemite National Park, bicycles are allowed only on paved roads and designated bike paths. In Sequoia and Kings Canyon parks, bicycles are allowed on paved and unpaved roads where cars are also permitted, and on paved recreational trails (e.g., connecting campgrounds). Bicycles are not allowed on hiking trails in the parks and may not go off-trail in wilderness areas. All riders under age 18 must wear a helmet. In Yosemite Valley, you can rent bicycles spring through fall (weather permitting) for an hour or a day from the Yosemite Valley Lodge or at Curry Village. Several mostly flat bike and pedestrian paths make biking a great way to explore Yosemite Valley without the hassle of traffic and parking.

Bus and Shuttle Travel

In Yosemite National Park, there are several park routes with **free shuttle buses**; all but one are seasonal (*see* the chart, *opposite*). Starting from Yosemite Valley, there are also **private shuttle buses** (*888/413–8869; www.travelyosemite.com*) that offer tours of Glacier

Yosemite's Shuttles

SHUTTLE SERVICE	ROUTE STOPS	HOURS OF OPERATION	TIME OF YEAR
Badger Pass Ski Area (free to in-park lodging guests)	Between Yosemite Valley and Badger Pass Ski Area	Departs Yosemite Valley twice each morning; departs Badger Pass Ski Area twice each afternoon	Ski season (usually from mid-December through March)
El Capitan (Free)	Yosemite Valley Visitor Center, El Capitan, and the Four-Mile trailhead	Daily 9 am–5 pm	Mid-June through early October
Glacier Point Tours ($28.50 one way; $57 round-trip)	Four-hour journey from Yosemite Valley to Glacier Point, offering panoramic views of Yosemite Falls, Nevada Falls, and Vernal Falls	Departs Yosemite Lodge at 8:30 am and 1:30 pm daily	Late spring to early fall
Tuolumne Meadows ($1 to $9 one way, depending on distance)	Tuolumne Meadows lodge, campground and store, visitor and wilderness centers, Tioga Pass, Olmsted Point, Tenaya Lake, and various trailheads	Daily 7 am–7 pm	Mid-June through Labor Day
Tioga Pass ($4 to $8 one way, depending on distance)	Tuolumne Meadows Lodge, Mono Pass, and Tioga Pass	Four daily round trips between 9 am and 5 pm	Mid-June to early September
Tuolumne Meadows Hikers Bus ($17 one way, $27 round-trip)	The all-day trip starts at Curry Village and winds its way to Crane Flat, White Wolf, May Lake Junction, Olmsted Point, Tenaya Lake, and Tuolumne Meadows before turning back.	Departs Curry Village one to three times daily	June or July through early September
South Entrance–Mariposa Grove (Free)	Between the Mariposa Grove Welcome Plaza, near South Entrance, to lower Mariposa Grove	Daily 8 am–7 pm (until 5 pm March to early April and mid-October to November)	Mid-March to November
Yosemite Valley (Free)	Major points of interest in eastern Yosemite Valley, including lodgings, stores, trailheads, and viewpoints.	Daily 7 am–10 pm	Year-round

Point for a fee. For the narrated four-hour tour to Glacier Point, buses usually depart the Yosemite Valley Lodge twice daily between late spring and early fall. The bus from Yosemite Valley to Tuolumne Meadows costs $17 one way, $27 round-trip; it departs one to three times a day from various spots in the Yosemite Valley roughly June through mid-September. These buses can serve hikers as well: if you are planning a one-way hiking or backpacking trip down into the Yosemite Valley, you should park your car in the valley, then use these buses to access trailheads off Glacier Point Road and Tioga Road. Reservations, which are especially recommended in summer, are accepted up to a month in advance for the trip to Glacier Point, while the bus to Tuolumne Meadows is first come, first served.

Yosemite Area Regional Transportation System (YARTS) public buses (*209/388–9589 or 877/989–2787; www.yarts.com*) travel along Tioga Road (Highway 120), connecting the Yosemite Valley Welcome Center with Crane Flat, White Wolf, Tuolumne Meadows, and Lee Vining, and Mammoth Lakes on the east side of the Sierra Nevada. This route operates once daily in each direction during July and August, weekends only in June and September, weather permitting.

In Sequoia and Kings Canyon national parks, **free shuttle buses** operate between late May and late September, including the gray route that loops from the Giant Forest Museum out to Moro Rock and Crescent Meadow. For route schedules, consult the free park newspaper *The Guide,* call *559/565–3341,* or visit *www.nps.gov/seki.*

Between the town of Visalia and the Giant Forest Museum, the **Sequoia Shuttle** (*877/287–4453; www.sequoiashuttle.com; $20 round-trip*), makes daily runs in each direction, stopping in Three Rivers and at the park's Foothills Visitor Center. The shuttle operates between Memorial Day and Labor Day. Advance reservations and prepayment are required.

CAR TRAVEL

Although the shuttles listed in the previous section eliminate parking hassles, most visitors drive themselves around the parks. Traffic jams are a common problem in summer, when there are long lines at park entrance stations and frequent delays along all of the main park roads. At peak times, some day-use **parking lots** at viewpoints and trailheads fill completely before noon, especially in the Giant Forest area of Sequoia National Park, and throughout Yosemite Valley and along Tioga Road near Tuolumne Meadows in Yosemite National Park.

In general, **navigating the parks is easy**, with the exception of Yosemite Valley, where a network of one-way roads can be confusing for first-time visitors (consulting the free park newspaper and map brochure will help you avoid backtracking). In Yosemite Valley, also keep an eye out for the well-marked bus lanes. The fine for driving in one is $250.

The **speed limit** varies on roads around the parks, ranging from 15 mph in congested areas up to 45 mph on highways such as Tioga Road (Highway 120). Other regulations limit the length of vehicles that may travel on narrow, twisting mountain roads, which are not recommended for RVs or trucks towing trailers.

If you're driving slowly to enjoy the scenery, **pay attention to other drivers on the road behind you**, and frequently pull over to let faster traffic pass on two-lane park roads. If you catch sight of wildlife, pull completely off the road instead of causing traffic jams and accidents by stopping suddenly in the middle of the highway. **Be cautious driving at night**, when wildlife is more apt to suddenly run across the road or stand in the middle of it. This is especially true on twisting, narrow park roads, such as the Kings Canyon Scenic Byway.

There are some **gas stations** in the parks, but only a few have 24-hour credit-card pumps. So it's best to fill up your car's gas tank before arriving in the parks. Gas stations are in Yosemite National Park at Crane Flat and Wawona. There is no gas in Yosemite Valley or along Tioga Pass, so plan accordingly. The **Yosemite Valley Garage** (*209/372–8320*) handles repairs, but there is no gas here. In national forest–service lands around Sequoia and Kings Canyon national parks, there are gas stations at Stony Creek, Hume Lake, and the Kings Canyon Lodge.

Because the winters are so severe in the Sierra Nevada, **frequent road construction is the norm inside the parks during the summer months**. In late spring and early fall, watch out for slushy, even icy, conditions on roads that have just been opened or are about to close for the season.

Winter road closures are common in all three parks (for details, *see* the special winter-travel features at the end of each national park chapter). In winter, always carry tire chains. For the latest road conditions in Yosemite National Park, call *209/372–0200*; for Sequoia and Kings Canyon national parks, call *559/565–3341*.

You also want to be sure that your car is in good condition before visiting the parks; towing services are time-consuming and costly, and the nearest pay phone may be miles away from where your car breaks down. Membership in an auto club like AAA (*www.aaa.com*) can help with roadside emergencies, including locking your keys in the car, running out of gas, or needing a tow.

GUIDED TOURS

Although the best way to get to know Yosemite is by strapping on a pack and heading out on a trail, guided bus and tram tours allow you to see a large number of the park's attractions in a relatively short period of time as well as give you the benefit of an expert's knowledge of Yosemite. Prices start around $38 for the shorter tours and go up to around $100 per person for the longer trips. For more information about departure times or to make reservations, call *209/372–4386* or

From Moro Rock's summit in Sequoia National Park you overlook the Great Western Divide.

visit any tour and activity desk in the park. All tours are contingent upon weather and road conditions.

In addition to the tours from Yosemite Valley to Glacier Point, there are several daily departures of the Valley Floor Tour, a two-hour bus excursion visiting the valley's top attractions (in an open-air tram, weather permitting). From mid-to-late summer the four-hour Glacier Point Stargazing Tour includes an hour of astronomy lessons under the stars at Glacier Point. And for four nights each month during full moons from May through October, the Moonlight Tour travels through the valley for two hours.

Private guided tours of Sequoia National Park are available year-round through Sequoia Sightseeing Tours, operated by longtime local tour guides and sponsored by the park's official concessionaire. Half-day tours depart from the Wuksachi Lodge and take in the General Sherman Tree, Tunnel Log, and Moro Rock. For those staying outside the park, full-day tours include transportation from Three Rivers.

From May to October, full-day tours of Kings Canyon National Park visit the General Grant Tree, Zumwalt Meadow, Grizzly Falls, and Roaring River Falls, as well as the Grant Grove Visitor Center. Tours depart from the John Muir Lodge in the park; pickup in Three Rivers is available for a small additional fee.

Half-day tours cost $650 for one to four people, plus $79 for each additional person (up to a maximum of 12 passengers). Full-day tours start at $875 for one to four people, with $159 for each additional person; again, group size is capped at 12. Make reservations online at *www.sequoiatours.com* or by calling *559/561-4189.*

⊛ HEALTH AND SAFETY

Even if you're planning a low-key trip in well-traveled areas of the parks, be prepared and familiarize yourself with the essential health and safety issues and tips. The advice given below is not intended to be a substitute for professional medical advice, which you should seek in the event of any illness or accident while visiting the parks. National Park Service rangers who are qualified as EMTs can offer free assistance to visitors.

As is true in most places in the United States, **for ambulance, fire, and police emergencies in the park, dial 911.**

ALTITUDE SICKNESS AND HANTAVIRUS

Commonly known as "altitude sickness," acute mountain sickness (AMS) can strike even if you have never experienced problems before at high altitudes (generally defined as above 8,000 feet). Although altitude sickness affects some park visitors in high places like Yosemite's Tuolumne Meadows or Mineral King in Sequoia National Park, AMS is more likely to affect backpackers and climbers. Symptoms, which typically appear within 10 hours after first arriving at high altitudes, include headaches, dizziness, loss of appetite, nausea (possibly vomiting), insomnia, and extreme fatigue. If symptoms do not resolve, or they worsen within the first 24 to 48 hours, get to a lower elevation immediately.

The best way to avoid altitude sickness is to allow yourself plenty of time to acclimatize before exerting yourself (e.g., sleeping at high elevations before hiking there the next day). To further lessen your chances of altitude sickness, drink plenty of water and either cut back on or avoid alcohol altogether.

In 2012 three died and several others fell ill after contracting hantavirus, a virus transmitted by infected deer mice, after staying at Yosemite, most of them in Curry Village. Symptoms of hantavirus pulmonary syndrome (HPS), which typically start from one to seven weeks after exposure, include fever, chills, and muscle aches, which are followed in four to ten days by coughing and difficulty breathing. If you develop any of these symptoms after a visit to Yosemite, you should tell your doctor about your potential exposure to hantavirus.

The park has destroyed the tent cabins involved and taken various measures to prevent a recurrence, but pay attention to brochures and bulletins around the park for minimizing your risk of infection, which include avoiding mice, either alive or dead, and avoiding contact with their feces, urine, or saliva. If you see rodent droppings or any other evidence of the presence of mice in your lodgings, alert the staff immediately and do not attempt to clean it up yourself.

HEAT EXHAUSTION AND HEATSTROKE

Protect yourself from the sun by wearing sunscreen and a hat, especially at higher elevations. Also, don't overexert yourself outdoors, especially on hot days, and be sure to stay well hydrated—always carry extra water with you on hikes. Dehydration can lead to heat cramps, heat exhaustion, and heatstroke.

Heat cramps occur when your muscles spasm after sweaty exertions; the best treatment is to rest, drink water, and gently stretch and massage the afflicted areas. Symptoms of heat exhaustion include headaches, nausea, dizziness, thirst, fatigue, and increased heart and respiratory rates. Move into the shade immediately, drink water, fan yourself, and pour water on your head while you rest. Heatstroke may give you flushed skin, a loss of coordination, an altered mental status, and seizures. It is potentially fatal and requires immediate cooling off and medical attention.

HYPOTHERMIA AND FROSTBITE

Hypothermia, which is when the body loses heat to the environment faster than it can produce it, may happen when you are exposed to cold, wet, and/or windy conditions. Early symptoms of hypothermia include the "umbles" (i.e., stumbling, fumbling, mumbling), which worsen as you lose motor control. Signs that the condition is progressing are uncontrollable shivering, increased heart and respiration rates, and cold, pale skin. If the hypothermia continues to advance, you eventually reach a severe state in which the shivering stops.

The best treatment for hypothermia is to change into dry clothes, adding insulating layers, and to take shelter from the elements. Drinking plain water and eating carbohydrates (e.g., energy bars) may help hasten your recovery, too. You may have heard that using direct body heat to warm hypothermic people and giving them hot beverages can help, but the results of recent medical studies suggest this isn't necessarily true. Wrapping them up warmly and giving them clean water and carbs to consume seems to work best.

Frostbite is another hazard in cold conditions. Always dress appropriately for cold weather and watch for any exposed skin that appears too white, waxy, numb, or cold. To treat superficial frostbite, do not massage the affected area. Instead, use skin-to-skin warming techniques (e.g., placing cold fingers under arms) and seek shelter in a warm place. Medical attention is necessary for all cases of frostbite.

LIGHTNING

Always check the weather forecast before setting out on any hike. Do not attempt to hike over mountain passes, tackle summits or peaks, or climb any granite domes when thunderstorms are approaching. If lightning flashes, descend immediately and get off any exposed ridges or high places. Also, avoid standing or being immersed in water. You want to make sure you are not the tallest thing in the immediate area, and you want to stay clear of all current-conducting materials. Throw all metal objects away from you, including hiking poles and backpacks that have metal stays. Many lightning-related fatalities occur from electricity running through the ground; sitting on a camping pad rolled up into a ball will help insulate you from this.

POISON OAK AND TICKS

Poison oak is a plant with distinctive tripartite leaves (remember "leaves of three, let them be"), although it can appear as a twiggy shrub. If you think you've been exposed, wash the affected areas immediately. Oral antihistamines and topical treatments may help relieve the itchy, oozing rash that often follows. For severe allergic reactions, seek medical help.

The best prevention for tick bites, which can lead to Lyme disease and other serious illnesses, is to use insect repellent containing DEET and to

If you see a black bear while in the parks, keep your distance and let it be. But if the bear threatens you, make noise and look big.

perform tick checks regularly while in the woods. Wearing light-colored clothing with your pants tucked into your socks will help. To remove a tick, pull slowly and steadily on the body of the tick with tweezers, being careful not to crush the tick or to pull too quickly and forcefully, and thus leave the tick's head inside the wound, as that may cause greater infection. With the patient application of slow and steady pressure, the insect will eventually back itself out and let go.

STREAMS, RIVERS, WATERFALLS, AND BRIDGES

Contracting giardia is always a risk in the Sierra Nevada, and it's better to be safe than sorry. Don't drink water from any natural (i.e., untreated) source without first bringing it to a rapid, rolling boil, filtering it with a pump, or treating it with purification tablets.

Streams and rivers are particularly dangerous places to swim in late spring and early summer, when winter snowmelt from the

Enjoy the sounds of running water alongside you while hiking in the parks—but don't drink it without purifying it first.

mountains causes extremely cold, fast-moving water that can sweep you away in an instant. Moving boulders and other underwater debris can pin down even strong swimmers.

Exercise caution when fording streams and rivers along hiking trails. Avoid water crossings above your knees. If you must cross, use a hiking pole while crossing at an angle to the current, preferably linking arms with your companions and loosening your backpack straps in case you need to disentangle yourself quickly. When waterfalls peak in late spring and early summer, nearby hiking trails can become dangerously slippery. Playing around water-

TAKE NOTHING BUT PICTURES, LEAVE NOTHING BUT FOOTPRINTS

When you visit national parks, the wild natural beauty around you easily inspires good deeds of eco-consciousness. A good way to start is to use the recycling bins in the parks to dispose of glass and aluminum containers.

In addition to recycling, you also need to pay attention to what you're throwing away and where you're throwing it. Littering is of course a no-no. But what some don't realize is that litter includes cigarette butts, which aren't very biodegradable and have been known to cause immensely destructive wildfires in the parks. Dispose of cigarette butts in trash cans located in developed areas of the parks. Additional smoking restrictions may apply in late summer, when wildfires are more likely due to dry tinder-box conditions in the forests and canyons. If a dumpster is full, look for an emptier one to leave your garbage in, and be sure to latch the dumpster securely before leaving—dumpsters that are overflowing or not latched securely will attract bears. Also, don't throw away any propane canisters in dumpsters; they are hazardous material, which you should instead take home with you and dispose of at the appropriate hazmat dump site in the town where you live.

You also do not want to feed or harass local wildlife, nor let your pets run wild. This is not only to protect the parks' natural ecosystems and to preserve wildlife-watching opportunities for all, but also to ensure the safety of your pets (*see* Pets in the Park).

It's important to be careful where you walk and drive in the parks. Avoid short-cutting trails, which can lead to erosion and landslides, and don't wander off-trail into fragile meadows, which can become easily trampled to death. Also do not drive off-road or park off the pavement; your car may damage tree-root systems and even start wildfires in dry, grassy areas. Bicycle on paved roads only. If you can, take advantage of park shuttles or walk wherever possible. This reduces traffic congestion as well as pollution.

Although it is tempting to pick wildflowers or gather pinecones to take home with you, it's illegal to remove any natural objects or cultural artifacts (such as Native American arrowheads and pioneer-era tools) from the parks.

If you're heading into the wilderness overnight, the park rangers who issue your wilderness permit will brief you on relevant regulations and Leave No Trace (LNT) principles of outdoor ethics. Here are a couple LNT guidelines that apply to day hikers as well:

• Always pack out what you pack in (that includes food scraps and toilet paper!).

• Do not dispose of human waste near any water sources, such as streams and rivers.

For more information on the Leave No Trace principles, see the website *www.lnt. org*.

falls is potentially fatal if you are swept over the top of the falls or caught in a whirlpool.

Exercise extreme caution when crossing bridges, and never cross a bridge when water is cascading over it. A number of experienced hikers have died as a result of unusually high late-season runoff.

WILD ANIMALS

Nothing is more important for visitors than to learn to share the park safely with wild animals. To avoid any potentially threatening encounters with wildlife in the park, it's good to follow a few simple guidelines. For instance, a good rule of thumb is to **never hike alone**.

In places where rattlesnakes might be hiding—for example in dense vegetation or around blind corners on hiking trails—stomping your feet (snakes are deaf, but they can feel vibrations through the ground) or gently poking through fallen foliage with a hiking pole from a safe distance, to roust any reptiles before you might accidentally step on them, are both good ideas.

Never feed a bear or any other wildlife, including birds and deer. It's important to keep any food or scented items (e.g., soap, candy, empty bottles, bags of garbage, sunscreen, coolers, even baby wipes and car seats) safely locked out of sight in the trunk of your vehicle. Better yet, use the food-storage lockers provided in parking lots inside the national parks. Doing so prevents bear break-ins, which not only cause extensive property damage to your car, but also hurt the wildlife. The same advice applies while camping in the parks. Keep a clean campsite, and you won't have any unwelcome visitors, whether deer, squirrels, Steller's jays, or black bears. It's worth noting that black bears that become habituated to humans eventually become more aggressive and have to be destroyed, which is why feeding wild animals is a federal offense. Remember: "A fed bear is a dead bear."

If you feel threatened by a black bear, stand your ground, gather any small children to your side, and make yourselves look as big as possible; then make as much noise as you can—shout and bang metal objects together, for example. But you need to do this only if the bear is doing something that makes you feel afraid. If the bear is just foraging for berries or tearing apart a log to get at the delicious ants underneath the bark, there's no need to scare it (or yourself). Just give the bear the right of way on the trail, for example, by moving off to the opposite side and waiting until it lumbers by. If a black bear does make a sudden move toward you, that's the time to react dramatically. Also note that there are no grizzlies anywhere in these parks, only black bears. (The last grizzly bear was extirpated from California in 1922.)

Mountain lions are most active at dawn and dusk, but you may encounter one anytime while hiking. Although it is rare to notice them before they notice you, if you do sight a mountain lion, make yourself look big and back away slowly from the animal (moving fast makes you look like prey instead). Other potentially harmful animals that hikers may encounter include spiders, most dangerously brown recluses and black widows. As noted above, **always watch where you step, sit, and place your hands outdoors**. And remember to check inside your shoes for critters before putting them back on your feet after swimming or tent camping.

If you run across pack mules and horses on trails, stand quietly on the uphill side of the trail and make eye contact with the riders, then follow any further directions they may have.

See also the Warning: Marmots Ahead box in the Sequoia National Park chapter.

⌖ PETS IN THE PARKS

Pets must be on a short leash (6 feet or less) at all times in the three national parks. They are typically allowed on paved roads and paved trails (e.g., in campgrounds) only in developed areas of the parks, but they're never allowed on hiking trails or anywhere in the wilderness. If you want to go hiking with your dog, leashed pets *are* allowed on hiking trails in the Sequoia National Forest around Kings Canyon and Sequoia National Parks.

⌖ TIME

California is on Pacific Standard Time (PST), which is eight hours behind Greenwich Mean Time (GMT), except during Daylight Saving Time (DST), when the clocks move ahead one hour, from the second Sunday in March until the first Sunday in November.

It's helpful to be aware of sunrise and sunset times while visiting the parks, so that you get an early enough start in the morning and, more important, so you don't get caught after dark on an unfamiliar hiking trail. To find out the times for sunrise and sunset, check the free park newspapers or ask at visitor centers.

⊕ VISITOR INFORMATION

At park entrance stations, rangers will hand you a glossy, foldout map providing a basic overview of the park. More detailed maps, as well as interpretive hiking-trail brochures, are sold at park visitor centers. Details of National Park Service visitor centers are given in each of the national park chapters.

In summer, rangers inside these visitor centers may be overwhelmed with visitors, so be patient. Or skip the wait entirely: the most common visitor questions are often answered on park websites and in the free park newspapers, *Yosemite Guide* in Yosemite, and *Visitor Guide* in Sequoia and Kings Canyon. Published seasonally, they contain the most accurate, up-to-date information that you may need during your visit, including hours of operation for all visitor facilities and services, schedules of ranger-guided programs and activities, maps of shuttle bus routes, and campground overviews.

In Yosemite Valley, visitor information is also available from the Sierra Club at Yosemite Conservation Heritage Center, open Wednesday to Sunday from May through September.

ONLINE RESOURCES AND APPS

National Parks Conservation Association: *www.npca.com.* The NPCA, a group that works to protect all of America's national parks, shares news, videos, and other resources on our parks.

NPS Sequoia & Kings Canyon mobile app: Released in 2020, the parks' mobile app offers self-guided tours and family-friendly suggestions in addition to helpful information about services and park events. Download offline content before you go and you'll be able to access it at the parks even without Wi-Fi.

NPS Yosemite app: Download the free NPS Yosemite app for planning tools, interactive maps, and an event calendar. Be sure to download the map before your visit, so you can use it when you're offline.

Sequoia and Kings Canyon National Parks: *www.nps.gov/seki.* These twin parks' official website covers all the visitor essentials, including helpful seasonal travel info, black bear safety tips, and road construction advisories. Be sure to visit the website's Soundscapes section (under Learn about the Park/Science & Research), where you can hear—and often see—the parks' resident creatures going about their business, from black bears ripping up bark and foraging in trees to the cacophony of Zumwalt Meadow at sunrise. The high-resolution recordings bring the parks to life in a new way; an interactive map allows you to track the locations as you plan your trip.

Sequoia Parks Conservancy: *www.sequoiaparksconservancy.org.* This nonprofit partners with the National Park Service to support education and conservation at Sequoia and Kings Canyon National Parks. Its natural history branch, the Sequoia Field Institute (*www. sequoiaparksconservancy.org/adventures.html*) offers an online bookstore, field seminar "EdVentures" in the park, and helpful links to partner agencies throughout the southern Sierra Nevadas.

Sierra Club: *www.sierraclub.org.* The national conservation organization's website explains its efforts to restore Yosemite's Hetch Hetchy and protect giant sequoias. It also has a good overview of the life and work of its founder and Yosemite savior, John Muir.

Yosemite Conservancy: *yosemite.org.* This website, presented by an organization dedicated to protecting Yosemite and enabling visitors to learn about it, has information about organized hikes, art and theater programs, kid-friendly activities, and docent-led experiences in the park.

Yosemite Hospitality: *www.travelyosemite.com.* Visit this site for lodging and activity info and reservations through the official park concessionaire. It's also a good place to find package deals.

Yosemite National Park: *www.nps.gov/yose.* The park's official website delves into everything you might want to know, including travel tips, current road conditions, and up-to-date park info, as well as video and audio podcasts.

USEFUL PHONE NUMBERS

Yosemite National Park: *209/372-0200.*
Sequoia and Kings Canyon National Parks: *559/565-3341.*
Recorded Road and Weather Conditions: *209/372-0200, ext. 1.*

RECOMMENDED READING

Dayton, Duncan, and Burns, Ken, *The National Parks: America's Best Idea,* 2009. Tied to a documentary of the same name, this book marries stunning text and mind-blowing images of the entire parks system. Yosemite, Sequoia, and Kings Canyon play big roles.

Frye, Michael, *The Photographer's Guide to Yosemite,* 2000. It has maps for shutterbugs looking to capture perfect images of Yosemite National Park in every season and at any time of day.

Huber, N. King, *Geological Ramblings in Yosemite,* 2008. This guide dives into the ancient geological forces that shaped what you see in the park today.

Klett, Mark, Solnit, Rebecca, and Wolfe, Byron, *Yosemite in Time: Ice Ages, Tree Clocks, Ghost Rivers,* 2005. Historic photographs by Ansel Adams, Eadweard Muybridge, and Edward Weston are juxtaposed with contemporary photos of the same scenery. Accompanied by essays, they provide a fascinating portrait of how Yosemite has changed . . . and how it has remained the same.

Lee, Gaylen D., *Walking Where We Lived: Memoirs of a Mono Indian Family,* 1999. Personal tale of how Native American ways of life in the eastern Sierra Nevada region have changed over generations.

Lee, Stetson, ed., *The Wild Muir: Twenty-Two of John Muir's Greatest Adventures,* 2008. Excerpts from early conservationist John Muir's most extreme outdoor adventures, with woodcut illustrations by Fiona King.

Muir, John, *The Yosemite,* 1912. Famous advocate for Yosemite National Park and the Sierra Nevada pens his observations of the region, dating from his first explorations in 1869. The Yosemite Association's 2002 edition includes color photographs by Galen Rowell.

Scott, Amy, ed., *Yosemite: Art of an American Icon,* 2006. Insightful essays accompany this museum-quality collection of artworks, ranging from Native American basketry to modern photography.

Secor, R. J., *The High Sierra: Peaks, Passes, and Trails,* 1999. An authoritative guide to mountaineering and trekking in the Sierra Nevada high country.

Storer, Tracy I., Usinger, Robert L., and Lukas, David, *Sierra Nevada Natural History,* 2004. A scientific field guide for amateur naturalists who want to learn more about the region, with color-plate inserts and helpful black-and-white illustrations.

Wiese, Karen, *Sierra Nevada Wildflowers,* 2nd edition, 2013. Perfect for beginning wildflower watchers, this handy identification guide covers 290 kinds of flora growing in the Sierra Nevada region.

Index

*Tuolumne Meadows in
June after a snowstorm.*

Acknowledgments

⊕ PHOTO CREDITS

All photographs in this book are by Chris Falkenstein unless noted below. 14, Library of Congress Prints & Photographs Division. **Best Experiences:** *21 (top) and 28–29, Robert Holmes.* **History of the Parks:** *40-41, Andrew S/Shutterstock. 42–43, 44, 46, 47, 50, and 51, Library of Congress Prints & Photographs Division. 52, Yosemite Research Library, National Park Service. 53 (top), Library of Congress Prints & Photographs Division. 53 (bottom), Porterville Public Library. 54 and 55, Library of Congress Prints & Photographs Division. 56, Christophe Testi/Shutterstock. 57, Yosemite Research Library, National Park Service. 61, Igor Karon/ Shutterstock. 68–69, Icompass/Dreamstime.com.* **Yosemite National Park:** *62-63, Stephen Moehle/Shutterstock. 92, Ian Dagnall Computing/Alamy Stock Photo. 122–123, Lokinthru/Dreamstime.com. 127, Bryan Brazil/ Shutterstock. 142, © Relais & Châteaux.* **Spotlight on Rock Climbing:** *161 (bottom left), Eric Limon/Shutterstock. 167 (top and bottom), Yosemite Climbing Association, www.yosemiteclimbing.org.* **Sequoia National Park:** *170–171, Stephen Moehle/Shutterstock. 172, John Seiler/iStockphoto. 173, Mia2you/Shutterstock. 174, Pierrette Guertin/iStockphoto. 180–181, 184– 185, 186, and 187 (top), Robert Holmes. 187 (bottom), Yevgen Timashov/ Shutterstock. 189 (top and bottom), 190–191, and 194–195, Robert Holmes. 198, Library of Congress Prints & Photographs Division. 200–201 (all), Robert Holmes. 202 and 203, Robert Holmes. 207, National Park Service. 210, Yenwen Lu/iStockphoto. 212 (left), Jens Stolt/Shutterstock. 212 (right), Newton Page/Shutterstock.* **Spotlight on Supersized Sights:** *218 (top right), Robert Holmes. 219 (left), Yenwen Lu/iStockphoto. 219 (top right), Nicole Paton/Shutterstock. 219 (bottom), Eric Foltz/iStockphoto. 220 (left), Alexandra Picavet/National Park Service. 221 (left), Christoph Rückert/Kirsten Auferkorte. 221 (right), Library of Congress Prints & Photographs Division. 227, Robert Holmes.* **Kings Canyon National Park:** *228–229, 231, 232, 233, 236, and 238, Robert Holmes. 230, Maislam/ iStockphoto. 241, Lisa Boulton/Sierra Nevada Recreation, caverns@ caverntours.com. 244, Robert Holmes. 247, 248, and 249, Robert Holmes. 250–251, Sarah Scott/Shutterstock. 253, 254–255, 257, 260–261, 262, and 267, Robert Holmes. 264, Astranger9/Dreamstime.* **Where to Stay and Eat:** *274, Victor Soares/Shutterstock. 277, Jgroup/Dreamstime. 287, W. Clanin/Relais & Châteaux. 289 (bottom), National Park Service Historic Photograph Collection, Harpers Ferry Center, photographer James V. Lloyd. 295, DNC Parks & Resorts at Yosemite. 301, and 302–303, Robert Holmes.* **Geology, Fauna, and Flora:** *320–321, AndrewSoundarajan/*

iStockphoto. 323, Robert Holmes. 326–327, Phase4Photography/ Shutterstock. 328, Tom Grundy/Shutterstock. 329, Neil Webster/ Shutterstock. 330 (left), Richard Sniezko/U.S. Forest Service. 330 (right), Nancy Nehring/iStockphoto. 331 (right), Craig Lovell/Eagle Visions Photography/Alamy. 332–333 and 334–335, Ronnie Howard/Shutterstock. 339, Liv Falvey/Shutterstock. 340 (left), BS Thurner Hof/wikipedia.org. 340 (right), Fimbriatus/Dreamstime.com. 341 (left), Dean Pennala/ Shutterstock. 341 (right), wikipedia.org. 342 (top), Nancy Nehring/iStockphoto. 342 (2nd from top), wikipedia.org. 342 (3rd from top), panasw/ iStockphoto. 342 (bottom), Sherri R. Camp/Shutterstock. 343, Rick & Nora Bowers/Alamy Stock Photo. 343 (center), U.S. Geological Survey. 343 (bottom), Calibas/wikipedia.org. **Practical Information:** 346, Robert Holmes. 349 (right), Jim Warner. 353, Robert Holmes. 355, Klara_Steffkova/ Shutterstock. 360, xeuphoriax/Shutterstock. 364, Frank Leung/iStockphoto. 365, Bryan Brazil/Shutterstock.

⊕ ABOUT THE WRITERS

Freelance journalist **Sara Benson,** who wrote the first edition of this book, has a natural affinity for the USA's national parks, which she has traveled in, volunteered for, and worked at for more than 15 years. The author of more than 30 travel and nonfiction books, Sara also writes for several popular websites. Her syndicated and feature travel articles have appeared in national and international newspapers and magazines, including the *San Francisco Chronicle, Los Angeles Times,* and *National Geographic Adventure.* She has served as a national parks volunteer in Hawaii and as a seasonal park ranger in the Sierra Nevada mountains. She first visited Yosemite National Park in 1995, when she keenly remembers sitting on a rock near the Happy Isles and gazing up in awe at the valley's waterfalls and Half Dome. She has returned to the Sierra Nevada mountains almost every year since then to go backpacking and hiking during summer, and cross-country skiing and snowshoeing in winter.

Native Californian **Cheryl Crabtree** has worked as a freelance writer since 1987. She contributes regularly to Fodor's *National Parks of the West* (including the Yosemite and Sequoia and Kings Canyon National Parks chapters), *California,* and *Oahu* guidebooks. Cheryl is editor of Montecito Magazine. She co-authors *The California Directory of*

Fine Wineries hardcover book series (Napa•Sonoma and Central Coast editions). Her articles have appeared in numerous regional and national publications, and she has also authored travel apps for mobile devices and content for travel websites.

⊶ ABOUT THE PHOTOGRAPHERS

Chris Falkenstein has lived in the Yosemite area since 1972. He has focused his lens on landscapes and adventure sports in all corners of Yosemite National Park. A mountaineering guide, Falkenstein has hundreds of Yosemite climbing ascents under his belt and coauthored *Rock Climbs of Tuolumne Meadows*, a thorough climbing guide to that region. His work has appeared in dozens of publications, including *Men's Journal* and *Climbing* magazines, catalogs for Patagonia and Black Diamond Equipment, and maps for *National Geographic*.

Robert Holmes launched his distinguished career covering the 1975 British Everest Expedition for the *London Daily Mail*. He has since traveled the world for major magazines, including *National Geographic*, *Islands*, and *Travel & Leisure*. He was also the photographer for *Fodor's Escape to the California Wine Country*. One of the world's foremost travel photographers, he was the first person to twice receive the Photographer of the Year award from the Society of American Travel Writers. For this book, he captured images of beautiful Sequoia and Kings Canyon national parks.